Dessert Circus

Dessert Circus

♦ ♦ ♦

Extraordinary Desserts You Can Make at Home

JACQUES TORRES

with Christina Wright and Kris Kruid

Dessert photography by John Uher

William Morrow and Company, Inc.

New York

It is the policy of William Morrow and Company, Inc., and its
imprints and affiliates, recognizing the importance of preserving
what has been written, to print the books we publish on acid-free
paper, and we exert our best efforts to that end.

Library of Congress Cataloging-in-Publication Data

Torres, Jacques.
    Dessert circus : extraordinary desserts you can make at home /
Jacques Torres with Christina Wright and Kris Kruid; photogra-
phy by John Uher.—1st ed.
        p.   cm.
    Includes index.
    ISBN 0-688-15654-1
    1. Desserts.   I. Wright, Christina.   II. Kruid, Kris.
III. Title.
TX773.T667 1998
641.8'6—dc21   97-28429
                                                            CIP

Printed in the United States of America

First Edition

1   2   3   4   5   6   7   8   9   10

BOOK DESIGN BY RICHARD ORIOLO

www.williammorrow.com

Dessert Circus is the companion cookbook to the public television
series *Dessert Circus with Jacques Torres*, produced by Maryland
Public Television and Frappé, Inc.

Acknowledgments

♦　♦　♦

KRIS ALWAYS SAYS EVERY day with me is an adventure, but I know these adventures would not be much fun if she were not part of the experience. I am grateful to share my life with her and appreciate her support and enthusiasm no matter how zany my ideas are or how much they will affect our lives. I thank her for keeping the panic I create to a minimum and for calming the waters in my wake. This project could not have happened without her.

I am not sure where I would be today without the complete and total support of Sirio Maccioni. He has generously given of his wisdom and guidance over the past eight years. I am grateful for the opportunity to be part of Le Cirque and Le Cirque 2000 but, more than that, Sirio has made me feel like a valuable member of his family. I am appreciative of the room he has given me to grow and for providing the most spectacular canvas on which to paint.

I would like to express my most sincere gratitude to Dorothy Cann Hamilton and Doug Hamilton, owners/founders of the French Culinary Institute. They have given me their support from the beginning of my time in New York. I have tremendous respect for Dorothy's knowledge, honesty, and dedication to the industry. I am especially appreciative of their generosity in making the FCI amphitheater available for my television series and for believing in me without question.

Team Torres began unofficially about five years ago when Kris and I met Tina Wright. Through all of the projects and opportunities that have come our way, Tina has been there to roll up her sleeves and donate her energy. She is a driving force that transforms my creativity into reality. I owe her my most sincere and heartfelt gratitude for her dedication, concentration, and enthusiasm. None of the projects I have undertaken over the last few years would have been possible without her. In addition to her responsibilities as cowriter, she personally tested every recipe; acted as associate producer of the television series, where literally nothing happened without her input; and worked by my side tirelessly through everything we have accomplished at the French Culinary Institute, from school design to writing the curriculum. I am certainly lucky she walked into my kitchen five years ago to volunteer her time as an apprentice and I am forever grateful to her.

Thank you to our television producer, Charlie Pinsky of Frappé Productions, for giving me artistic license and for letting my vision become a reality. He trusted me from the beginning and had the energy to put me on television. He empowered us to do so much on our own. Working with the talented team of Lewis Rothenberg, Pete McEntyre, Bobbi Benedetti, Jeff Cirbes, Craig Haft, and Theresa Lopez was a pleasure.

We have been blessed with the most generous sponsors. Thank you to:

- Michel Roux, Chairman of the Grand Marnier Foundation; Michel is a fellow Frenchman whose mind moves faster than my computer's. His generosity knows no bounds, and I sincerely appreciate his total support of our entire project. He taught me, "The most important dollar is not the first dollar you make. It's the first dollar you give." Thank you.

- Stolichnaya Vodka
- Callebaut Chocolate of Belgium and Vincent de Clippele
- Frank and Brinna Sands and the entire King Arthur Flour family
- Francine "Martine" Kowalsky and Frederick Wildman and Sons, Ltd.

We are grateful to the following companies for providing equipment: The Edlund Company (scales); Braun Inc. (immersion blenders, hand-held mixers); Bourgeat (copper pans); KitchenAid (stand mixers); Amco, a Leggett & Platt Company (measuring cups and spoons); Wüsthof-Trident of America, Inc. (knives); and Paige Watson at Broadway Panhandler.

We also thank the following companies for generously providing the use of beautiful china, flatware, and tableware: Annieglass, Christofle Silver, Inc., Hermès, Villeroy & Boch, Rosenthal U.S.A., Bernardaud, Matter & Sense, and The LS Collection.

We extend a special thank you to Lars Malmberg and Gunther Scheible from PACOJET for giving us the machines we used for making ice creams and sorbets.

I would like to thank my parents for their unfaltering love and support in everything I have done. *Merci, Maman et Papa: Vous me manquez beaucoup et vous me donnez le courage et la volonté de faire plus tous les jours.*

Louis Franchain, my teacher and mentor, has been like a second father to me through all of the years. I am grateful for his encouragement and for his generous gifts of knowledge.

My dearest friends Glenn and Euphrasia Dopf have given me more friendship than would seem humanly possible. Glenn has touched almost every aspect of this whole project and I thank him for his legal advice, for negotiating all of my deals, and for introducing me to our producer, and the Family Dopf for their never-ending enthusiasm and support.

Team Torres sincerely thanks Linda Kuipers, who has earned the title "satellite editor, recipe tester, and healer." As she always does, Linda gave generously of her time, advice, and knowledge. She is the official "worrier" of Team Torres and is always there to cater to every emotional need. We love you and John and thank you both for your untiring support.

Thank you to Drew Shotts for being so committed to our entire project. His help in the prep kitchen during the television taping and his dedication during the photo shoot was invaluable. No matter what we needed, he met every challenge.

Adam Tihany is the most amazing designer I have ever had the opportunity to meet. He is not afraid to push the limits of every idea and sets the trends so far ahead that he leaves us all behind in the wake of his talent.

Team Torres gratefully acknowledges Peter Marengi for bringing our project to the attention of William Morrow and for being such a true and wonderful friend.

We would like to thank our editor, Pam Hoenig, for her sense of humor through the editing process of this arduous project, for her continuous leaps of faith, for bending to do it our way, and for guiding us out of the kitchen and onto the page. Thanks to everyone at William Morrow for dropping everything and rushing the project to meet our deadline.

Our photographer, John Uher, made what could have been difficult photo sessions lots of fun. Aside from his phenomenal talent, we thank him for his total flexibility in accommodating our schedule, for his vision, and for his dedication to making every dessert look spectacular.

Fern Berman coordinated and directed our public relations and promotions campaign and made it look like it was a piece of cake. Thank you, Fern, for your tremendous energy, for thinking of every angle, and for being brilliant.

To our photographer friends, Lou Manna and Matthew Septimus, thank you for dropping everything to be at the show tapings to capture the casual shots.

Thank you to my trusted colleagues: Sottha Khunn, Benito Savarin, Keitaro Goto, Francisco Gutierrez, Hiroko Asada, Clare Perez, and all of the talented chefs with whom I have worked. I am especially grateful to Lillian Masamitsu-Hartmann for designing and creating the wedding cake featured in this book.

Thank you to Richard Cotter and the entire crew at the New York Palace. I appreciate Mr. Cotter's support and generosity and the way the staff at the hotel graciously accepted me as part of their family. A special thank you to Brett Traussi, director of food and beverage at the hotel.

Thank you to Maryland Public Television, John Potthast, and Margaret Sullivan.

Special thanks to:

- Sue Reinius Pacifico for all of her help and for the smile with which she does it
- Gordon Anthony, Scott Cohen, and the team at LMG for endless technical advice, friendship, and for taking our Web page to the next dimension
- Marc and Kelli Minker for sound business and financial advice and for their tremendous moral support
- Ray and Erika Wright for raising a great daughter and for having faith this all would happen
- Greg "Guru" Poulos for paving the way to global communications by getting our Web page up and running

During the taping of the show, we would have been lost without Chef Dieter Schorner, Ted Matern, Anthony Del Tufo, Cheryl Ledet, and Alison Bowers and the entire FCI family.

Thank you to Jacques Pépin and André Soltner. These two talented chefs provide inspiration to all aspiring chefs. They generously share their knowledge and encouragement and set the example for professionalism in our industry.

To all of our friends who have not only endured hearing us talk about this project for what must seem like years but have also waited patiently for us to finish it so we can return their phone calls and resume our friendship: Thank you also to Birgitt Stepanow, Bea Flammia, Laura Fastie, Patty Hunstein, Laurie Rosatone, Anne Traynor, André Renard, Claude Solliard, Claude and Nicole Franques, Patrice Caillot, Gigi Wright, Ed Gabriels, Nancy "9C" Stark, Remi Lauvant, Tanya Olenik, Jean Pierre Dubray, and John and Laura Ressner.

Contents

♦   ♦   ♦

Introduction

◆　◆　◆

WHEN I WAS FOURTEEN years old, I decided to follow in the culinary footsteps of my brother and asked him if he would help me find a job in a kitchen. He suggested that I look for work in a pastry shop. I spent the next one and a half years trying my hand at a local pastry shop. I accepted a formal apprenticeship appointment at the age of sixteen and, after two years, graduated first in my region. A little later, I was in Nice visiting a friend and found myself standing in front of the Hotel Negresco. On a bet, I went in and asked Chef Jacques Maximin for a job. As luck would have it, he had just dismissed the pastry chef. He asked me how quickly I could return with my chef's jacket and one hour later, I began an eight-year adventure that took me around the world. In 1986, I competed in the Meilleur Ouvrier de France and became the youngest chef at the time to earn the honorable distinction. That was how I got started in this field almost twenty-four years ago.

In 1988, I met my friend Jean Pierre Dubray on the beach; he worked in America. The next thing I knew, I was on my way to Palm Springs to open a new Ritz-Carlton Hotel. I met Kris almost immediately upon my arrival. In 1989, I received a call from Le Cirque offering me the opportunity to move to New York and work in one of the finest restaurants in the world. At the time, I had no idea of the journey I was about to begin. Working for Mr. Maccioni has exposed me to some of the most wonderful experiences and has opened a lot of doors that have led down some exciting paths. In 1996, the legendary Le Cirque closed its doors, only to reopen nine months later as the new Le Cirque 2000. Mr. Maccioni built the pastry kitchen of my dreams. I now have every toy and tool available and I am very proud to be working in one of the most coveted kitchens in the industry. In all of this time, I have made a lot of mistakes but I have also learned how to fix them!

I am very dedicated to sharing my craft with others. In 1995, Dorothy Cann Hamilton gave me the stage for that dedication by inviting me to be part of the French Culinary Institute. She said she wanted to build the best pastry school in the world and asked me to help make that dream a reality. Part of Dorothy's plan included a state-of-the-art amphitheater, which she generously allowed us to use for our television series. With a host of fellow pastry chefs, friends, and industry colleagues, we designed the entire pastry school, from kitchens to classrooms. Tina and I wrote the curriculum in every spare moment. (Kris has lots of pictures of our vacations, but all of them feature Tina and me busy on our laptops!)

When Charlie Pinsky and I first started talking about doing a television series, I knew I wanted to combine entertainment and teaching. My hope was to make it fun and educational. The F.C.I. provided the perfect setting. The idea behind the series was to cater to all levels of ability.

Each recipe in this book is also rated according to its level of difficulty:

◆ means the recipe is simple and requires no previous kitchen experience. I call these the confidence builders. Mastering these recipes will help you form the basic skills necessary for making your own creations.

◆◆ means the recipe uses the skills most home cooks probably already possess. If you own basic kitchen equipment and have been anxious to use it, these recipes will help you fine-tune your talents.

◆◆◆ means the recipe is moderately challenging and/or time-consuming.

I think all of the recipes are attainable for anyone who has the desire and motivation to make them. Please read any recipe all the way through before you begin. The notes and variations at the end of the recipes contain ideas and information you should find useful. I have found that if I always have everything weighed and measured before I begin, I am less likely to make a mistake.

Growing up in the South of France, I was taught the value of all of our natural resources. I try very hard to recycle both material and edible items. I have tried to give you recipes that do not cause you to make more than you need, but I do hope you share my belief that sometimes it is good to have some extra cake or ice cream in the house for last-minute entertaining.

Pastry is really very logical. Once you learn the basic building blocks, you can use them to create simple designs or spectacular creations. With this book, I hope to demystify pastry and encourage you to develop your own creations.

I hope you will share what you learn as you make these recipes. Please feel free to leave me a message on my Web site at http://www.jacquestorres.com. While you are there, look for specialty tools or hard-to-find ingredients. I will also keep you posted on my schedule—when I will be giving demonstrations or offering classes, sharing what is new at Le Cirque, and other projects on which I am working. If you prefer, drop me a line in care of Team Torres, P.O. Box 303, New York, New York 10101–0303. I look forward to hearing from you, but until then, order dessert first!

Getting Started: Equipment, Ingredients, and Terms

◆   ◆   ◆

I CAN'T STRESS ENOUGH how important it is to use the best ingredients possible when preparing desserts. If you start with an inferior product, no matter what you do you cannot make it fantastic. Buy the freshest, ripest fruit, for example, even if you have to spend a little more. I very rarely use anything except high-quality bittersweet chocolate. I prefer its flavor and the way that flavor stands up to the other flavors in any dessert. I always use fresh, unsalted butter and would never attempt any of these creations with any kind of butter substitute. I also have learned a lot about flour and strongly suggest that you always use unbleached, unbromated flour.

The owner of the Hotel Negresco in Nice once told me, "You are never too rich to be cheap." She meant that I should always buy the best equipment and the best ingredients I could afford. I have really learned the value of her advice. If you buy cheap pastry tools, they will break over time and you will have to buy others later. So buy the best quality from the start!

Since pastry making is an exact science, I use an electronic scale to weigh everything. It makes a big difference, since weight is the only true measure. For example, when you measure flour in a cup, it can weigh out differently, depending on how it was stored or how tightly it is packed in the cup. In this book, I started with the metric weight of ingredients and converted it as closely as possible to the American measurements of cups and teaspoons. All of the recipes have been tested using the basic tools most people are likely to have.

Equipment

Acetate: This is a clear plastic found in art supply stores or florist shops. I use a medium weight (.003). It imparts a nice shine to tempered chocolate. It can be purchased by the roll or in sheets. For the recipes in this book, the acetate sheets are 12 × 18 inches.

Baking sheet: For the recipes in this book, I used professional baking sheets that are 12 × 18 × 1 inch. They are similar in size and shape to jelly-roll pans.

Candy thermometer: These usually measure temperatures ranging from 176° to 320°F (80° to 160°C). I use one that is positioned inside a metal cage, which makes it sturdier. Always keep the thermometer upright as it cools, or the mercury will separate and the thermometer will be useless. It's a good idea to hang the thermometer when stored. When you get a new thermometer, always place in it boiling water for about 5 minutes to test whether or not it reads 212°F (100°C) at the boiling point. This way you will know the exact reading of your thermometer, and you can make adjustments if necessary.

Chef's knife: My knives are from Wüsthof-Trident. The ones I use the most are an 8- or 10-inch chef's knife, a paring knife, and a 10- to 12-inch serrated knife.

Chinois: A chinois (also known as a china cap) is a deep conical strainer. It comes in various grades from fine to coarse and is used only for liquid ingredients (never to sift dry ingredients). When you need to push a mixture through it, use the back of a ladle so you do not rip or pierce the mesh.

Cutting board: I usually use white plastic cutting boards. Wooden boards can hold oils and odors that fruit or sugar will absorb.

Decorating tips: I use the Inox (stainless steel) tips that come thirteen to a set. They are very strong and will hold up over time.

Dome mold: I use these 4-ounce molds for many of my desserts. They come in plastic or aluminum and can be found in most baking supply stores.

Double boiler: This is used to heat ingredients consistently and safely without exposing them to the direct heat of the burner. In this book, a double boiler is most often used to melt chocolate. To make a double boiler, if you don't own one, place a saucepan half-filled with water over medium heat and cover with a heatproof mixing bowl large enough to snugly rest on the rim of the saucepan. The water in the saucepan and the bottom of the bowl should never come in contact with each other. If steam escapes from the seal between the pan and the bowl, either the bowl does not fit the pan properly or the water is too hot and you should lower the heat slightly.

Ice bath: I use ice baths often to cool down mixtures quickly, which saves time. To prepare an ice bath, pour ice cubes into a 4-quart bowl. Generously sprinkle salt over the ice and add water to cover the ice. Place a clean, dry 2-quart bowl in the ice bath.

Immersion blender: I can't live without my Braun immersion blender. I use it for everything, from mixing purees to tempering chocolate.

Mandoline: This is a very sharp hand-operated slicer used especially for making very thin slices. It usually comes with a variety of blades. Professional kitchens use stainless steel mandolines.

Measures: For all the dry measures given in the recipes, I used an Amco stainless steel set of cups and measuring spoons.

Mixer: I always use a heavy-duty stand mixer but most of these recipes were also tested with a hand-held mixer. I can't imagine making anything without a stand mixer. Mine has three attachments: paddle, whip, and dough hook. I prefer the 5-quart professional version.

Offset spatula: I like one that is fairly firm, not very flexible. These are available in different sizes and are very strong.

8-inch, 10-inch, 12-inch cake pans

Frying pan

Loaf pan

Soufflé mold

Muffin tin

Mini muffin tin

Saucepans in assorted sizes

Fluted tart pan with removable bottom

individual soufflé mold

Crème brûlée mold

Tartlet pan

Savarin mold

Mandoline

Cutting board

Aluminum dome molds

Box grater

Assorted cutters, plain and fluted

Chinois

Heart mold (for Frozen Strawberry Parfait)

Charlotte mold

Revolving metal cake stand

Plastic dome mold

Sieve

Disposable aluminum molds

Stove mold

Heart-shaped cutters

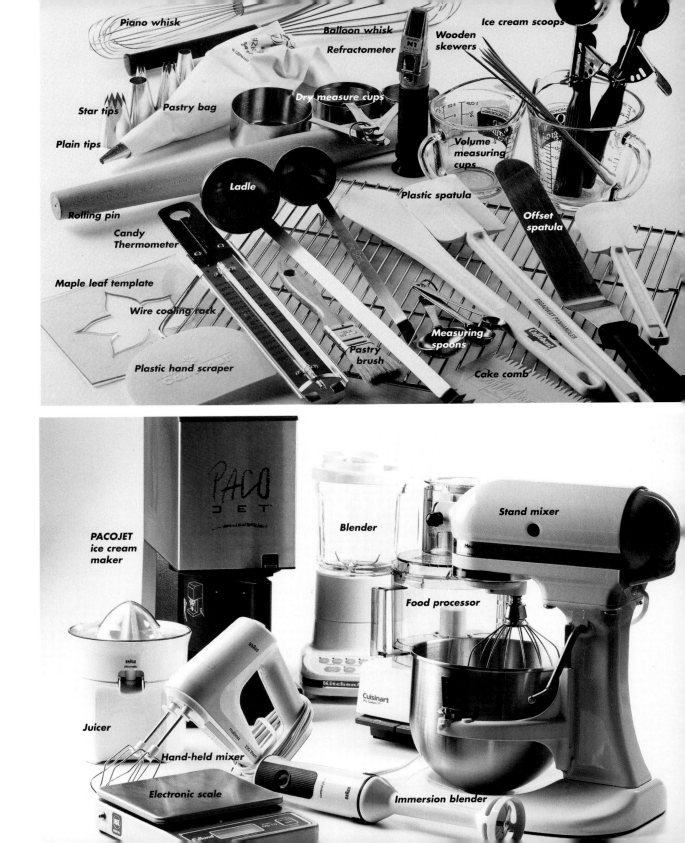

Piano whisk

Balloon whisk

Refractometer

Ice cream scoops

Wooden skewers

Dry measure cups

Star tips

Pastry bag

Volume measuring cups

Plain tips

Ladle

Plastic spatula

Offset spatula

Rolling pin

Candy Thermometer

Maple leaf template

Wire cooling rack

Measuring spoons

Pastry brush

Plastic hand scraper

Cake comb

PACOJET ice cream maker

Blender

Stand mixer

Food processor

Juicer

Hand-held mixer

Electronic scale

Immersion blender

Ovens: In a conventional oven, it is a good idea to keep an oven thermometer inside your oven to check the accuracy of the temperature. A convection oven cuts the baking time by allowing air to circulate, which makes the baking much more even. No matter what kind of oven you have, always rotate your baking sheets onto the different racks during baking to avoid any hot spots.

Parchment paper: I use parchment paper, also called baking paper, for almost every recipe because it is clean, never sticks, and avoids the need for adding fat to a recipe. It is very fast, convenient, and cheap. The sheets I use are 12 × 18 inches.

Pastry bag: I use plastic disposable pastry bags so I don't have to worry about bacteria (cloth bags hold bacteria). If you prefer, you can buy cloth bags in specific sizes in most baking supply stores.

Plastic scraper: This is one of the most useful tools in my kitchen. I always have several in the pocket of my chef's coat. I use them for everything from mixing to scooping.

Refractometer: This expensive tool is used to balance the sweetness of sorbet. It measures the total sugar content of a sorbet base. If you plan to make sorbet often, a refractometer is a good investment because it provides an easy and accurate measurement.

Rubber spatulas: I use white heavy-duty spatulas.

Saucepans: I always use heavy-bottomed saucepans like All-Clad. They allow the food to cook evenly and help keep milk products from burning.

Scale: I use a scale to weigh everything. Pastry making is a relatively exact science and the volume measure of cups is very inaccurate. For example, 1 cup of flour can weigh from 4 to 7 ounces, depending on how it is packed in the cup. I use an Edlund digital scale, DS-10, that weighs measures from 0.1 ounce to 10 pounds, or 2 to 5000 grams. They cost about $300 but for a professional kitchen, this type of scale is necessary. Less expensive scales are widely available. If you are going to use dry-cup measures, keep in mind that during testing I used the cup to scoop up the ingredient and then leveled the top with an offset spatula. I did not pack it or tap it down. Whenever an ingredient is sifted, I always weigh it before I sift it. In our tables of ingredients, ounces refer to weight, not volume.

Whisks: I prefer to use the black-handled balloon whisks by Matfer.

Ingredients

Almonds: You can buy them skins on, blanched (skins off), whole, halved, slivered, granulated, or ground. Slivered and granulated almonds are generally sold blanched. I use them all!

Almond flour: A flour made of finely ground almonds. Available in specialty gourmet stores and health food stores.

Almond paste: Almond paste is made from equal amounts of powdered sugar and finely ground almonds mixed together with corn syrup. It differs from marzipan, which is 33 percent ground almonds and 67 percent cooked sugar. Almond paste brings a lot of moisture to a cake because almonds contain a lot of fat. Almond paste can be stored well wrapped in the refrigerator for up to six months.

Anise seeds: Derived from an herb that is a member of the carrot family, anise seeds have a licorice taste. They are found in the spice rack at most grocery stores.

Baking powder: A chemical leavener, it is a mixture of baking soda and an acid (salt crystals). A little cornstarch is also added as a stabilizer. Double-acting baking powder is the easiest to find and the most popular. "Double-acting" means it has two reactions—first, when it comes in contact with the wet ingredients (it forms small gas cells or air pockets), and second, when it comes in contact with the heat of the oven (the gas cells or air pockets expand, causing the product to rise). Single-acting baking powder reacts only once, when combined with liquid. Store baking powder in a cool, dry place and replace it every six months. To determine freshness, check the expiration date on the package or add one teaspoon of the baking powder to about half a cup of hot water. If it bubbles a lot, it is still good.

Baking spray: I often use a baking spray such as PAM.

Butter: In baking, I always use unsalted butter in bars. Whipped butter contains air and if you use it your butter measurements will not be accurate. In the United States, butter must contain at least 80 percent butterfat. In French butters, the butterfat content is often higher. Keep unsalted butter in the refrigerator well wrapped in plastic wrap, because it will absorb other odors. Keep it in the freezer if you need to store it for more than a week or two.

Butter, clarified: Clarified butter has had the milk solids removed; it has a higher burning point than regular butter (see page 173 for instructions on how to clarify).

Candied chestnuts: Called *marrons glacés* in French, these are cooked chestnuts preserved in a sweet syrup. They are found in specialty gourmet stores such as Dean & DeLuca (see Sources, page 325).

Cassis: Small berries from the south of France that resemble miniature blueberries; they are sometimes available in specialty markets. In a recipe, substitute blueberries if you can't find them.

Chocolate: Chocolate begins with the cocoa tree. Cocoa trees begin to produce fruit at four to five years of age. The fruits, or pods, open three to four days after being harvested. The beans are extracted from the pods and fermented for five to seven days. Fermentation helps to remove the white pulp around the bean, to destroy the germ, and to enhance the brown color. The beans are then dried, naturally or mechanically, for eight to fifteen days as a preservative measure. Drying also enhances the cocoa aroma. At this point, the beans are sent to the factories to be cleaned and processed. They are sifted twice, once to remove foreign particles and then to remove the shells or husks. Then the cocoa beans are roasted to fully develop their aroma. Once cooled, they are crushed to produce a paste called "chocolate liquor" or "cocoa paste." When this paste is tempered, it is sold as unsweetened chocolate. If the cocoa butter is extracted from the liquor, the remaining paste is used to produce cocoa powder. When left as is, the paste is used to produce chocolate.

To make cocoa powder, the paste is finely ground. If it is treated with an alkaline solution (potassium carbonate), it is called Dutch-processed cocoa. The alkaline solution raises the pH level of the chocolate, which darkens the color and makes the flavor milder and the powder easier to dissolve. When it is untreated, cocoa has a slightly acidic taste. I always use Dutch-processed unsweetened cocoa powder.

Unsweetened chocolate is pure cocoa paste (chocolate liquor), with 53 percent cocoa butter and 47 percent cocoa solids. This type of chocolate contains no sugar and is generally used in desserts and baked goods having other sources of sweetness.

Bittersweet chocolate consists of 27 percent cocoa butter and 35 percent cocoa paste. This type of chocolate has a strong, pronounced flavor and is slightly less sweet than other sweetened chocolates. It should not be confused with unsweetened chocolate.

Semisweet chocolate consists of 27 percent cocoa butter and 15 percent cocoa paste. It is slightly sweeter than bittersweet chocolate but the two can be used interchangeably, according to personal taste.

Milk chocolate contains milk solids, which create a milder, sweeter chocolate. This chocolate is best used in recipes requiring minimal heat, as the milk makes it heat-sensitive.

White chocolate is not considered chocolate because it does not contain cocoa solids. It derives its ivory or cream color from cocoa butter. Like milk chocolate, white chocolate is sensitive to heat and should be used where its taste and texture can be fully enjoyed. Always use white chocolate that contains cocoa butter, not vegetable fat.

I almost always use Callebaut bittersweet chocolate for recipes that call for dark chocolate because I prefer its taste. Most specialty gourmet shops carry it. Always buy the best-quality chocolate available. Taste a few different chocolates to find the one that pleases your palate. The taste will not change when it is baked, heated, or tempered.

Melting chocolate: Chocolate melts best at a temperature between 104° and 113°F (40° and 45°C). *Never melt chocolate directly over a heat source.* Use an indirect heat source like a hot water bath.

Tempering chocolate: Tempering is important because it determines the final gloss, hardness, and contraction of chocolate. When you melt chocolate, the molecules of fat separate. In order to put them back together, you must temper it. There are a variety of ways to do it but the result is always the same. Chocolate is tempered when its temperature is between 84° and 88°F (29° and 31°C).

One of the easiest ways to temper it is to place it in the microwave for thirty seconds at a time on high power until the chocolate is melted. Be very careful not to overheat it: The chocolate may not look as if it has completely melted, because it retains its shape. The chocolate should be only slightly warmer than your bottom lip. You may still see lumps in it once you've stirred it, but don't worry; the residual heat of the chocolate will melt them. You can also use an immersion blender to break up the lumps and start the recrystallization process. Usually the chocolate begins to set (recrystallize) along the side of the bowl. As it begins to crystallize, mix those crystals into the melted chocolate and they will begin the recrystallization process. I like to use a glass bowl because it retains the heat and keeps the chocolate tempered for a long time.

Another way to temper chocolate is a technique called seeding. In this method, tempering is achieved by adding small pieces of unmelted chocolate to melted chocolate. The amount of unmelted chocolate to be added depends on the temperature of the melted chocolate, but it is usually one fourth of the total amount. I usually use an immersion blender to mix the two together.

The classic way to temper chocolate is called *tabliering*. Chocolate is melted over a hot water bath to a temperature between 88° and 90°F (31° and 34°C). (White and milk chocolates melt at a temperature approximately 2°F less because of the amount of lactose they contain.) Two thirds of the melted chocolate is poured onto marble or another cold work surface. The chocolate is spread out and worked with a spatula until its temperature is approximately 81°F (27°C). At this stage, it is thick and begins to set. This tempered chocolate is then added to the remaining nontempered chocolate and mixed thoroughly until the mass has a completely uniform temperature. If the temperature is still too high, part of the chocolate is worked further on the cold surface until the correct temperature is reached. This is a lot of work, requires a lot of room, and makes a big mess.

Checking tempering: A simple method of checking tempering is to apply a small quantity of chocolate to a piece of paper or to the point of a knife. If the chocolate has been correctly tempered, it will harden evenly and show a good gloss within five minutes.

Storing chocolate: You need to use enough chocolate to make it easy to work with, so you will always have some left over after molding in most of these recipes. Chocolate is susceptible to moisture and absorbs external odors. It is also important to protect it from light and air. Store it in a cool, dry place in sealed packaging. The ideal temperature for storing chocolate is between 54° and 68°F (12° and 20°C). Do not store chocolate in the refrigerator, because the humidity (moisture) will affect it (see below).

Fat bloom is a soft, white layer that forms on the surface of chocolate and is comprised of a thin layer of fat crystals. Storage at a constant temperature will delay the appearance of fat bloom.

Sugar bloom is a rough irregular layer on top of chocolate caused by condensation (for example, when chocolate is taken out of the refrigerator). This moisture dissolves the sugar in the chocolate. When the water evaporates, the sugar recrystallizes into rough, irregular crystals on the surface and gives the chocolate an unpleasant look. Prevent sugar bloom by avoiding temperature shocks.

Coco Lopez: Sweetened coconut juice most often used for making piña coladas. It can be found in most grocery stores or in liquor stores in the mix section.

Coconut flakes: Come sweetened and unsweetened; I usually use sweetened.

Coffee extract: Concentrated coffee flavoring. The brand I use is Trablit.

Cornstarch: A thickening agent derived from corn. Also contained in powdered sugar.

Cream: The part of milk with the highest concentration of fat. The fat allows whipping cream to hold its shape when whipped. Cream comes in three grades: Light cream is 18 to 30 percent butterfat, light whipping cream is 30 to 36 percent butterfat, and heavy whipping cream 36 to 40 percent butterfat. I usually use heavy whipping cream.

Crème fraîche: A French variation of sour cream, it can be universally substituted for sour cream.

Eggs: Grade AA eggs have a thicker white and a stronger yolk. Grade A eggs have thinner albumen (not as strong) or white, and a weaker yolk membrane (which breaks more easily). The egg white is comprised mostly of water and some protein. The yolks contain vitamins, minerals, cholesterol, fat, and protein. I usually use large eggs. The color of the shell, brown or white, has nothing to do with the flavor or quality. Eggs are a natural emulsifier, which is why they are often used to make a sauce smooth and thick.

Flour: It is *really* important to use the right flour in a recipe to achieve the desired results. Some commercially processed flours contain toxic chemicals that are used to whiten and oxidize them (see below). I have found that these chemicals significantly affect the outcome of certain recipes and prefer to use a pure flour that does not contain any unnecessary additives. For this reason, I always use King Arthur flours both at home and at the restaurant. I hope the following information helps you to choose the right flour for the recipe you want to make.

First, let's take a look at the wheat berry itself. In simplest terms, it is composed of the following:

- The bran: the protective outside coating that holds the berry together
- The germ: the embryo of a new wheat seedling were it to germinate
- The endosperm: the remaining part of the berry, which is the food or nutritive source for the growing wheat seedling

What is gluten and what does it do? The endosperm contains two proteins, glutenin and gliadin, that will, when mixed with a liquid, produce a substance called gluten. Gluten will stretch, and eventually stops trying to snap back to its original shape, staying put in its new configuration. These two characteristics are what allow bread dough to capture, expand, and contain the carbon dioxide bubbles produced by yeast as it grows and divides. (It is also what allows you to roll out pastry into thin sheets that don't shrink back or fall apart.) Wheat is the only grain that contains significant amounts of these proteins, meaning that doughs made from wheat flours are the only ones that can truly be leavened.

What is enriched flour? In the 1940s, the Food and Drug Administration mandated that every all-purpose flour be "enriched," so small amounts of iron, niacin, thiamin and riboflavin are added. In the future, folic acid, a member of the vitamin B complex, will be added to this list.

What else is added to flour? A small amount of malted barley flour is usually added to all-purpose flour to increase the level of enzyme activity in the flour. Malted barley flour is made from sprouted barley that is dried and ground. This sprouting stimulates the production of enzymes that break starch into sugars, on which the yeast feeds.

What is bleached flour? Some companies add bleaching and oxidizing chemicals to flour. It is legal to add a number of chemicals, many of which are toxic, to whiten flour and to oxidize it instantly rather than to allow it to age naturally. (Flour that is oxidized, or aged, has better baking qualities.) Potassium bromate, a potentially carcinogenic chemical, has been used extensively as both an oxidizer and a conditioner. (In California, any food containing potassium bromate must carry a warning label.)

There are other permissible chemical additives used to whiten and oxidize flour such as chlorine dioxide, benzoyl peroxide, and chlorine gas. People with especially sensitive palates can detect a bitter aftertaste from flours treated with these chemicals, which leave a residue of benzoic acid and hydrochloric acid after baking.

What are the types of flours used most often in this book?

- *King Arthur Unbleached All-Purpose Flour* is milled from hard red winter wheat and has a protein level, after milling, of about 11.7 percent. It is the closest I have found to the flour used in France. This type of flour is the most widely available.
- *King Arthur Round Table Pastry Flour* makes exceptionally tender pastry. I also use it in combination with all-purpose flour to make French-type breads. It is milled from soft white wheat and contains 9.2 percent protein. It is available through the King Arthur Flour Baker's Catalogue (see Sources, page 325) and should be in stores sometime in 1998.
- *King Arthur Special* is a bread flour, designed for yeast baking. It is milled from hard red spring wheat and has a high protein level of 12.7 percent. It is available through the King Arthur Flour Baker's Catalogue and from select grocery stores.

How should flour be stored? Flours that do not contain the germ, i.e., unbleached all-purpose, bread, pastry, cake, white or medium ryes, etc., can all be stored in a cool, dry place for an indefinite period of time. Whole-grain flours (containing the oil-rich germ) will slowly become rancid. They will keep for about three months if stored where it is cool and dry. Place them in the refrigerator in an airtight container to store them for up to six months. Freezing flour will allow it to last even longer. Tuck a bay leaf into any flour stored at room temperature to discourage "visitors."

Framboise liqueur: I usually use either Stoli Razberi vodka for its natural raspberry flavor or raspberry eau de vie.

Gelatin: A gelling agent that can be found in the form of sheets or powder (envelopes). Most brands weigh 2 to 3 grams per sheet or 7 grams per envelope. In the United States, grocery stores sell the powder form; in Europe the sheets are more common. I prefer the sheets because they are easier to measure. They can be found in gourmet food stores and specialty baking stores. One envelope equals three sheets, and a teaspoon of powdered gelatin equals one sheet.

Before gelatin—sheet or powder—can be used, it needs to be hydrated in a liquid, generally water. With sheet gelatin, always use cold water; hot water will cause it to absorb too much water. Use enough water to completely submerge the sheets. Squeeze the excess water from the sheets once softened. For powdered gelatin, see the instructions on the box.

Gold leaf: Very thin sheets of gold available through gourmet food shops. I use it for decoration, and it is edible!

Half-and-half: Half cream, half milk. Found in the dairy section of any grocery store.

Halvah: Ground sesame seeds and sugar or honey. Usually sold in individually wrapped bars in ethnic markets or gourmet food stores.

Lecithin: An emulsifier found in egg yolks (30 percent of a yolk) and some vegetables. It helps make chocolate smooth and moist and acts as a stabilizer.

Mascarpone cheese: A soft, sweet Italian cheese similar to cream cheese. It is made from cow's milk and has a very high butterfat content.

Meringue powder: A powder that contains dried egg whites, sugar, vanillin, and salt. The dried albumin adds strength to egg whites, which helps a meringue to hold. It can be used without fear of salmonella.

Milk: I always use Grade A whole milk (about 4 percent milk fat), homogenized and pasteurized.

Oil: Unless otherwise specified, I always use neutral-flavored oil like canola or vegetable oil.

Phyllo dough: Paper-thin sheets of dough made from flour and water, originally from Greece. Phyllo dough must be baked. It is often used as a wrapping because it bakes to a crunchy texture and keeps its contents moist. Be sure to keep it covered, or it will dry out and be unusable. It can be found in the freezer section of most grocery stores. Always thaw before using.

Pignoli nuts: Also known as pine nuts. They are the seed of a pine cone. Usually, they are bought shelled and skinned. They are extremely expensive, so store them in the refrigerator or freezer to prevent the oil in the nuts from becoming rancid. Look for them in health food stores, nut shops, or gourmet food stores.

Pistachio nuts: Try to buy them raw, unsalted, shelled, and skinned. Keep them in the refrigerator or freezer to keep the oil in the nuts from becoming rancid.

Pistachio paste: Contains sugar, almonds, ground pistachios, vegetable oil, emulsifier, and lecithin. Available in some gourmet food stores.

Port wine: I like to use Cockburn's Special Reserve.

Praline paste: Usually a mixture of ground almonds and hazelnuts with sugar, but can also be found as pure hazelnuts with sugar. When the nuts are ground, they release their oils and form an oily paste with a consistency like smooth, old-fashioned peanut butter. It is always made commercially because it is impossible to grind the nuts finely enough without special equipment. When stored, the oil often separates. Just mix it together before using. Store it in the refrigerator. It is hard to find—check with a gourmet store or food distributor.

Rolling fondant: A cake covering primarily made from powdered sugar, water, and corn syrup. You can make your own, but I usually buy it.

Rum: I always use dark rum from the Caribbean, and I prefer Rhum Barbancourt from Haiti.

Sauternes: a sweet dessert wine.

Sesame seeds: Come in black, brown, or ivory (or white). I use ivory. Sesame seeds are about 50 percent oil and will quickly become rancid. Store them in an airtight container in the refrigerator or freezer.

Sour cream: Cream to which an acid (e.g., lactic acid, lemon juice, or vinegar) has been added. The mixture is allowed to stand for several hours until the cream curdles. You can buy fat-free or low-fat versions but I always use the regular sour cream. It can be universally substituted for crème fraîche.

Sugar and other sweeteners: The sweeteners I use in this book are granulated sugar, light brown sugar, powdered (confectioners' or 10-X) sugar, corn syrup, and honey. Granulated sugar is available in about five categories of "fineness" but I always use "regular," which is fine.

In many of the recipes in this book, cooked sugar is added to beaten eggs to make a *pâte à bombe* (egg yolks) or an Italian meringue (egg whites). I usually suggest that you start cooking the sugar and then go on to the next step. As the sugar cooks, the water added to it evaporates. If you are not ready to use the sugar when it reaches the proper temperature, simply add a few tablespoons of water and allow it to continue to cook. This way you can "hold" the sugar until you are ready.

When sugar is cooked to 250°F (121°C) on a candy thermometer, it is cooked to the soft ball stage. In a professional kitchen, we test it by hand as described on page 32. This method is definitely *not* recommended for anyone other than an expert confectioner. Sugar cooked to the soft ball stage is used when making a *pâte à bombe* or Italian meringue.

When sugar is cooked to 300° to 311°F (148° to 155°C), it is cooked to the hard crack stage. Sugar cooked to this stage is used to make Angel Hair (page 48) or the Sugar Cage (page 311).

Stages of Sugar	Temperature Range
Thread	230°–235°F/110°–112°C
Soft ball	240°–250°F/115°–121°C
Hard ball	255°–265°F/124°–129°C
Soft crack	270°–290°F/132°–143°C
Hard crack	300°–311°F/148°–155°C
Caramel	320°–350°F/160°–176°C

Using an invert sugar allows you to use half the amount of regular sugar called for in a recipe. Examples of invert sugars are honey, glucose, and trimoline.

Powdered sugar: Also known as confectioners' sugar or 10–X, this is granulated sugar ground to a powder. You can't make it at home because no home processor will grind it to that powdery texture. It is used to sweeten because it dissolves more easily than granulated sugar. It is also used to thicken because it usually contains cornstarch.

Brown sugar: Brown sugar is either light or dark. I usually use light brown sugar, but for Crème Brûlée (page 133) it doesn't matter. Brown sugar is a mixture of granulated sugar and molasses. You can substitute brown sugar for granulated sugar any time the flavor of the recipe will not be altered by a slight taste of molasses.

Corn syrup: This is starch extracted from corn kernels and treated with an acid or enzyme to create a sweet syrup. Its presence will keep sugars from crystallizing. It helps baked goods retain their moisture and increases shelf life. I always use light corn syrup, which lasts indefinitely in an airtight container.

Honey: Honey is an invert sugar used to add sweetness and moistness to baked goods. It also helps to extend shelf life because it releases its moisture slowly and absorbs humidity. The darker the color, the stronger the flavor.

Vanilla sugar: This is granulated sugar to which dried vanilla bean has been added. It can be stored indefinitely at room temperature in an airtight container. See page 168 for directions on how to make it.

Sure-Jell (powdered pectin): Fruit pectin for homemade jams and jellies. It contains dextrose (corn syrup), fruit pectin, and fumaric acid (which assists in the jelling process). Most grocery stores carry it. I use regular Sure-Jell, but it is also available as Sure-Jell Light or Slim-Set.

Vanilla bean: A pod fruit from a climbing vine in the orchid family. Usually comes from Tahiti (these are larger and more aromatic) or Madagascar (also known as Bourbon vanilla). The pods contain vanillin, which is the source of the fragrant flavor and aroma. The seeds from the vanilla bean are stronger in flavor than vanilla extract. I strongly recommend using vanilla beans over extract whenever possible. Store vanilla beans in a zippered-top plastic bag in the refrigerator for up to a week or in the freezer for longer.

Yeast: Compressed and dry yeasts are the two most common forms of yeast in baking. They have different traits but are from the same species. Compressed yeast is partly dried, then pressed into solid cakes. It should be slightly moist and cakey, and it should crumble easily. Unlike dry yeast, compressed yeast shows little activity when dissolved in water before being added to flour, because it needs sugar on which to feed. Store it in the freezer and it will lose less activity than if stored in the refrigerator. If it is too old, it will have a strong smell. Dry yeast has about a tenth of the moisture of compressed yeast. It needs to be hydrated in very warm water (105° to 110°F; 40° to 43°C). If you hydrate it at lower or higher temperatures, it will lose most of its fermentation power. If it is still active, you will see it bubbling in water as it hydrates.

It is best to store dry yeast in the freezer. I don't use dry yeast because I think it is unreliable. If you can't find compressed yeast, however, you can substitute one third as much dry yeast.

In general, yeast activity (fermentation) is dependent on temperature. The ideal temperature is 95°F (35°C). Sugar is also needed for fermentation to occur. Salt inhibits yeast activity and if too much is added, it can actually kill the yeast.

Yogurt: Generally contains active cultures. It can be made from skim or whole milk. I usually use plain or unflavored regular yogurt, but you can also use low-fat or non-fat varieties.

Substitutions

Ingredients	Substitute
1 cup firmly packed light brown sugar	1 cup granulated sugar + ¼ cup molasses
1 cup firmly packed dark brown sugar	1 cup granulated sugar + ½ cup molasses
3 sheets gelatin	1 envelope powdered gelatin
1 sheet gelatin	1 teaspoon powdered gelatin
1 package dry yeast (0.25 ounce)	1 generous tablespoon (0.75 ounce) compressed fresh yeast
1 teaspoon baking powder	¼ teaspoon baking soda + ½ teaspoon cream of tartar
1 cup pastry flour	Place 1½ tablespoons cornstarch in a cup measure and fill the cup with all-purpose flour
All-purpose flour	Equal parts bread flour and cake flour
Half-and-half	Equal parts milk and cream
Bittersweet chocolate	Semisweet chocolate
Crème fraîche	Sour cream
Meringue powder	Dried egg whites

Terms

Albumin: The protein content of the white of an egg.

Aspic: A jelly made of liquid that is often molded.

Bavarian: A creamy mixture that can be either fruit-based or crème anglaise–based. It always contains whipped cream.

Bloom: Refers to hydrating powdered gelatin. Can also refer to the white coating that appears on chocolate that is not tempered properly.

Cornet: A small piping bag made from parchment paper. It is usually used to make fine decorations. Every chef makes his or her cornet differently. This is how I make mine: Cut an $8 \times 12 \times 14\frac{1}{2}$-inch triangle from a sheet of parchment paper. Hold the middle of the long side of the triangle between two fingers of one hand. Take the tip of the triangle on the short, wide end and roll it toward the other tip of that same end while simultaneously pulling it in an upward motion. The tip of a cone will form where your thumb and finger hold it on the long side. Release your grip from the long side so you are now holding the two corners where they meet. The paper will already resemble a partially formed cone. Then just roll the remaining tail until it is completely rolled into a cone. There will be one point sticking up from the open end. Fold it inside toward the center and crease the fold. Now you should have a cornet. When you fold a filled cornet to close it, fold it away from the seam; this will keep the seam from opening. Use a pair of scissors or a sharp paring knife to cut an opening at the tip of the cornet to the desired size.

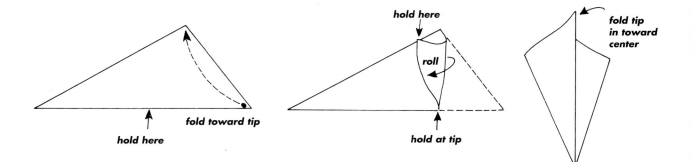

Dock: To pierce lightly with a fork, or a docker, to make small holes in dough that will let steam escape during baking. This helps the dough to remain flat and even. A docker looks like a spiked paint roller.

Emulsion: A mixture of two liquids, such as oil and water, that don't naturally combine smoothly. An emulsion is formed by the suspension of one liquid in the other. Butter is an emulsion.

Fermentation: A process that happens in any dough containing yeast. It begins as soon as the ingredients are mixed together and continues until the dough reaches an internal temperature of 138° to 140°F (58° to 60°C) during baking, at which point the yeast dies. The ideal proofing environment is 80° to 98°F (27° to 36°C), with 80 to 85 percent humidity. The temperature of the added water determines the rate of fermentation (warm = fast; cold = slow). As the yeast eats the added sugar and the sugar already contained in the flour, carbon dioxide is released. Salt also helps control the rate of fermentation (too little and the yeast is overactivated, too much and the yeast is killed).

French meringue: Egg whites are first whipped until foamy, then sugar (granulated or powdered) is added and the whites are whipped until they form stiff glossy peaks and triple in volume. It is important to add the sugar slowly and at the beginning so it has time to dissolve in the egg whites. Otherwise, the meringue will be grainy. Adding sugar slowly gives strength to the egg whites, which helps them hold as they are whipped.

Ganache: A mixture of hot heavy cream and chopped chocolate. The cream melts the chocolate and an emulsion is formed as they are whisked together. In this book, ganache is generally used as a filling, but by altering the proportion of chocolate to heavy cream, it can also be used as a glaze.

Gluten: See page 12.

Italian meringue: Egg whites whipped to stiff peaks to which cooked sugar (at the soft ball stage) is added. The mixture is then whipped until cool. It becomes thick and glossy and doubles in volume. This is the most stable type of meringue.

Macerate: Generally used to describe marinating fruit in liquid (alcohol, juice, syrup, etc.) to enhance the flavor of the fruit.

Nonreactive: Refers to a pan that is not lined with aluminum, which can react with certain ingredients like acids. I use All-Clad or Bourgeat pans.

Oxidation: The union of a substance and oxygen; fruit exposed to oxygen will often turn brown.

Pain de gênes: An almond cake similar to American pound cake in which almond paste is substituted for some of the butter.

Parfait: A whipped cooked sugar-and-egg yolk mixture (*pâte à bombe*) folded together with whipped cream and then flavored. Can be served frozen.

Pâte à bombe: Whipped yolks to which cooked sugar (at the soft ball stage) is added; the mixture is then whipped until lukewarm, thick, and doubled in volume. Used as a base for a parfait.

Pâton: Term used when making puff pastry. A *pâton* is dough to which butter has been added.

Proofing: A term that describes the action of a yeast dough as it ferments and rises.

Quenelles: Oval-shaped scoops of any mixture (mousse, Bavarian, meringue, etc.) generally formed using two spoons.

Seize: Used in reference to chocolate to describe what happens when liquid chocolate suddenly contracts and hardens upon coming in contact with water or being mixed with another ingredient that is too cold.

Soft peaks: In this book, used in reference to whipped cream. When the beaters are lifted from the whipped cream, peaks are briefly formed, but they do not hold their shape. This is the stage at which whipped cream has the most volume.

Stiff peaks: In this book, used in reference to egg whites. When the beaters are lifted from the egg whites, peaks that hold their shape are formed. When egg whites have reached the stiff peak stage, they are opaque, thick, and shiny, or glossy.

Temper: To bring the temperature of one mixture closer to that of another until the desired temperature is reached.

The Basics

◆ ◆ ◆

SOMETIMES IT CAN BE more interesting to make a fruit tart than an elaborate dessert. In a simple recipe, each flavor and technique is transparent, meaning that there is nothing to hide behind, so you work harder to enhance the recipe and develop all of the flavors. For this reason, you will achieve the best results if you begin with the highest-quality ingredients. In order to be able to "fix" or enhance a recipe, you need to understand what each of its components is and what it does. I am often quoted as saying, "Pastry is like mathematics. Everything is logical. If you know the basic building blocks, you can make anything." The recipes and techniques outlined in this chapter will set you on the right path for building a good foundation in pastry making. Mastery of them will give you the knowledge and confidence to make your own creations.

Crème Anglaise

3 CUPS (25 OUNCES; 700 GRAMS)

The technique for making crème anglaise is one of the true building blocks in pastry. Variations of this technique can be found in recipes for pastry cream, Bavarian creams, and mousses. I make crème anglaise to use as a sauce and as a base for ice cream.

The trick to making crème anglaise is how long you cook it. There is a very fine line between done and overcooked. If it's overcooked, you end up with bits of scrambled eggs. With practice, you will learn to tell when the crème anglaise is finished by the way it moves in the pan and how it coats a spoon. For your first attempt, you might want to use a candy thermometer and cook the mixture to 182°F (83°C).

You will need to prepare an ice bath (page 3) before you begin. When the crème anglaise has finished cooking, it is important to cool it as quickly as possible; otherwise, the mixture will retain heat and continue to cook.

In this recipe you will learn how to temper eggs. Tempering eggs means bringing the temperature of the eggs closer to the temperature of the boiled milk or cream to which they are added. If the eggs are not tempered, the thermal shock of hot liquid added to cold eggs will scramble the eggs.

Granulated sugar	*½ cup + 2 tablespoons*	*4.5 ounces*	*125 grams*
7 large egg yolks			
Whole milk	*2 cups + 1 tablespoon*	*17.6 ounces*	*500 grams*
Heavy cream	*½ cup*	*4 ounces*	*115 grams*
Honey	*1½ tablespoons*	*0.8 ounce*	*30 grams*
1 vanilla bean			

Pour half of the sugar into a large mixing bowl and set the remaining sugar aside. Add the egg yolks and whisk until well combined. The mixture should be thick, smooth, and homogenous.

Pour the milk, heavy cream, honey, and the remaining sugar into a nonreactive 3-quart heavy-bottomed saucepan and place it over medium-high heat. Use a sharp knife to slice the vanilla bean in half lengthwise. Separate the seeds from the skin by scraping the blade of the knife along the inside of the bean. Add the seeds and the skin to the mixture and bring to a boil. Remove the saucepan from the heat.

Temper the egg mixture with the hot milk mixture by carefully pouring about one third of the milk into the egg mixture. Whisk immediately to keep the eggs from scrambling. Pour the tempered egg mixture into the saucepan, place over medium heat, and cook, stirring constantly with a heatproof rubber spatula. The liquid will begin to thicken. When it reaches 182°F (83°C) and is thick enough to coat the back of a spoon, it is finished and should be removed from the heat. If you do not have a thermometer, you can tell that the crème anglaise is ready by using the following method: In one quick motion, dip the spatula into the crème anglaise and hold it horizontally in front of you. With the tip of your finger, wipe a clean line down the center of the spatula. If the trail keeps its shape, the crème anglaise is ready. If the trail fills with liquid, cook it for another minute and repeat the test. The objective is to remove the crème anglaise from the heat just *before* it boils.

If the crème anglaise boils, the egg yolks will scramble. If this happens, you can still use the mixture as an ice cream base if you blend it with an immersion blender, food processor, or a blender; you need a blade to liquefy the scrambled egg pieces. You will not be able to use it as a sauce, because once the eggs are scrambled, they lose their ability to hold a sauce together.

Strain the crème anglaise through a chinois or fine-mesh sieve into the bowl placed in the ice bath, to remove the vanilla bean and any cooked egg. Stir occasionally to allow the crème anglaise to cool evenly. Once it has cooled completely, pour it into a clean container. Place plastic wrap directly on top of the crème anglaise to prevent a skin from forming and store in the refrigerator for up to three days.

Variation: It is very easy to flavor crème anglaise. Just add a tablespoon (more or less to taste) of any flavored liqueur, coffee extract, or nut paste at any stage in the recipe. I recommend that you add your flavoring when the crème anglaise has finished cooking. You can divide it into smaller portions and flavor each differently.

As in an ice bath, salt blocks the temperature exchange between two objects of different temperatures (e.g., water and ice). When two objects of different temperatures come together, the colder one becomes warmer. Ice is colder than water. The addition of salt inverts that catalytic effect. When you pour salt over ice and water, the water becomes colder.

Pastry Cream

2½ CUPS (25 OUNCES; 700 GRAMS)

astry cream is one of the first recipes I learned as an apprentice in Provence. At my first job, I had to make huge quantities of it every day. Only fifteen years old at the time, I had to stand on a box to reach inside the pot to stir it. I still make pastry cream every day, but I no longer need to stand on a box.

I always add some butter after the pastry cream has finished cooking because it really enhances the taste and texture. Pastry cream can be used in combination with fruits, whipped cream, almond cream, flavored liqueurs, praline paste, and chocolate.

The technique of tempering eggs is the same as in making crème anglaise and lemon curd.

2 large eggs			
2 large egg yolks			
Granulated sugar	*½ cup + 2 tablespoons*	*4.5 ounces*	*125 grams*
Pastry flour	*3 tablespoons*	*0.9 ounce*	*25 grams*
Cornstarch	*2 tablespoons + 1 teaspoon*	*0.8 ounce*	*25 grams*
Whole milk	*2 cups + 1 tablespoon*	*17.6 ounces*	*500 grams*
½ vanilla bean			
Unsalted butter (optional)	*3½ tablespoons*	*1.75 ounces*	*50 grams*

Place the whole eggs, egg yolks, sugar, flour, and cornstarch in a medium-size mixing bowl and whisk until well combined. It is especially important to remove any cornstarch lumps. The mixture should be thick, smooth, and homogenous.

Pour the milk into a nonreactive 2-quart heavy-bottomed saucepan and place over medium-high heat. You want to use a large saucepan because the pastry cream gains in volume as it cooks and you will need enough room to be able to whisk vigorously without spilling. While the milk is heating, use a sharp knife to slice the vanilla bean in half again, this time lengthwise. Separate the seeds from the skin by scraping the blade of the knife along the inside of the bean. Add the seeds and the skin to the heating milk and bring to a boil.

Temper the egg mixture with the hot milk by carefully pouring approximately half of the milk into the egg mixture. Immediately whisk to prevent the eggs from scrambling. Pour the tempered egg mixture into the saucepan and continue to whisk, remembering to whisk into the edge of the saucepan, where the pastry cream can stick and burn. As the temperature rises, the mixture will slowly start to thicken. The pastry cream will become very thick very quickly just before it boils. (The eggs and starch cause it to thicken.) Continuously whisk to ensure that the mixture cooks evenly. Once the pastry cream has come to a boil, continue to whisk and cook for another 2 minutes to fully develop the flavor and to cook out the flavor of the starch. Remove the pan from the heat.

If you would like to add butter, and I always do, this is the time to do so. I just cut the butter into small chunks and stir it in until it is well incorporated. Pour the pastry cream into a clean, airtight container and place a piece of plastic wrap directly on top of the pastry cream to prevent a skin from forming. Let the pastry cream cool at room temperature, then store it in the refrigerator for up to three days, until ready to use. Before using the pastry cream, be sure to remove the vanilla bean skin and save it to make vanilla sugar (page 168).

Variation: It is very easy to flavor pastry cream to complement the dessert you are making. With a whisk or spatula, fold about 1 tablespoon of any flavored liqueur into the pastry cream at any point in the recipe. I usually add it right before I use the pastry cream; that way I can flavor only the amount I need for a specific dessert. Be sure to add the liqueur slowly and taste often. If you add too much, the pastry cream will become runny and lose its ability to hold its shape. If you prefer to add flavor without alcohol, you will need to do so at the beginning of the recipe. Place the grated zest of 2 oranges in the heating milk to infuse it with the flavor of the orange.

When you use a vanilla bean, split it in half with a sharp knife. The flavor comes from all of the tiny seeds that are inside. You can put it in milk and make an infusion to strengthen the taste.

Almond Cream

1¾ CUPS (16 OUNCES; 425 GRAMS)

I think almond cream is one of the most heavenly batters in pastry. All the flavors in this recipe are well balanced and complement one another.

Almond cream is always baked to a spongy, cakelike texture and can be used by itself or in combination with nuts or fruits. The addition of starch to this recipe ensures that it will not run out of a pastry shell during the cooking process. Its moist and flavorful qualities make it perfect for use as a filling in cookies, tarts, and puff pastries.

The format of the recipe is easy to remember: one part butter, one part almond flour, one part sugar, one-fifth part eggs, one-seventh part all-purpose flour. With those ratios in mind, you can make as much or as little of it as you like.

Room temperature unsalted butter	**½ cup + 1 tablespoon**	**4.5 ounces**	**125 grams**
Granulated sugar	**½ cup + 2 tablespoons**	**4.5 ounces**	**125 grams**
Almond flour	**1 cup**	**4.5 ounces**	**125 grams**
1 large egg			
All-purpose flour	**Scant ¼ cup**	**0.75 ounce**	**20 grams**

Place the butter, sugar, and almond flour in a medium-size mixing bowl and beat with an electric mixer on medium speed until light and fluffy, about 5 minutes. The mixture will be dry and sandy until the butter begins to be incorporated. Add the egg and mix well. Use a rubber spatula to scrape down the side of the bowl as needed. The egg is well incorporated when the mixture becomes light and creamy, after about 3 minutes. The batter lightens in color and increases in volume because of the incorporation of air by the mixer. It is important to allow time to beat in air, or the almond cream will be too heavy and will not have as great a rise when baked, causing the texture to be dense.

Add the flour and beat on low speed just until it is no longer visible, about 30 seconds. If you overmix, gluten (page 12) will overdevelop and the almond cream will lose its delicate texture when baked.

Pour the almond cream into an airtight container, cover, and store in the refrigerator for up to five days, until ready to use. The almond cream will darken in color and lose some of its volume; this happens because the butter hardens and the incorporated air escapes. You can also freeze the almond cream for several weeks. In either case, allow it to come to room temperature before using and beat it lightly with an electric mixer on medium speed until it returns to its initial volume and is once again light in texture and color.

Lemon Curd

2 ½ CUPS (22.6 OUNCES; 650 GRAMS)

emon curd is a custard filling used for cookies, tarts, cakes, and puff pastries. I like the citrus zing it adds to a dessert. Lemon curd is traditionally found at teatime served with scones.

The egg tempering technique used in this recipe is also used when making pastry cream and crème anglaise.

4 large eggs			
Granulated sugar	**½ cup + 2 tablespoons**	**4.5 ounces**	**125 grams**
Grated zest of 6 lemons			
Juice of 6 lemons, strained	**⅔ cup**	**5.4 ounces**	**160 grams**
Cold unsalted butter, cubed	**¾ cup + 2 tablespoons**	**7 ounces**	**200 grams**

Place the eggs and sugar in a medium-size mixing bowl and whisk until well combined. The mixture should be thick, smooth, and homogenous.

Place the lemon zest and juice in a nonreactive 2-quart heavy-bottomed saucepan, place it over medium-high heat, and bring to a boil. (A nonreactive pan will keep the eggs from turning green because of the reaction that would occur between the citric acid of the lemon and an aluminum pan.) When the lemon juice boils, temper the egg mixture by carefully pouring about half of the hot juice into the eggs. Whisk immediately to prevent the eggs from scrambling. Use a rubber spatula to scrape all of the tempered mixture into the saucepan and continue to whisk, remembering to whisk into the edge of the saucepan, where the lemon curd can stick and burn. The closer the mixture gets to the boiling point, the thicker it will become. As with pastry cream, the eggs act as the thickening agent. When the lemon curd boils, remove it from the heat and pour into a deep mixing bowl. Let it cool for about 7 minutes, stirring occasionally.

When the outside of the bowl is still quite warm but not hot, add the cubed butter. It is best to use an immersion blender or electric mixer for this; blend until the curd is smooth. If the lemon curd becomes grainy immediately after the butter is added, the mixture was probably too cool. To fix it, place it over a double boiler (page 3) and whisk until the graininess disappears. If the lemon curd is too hot when the butter is added, it will become very runny. To fix it, just put the mixture in the refrigerator and whisk it every 10 minutes. It will return to a creamy state in 20 to 30 minutes. In either case, it is the emulsion (page 20) in butter that helps bring the lemon curd back to a homogenous state.

The finished lemon curd should be smooth, creamy, and homogenous. Place it in a bowl, cover with plastic wrap, and let cool in the refrigerator for a few hours. This allows the butter to solidify, which will cause the lemon curd to thicken. It will keep in the refrigerator for up to one week if stored in an airtight container. Lemon curd is usually served cold. Do not whisk it before serving, or it will become loose.

Cream often burns on the bottom and side of a saucepan. To help keep this from happening, always stir to the bottom of the pan and use a saucepan with a rounded edge. If you notice any brown specks in the lemon curd (this is burned residue from the side of the pan), to remove them, use a fine-mesh sieve to strain the lemon curd as soon as it has finished cooking.

Basic Buttercream 1

**6 CUPS (43 OUNCES; 1,230 GRAMS); ENOUGH TO FILL
AND FROST TWO 8-INCH ROUND CAKES**

 like this buttercream recipe because it is easy to make. It is richer than Buttercream 2 (page 32) because it contains egg yolks instead of egg whites, which results in a creamier texture. The color will be slightly yellow. I like to use it for fillings, frostings, and decorating. One of the techniques used in this recipe is making what the French call a *pâte à bombe*.

1 large egg			
5 large egg yolks			
Water	*²/₃ cup*	*5.3 ounces*	*150 grams*
Granulated sugar	*2 cups*	*14 ounces*	*400 grams*
Cold unsalted butter, cubed	*3 cups + 2 tablespoons*	*25 ounces*	*700 grams*

Place the whole eggs and egg yolks in a large mixing bowl and whip with an electric mixer on medium-high speed until thick, light, and tripled in volume, 5 to 7 minutes. Continue to whip the eggs while you cook the sugar.

Pour the water and sugar into a 1-quart heavy-bottomed saucepan and place over medium heat. Insert a candy thermometer into the mixture. The sugar is ready when it reaches 250°F (121°C), what is known as the soft ball stage (see below). Make a *pâte à bombe* by pouring the cooked sugar down the side of the bowl as you continue whipping the eggs. Do not pour the hot sugar onto the beaters, or it will splatter. Continue whipping the *pâte à bombe* until the outside of the bowl is warm but not hot, 2 to 3 minutes. Add the butter all at once and beat on medium speed until incorporated. Increase the mixer speed to medium-high and whip until the buttercream is thick, smooth, and shiny, about 10 minutes. At this stage, you can add flavoring, if you wish. If you are not going to use all of the buttercream for your recipe, flavor only the amount you will use and store the rest to be flavored differently tomorrow.

The buttercream can be used immediately or can be stored in an airtight container in the refrigerator for three to four days or in the freezer for several weeks. If it has been chilled or frozen, allow the buttercream to come to room temperature, then whip it with an electric mixer on medium speed until it returns to its initial volume and is once again thick, smooth, and shiny.

When sugar is cooked to 250°F (121°C), it has reached what is called the soft ball stage. In a professional kitchen, we test the sugar by hand. I don't recommend that you try it, but I will tell you how I do it: First, I place a small bowl of ice-cold water next to the stove. Once the sugar begins to boil, I dip my thumb and first two fingers in the cold water. In one quick motion, I dip my fingers into the hot sugar (yes, you read that correctly), grab a small bit of the sugar, and immediately return my fingers to the bowl of cold water. When I can form the sugar into a small, malleable ball, it has reached the proper temperature. If it hardens as soon as it hits the cold water and cannot be formed into a ball, it is overcooked and has reached what is called the hard crack stage. To fix this, I add about 2 tablespoons of water to the cooking sugar and try again. If, on the other hand, the sugar feels like egg whites, it is not cooked enough but it is very close. I wait 30 seconds and try again.

Basic Buttercream 2

6 CUPS (40 OUNCES; 1,138 GRAMS); ENOUGH TO FILL AND FROST TWO 8-INCH ROUND CAKES

 borrowed this recipe from my friend Chef Dieter Schorner who was one of Le Cirque's first pastry chefs. His recipe is especially handy as a frosting for wedding cakes because it is very white. It is smooth, creamy, light, and easy to handle. When color is not a concern, this buttercream may be flavored in a variety of ways—with coffee extract, jam, nut paste, ganache, zest, etc.

One of the techniques used in this recipe is that of making an Italian meringue. I like to make an Italian meringue because the heat of the sugar kills any bacteria in the eggs.

Water	**Scant ¹/₂ cup**	**3.7 ounces**	**106 grams**
Granulated sugar	**2¹/₄ cups + 3 tablespoons**	**17 ounces**	**485 grams**
5 large egg whites			
Cold unsalted butter, cubed	**2¹/₄ cups + 1 tablespoon**	**18.5 ounces**	**520 grams**

The first step is to start cooking the sugar. Pour the water and sugar into a 1-quart heavy-bottomed saucepan and place over medium-high heat. When bubbles start to form around the edge of the pan, insert a candy thermometer in the mixture. When the sugar reaches 245°F (118°C), begin to whip the egg whites.

Place the egg whites in a large mixing bowl and whip with an electric mixer on medium-high speed until foamy and slightly soft peaks.

The sugar is ready when it reaches 250°F (121°C), what is known as the soft ball stage (see above). Make an Italian meringue by pouring the cooked sugar down the side of the bowl while you continue to whip the egg whites. Do not pour the hot sugar onto the beaters, or it will splatter. Continue whipping the meringue on medium-high speed until the outside of the bowl is warm but not hot, about 5 minutes. Add the butter all at once and beat on medium speed until incorporated. Increase the mixer speed to medium-high and whip until the buttercream is thick, smooth, and shiny, about 10 minutes. At this stage, you can add flavoring, if desired. If you are not going to use all of the buttercream for your recipe, flavor only the amount you will use.

The buttercream can be used immediately or can be stored in the refrigerator for three to four days or in the freezer for several weeks if held in an airtight container. If it has been chilled or frozen, allow the buttercream to come to room temperature before using, then whip it with an electric mixer on medium speed until it returns to its initial volume and is once again thick, smooth, and shiny.

Sugar Dough

This dough is easy to work with and makes a great tart crust. When baked, it is light and delicate. I love this recipe because it is so quick and all I need is nice fruit to make a spectacular dessert.

The best advice I can give you is not to overwork the dough, or the crust will be tough. I prefer to use powdered sugar rather than granulated because it dissolves instantly. Start with cold butter to keep the dough from becoming difficult to roll out and too soft. Baking powder gives it a little extra lightness.

Cold unsalted butter, cubed	**6 tablespoons**	**3 ounces**	**83 grams**
1 large egg			
Powdered sugar	**⅓ cup**	**1.5 ounces**	**42 grams**
Pastry flour	**1¼ cups**	**6 ounces**	**166 grams**
Baking powder	**1½ teaspoons**	**0.3 ounce**	**8 grams**

Place the cubed butter and egg in a large mixing bowl and beat with an electric mixer on medium speed until the butter is reduced to small pieces and the mixture looks like scrambled eggs, 2 to 3 minutes. Add the sugar and continue to beat until it is well incorporated, about 30 seconds. Don't worry; the mixture will be lumpy and may separate. This is normal and occurs because there are not enough dry ingredients to hold the mixture together at this stage. Continue mixing on medium speed and add the flour and baking powder. Stop mixing when the dough is smooth and holds together. If you are using a hand-held mixer, stop mixing as soon as it starts to clump; you will need to finish the dough by very gently kneading it until it holds together. At this stage, you may still see small pieces of butter in the dough. Remove from the mixing bowl and pat into a ball.

Use the dough immediately or store it in the refrigerator. If it has been stored in the refrigerator, you will need to give the cold dough four or five quick raps with a rolling pin before proceeding, to break up the cold butter. Roll out the dough to the desired size on a lightly floured work surface.

Baking instructions vary and will be specified in any recipe using sugar dough.

The sugar dough will keep if well wrapped in plastic wrap in the refrigerator for one week or in the freezer for one month. Thaw the dough in the refrigerator until ready to use. You can also store the dough already rolled into a tart pan, wrapped in plastic wrap.

Quick Puff Pastry

40.4 OUNCES (1,150 GRAMS)

uff pastry is something magical. It rises to about ten times its initial size without the help of yeast or chemical leaveners. The long baking process causes the butter to brown and develop the deep, rich flavor that makes puff pastry so popular. The layers are formed when the dough is repeatedly rolled, folded, and rested. I love its light, crunchy texture.

I like this recipe because it is quick to make compared to the traditional puff pastry method. You can do a few steps, store it, and come back to it later to finish it. This recipe can be used with sweet or savory fillings.

If you do not have a stand mixer, it might be better to incorporate the frozen butter with your hands, as you might burn out the motor of a hand-held mixer attempting it.

Unsalted butter	**7 tablespoons**	**3.5 ounces**	**100 grams**
All-purpose flour	**4 cups**	**17.8 ounces**	**500 grams**
Salt	**2½ teaspoons**	**0.6 ounce**	**15 grams**
Water	**Scant 1 cup**	**8 ounces**	**220 grams**
Unsalted butter, cut into ½-inch cubes and frozen	**1¼ cups + 1½ tablespoons**	**10.75 ounces**	**300 grams**

The first step is to melt the 7 tablespoons (3.5 ounces; 100 grams) of butter in a 1-quart saucepan over low heat. Allow the butter to cool to room temperature. It will appear milky and should be pourable and warm to the touch.

Place the melted butter, flour, salt, and water in the bowl of a stand mixer fitted with the paddle attachment. Set the mixer on the second speed (medium speed on

You should still be able to see large pieces of frozen butter in the dough.

Give the dough a book fold, or double fold, by folding the short ends to the middle until they meet, without allowing them to overlap. Then fold one half over the other half.

Mark the dough with your fingertips as a reminder.

a hand-held mixer) and mix for about 1 minute. Stop the mixer as soon as the ingredients begin to form a dough and pull away from the side of the bowl. Add the frozen butter cubes all at once and mix on low speed only long enough to distribute them throughout the dough, about 15 seconds. When you stop mixing, you will still see large pieces of frozen butter.

Remove the dough from the mixer and pat it into an 8 × 10-inch rectangle about 1 inch thick. Make sure the pieces of butter are evenly dispersed throughout the dough. Wrap the dough completely in plastic wrap and let it rest in the refrigerator for a minimum of 1 hour and a maximum of 12 hours. The resting period allows any gluten strands (page 12) that have developed to relax.

Remove the dough from the refrigerator and place it on a lightly floured work surface. It is important not to add too much flour to the dough at this point, or it will be tough. Roll out the dough lengthwise into a 10 × 23-inch rectangle. Try to keep it an even thickness. You will be able to see pieces of butter as you roll out the dough. If the dough starts to break, stop rolling and place it in the refrigerator for about 15 minutes to allow the gluten to relax. Give the rolled-out dough what is known as a book fold or double fold by folding each short end to the middle so they meet but do not overlap. Then, fold one half over the other half. Rotate the dough so the seam is on your right. You have completed fold #1. (The process is called a book fold because the folded dough resembles a book and a double fold because the dough is folded onto itself two times.)

Repeat the folding process by rolling out the dough into a 10 × 23-inch rectangle again and folding it again exactly as described in the above paragraph. When you have completed the second book fold, wrap the dough well in plastic wrap and let it rest in the refrigerator for a minimum of 1 hour. To remind myself that I have folded the dough two times, I make two indentations in the dough with my fingertips. (At this stage, the puff pastry can be kept well wrapped in the refrigerator for one day or in the freezer for up to two months. If it has been kept in the freezer, let it thaw in the refrigerator before taking the dough to the next step.)

Remove the dough from the refrigerator. Give the dough two more book folds, starting each time with the 10 × 23-inch rectangle. After the fourth and final fold, let the dough rest in the refrigerator for 1 hour well wrapped in plastic wrap. As a reminder, I make four indentations in the dough. (At this point, it can still be stored in the refrigerator for another day or returned to the freezer.)

To use the puff pastry, roll it out to the thickness and shape specified in the recipe you are using. Usually puff pastry is baked at a high temperature (about 400°F/200°C) for the first 15 minutes of baking to produce steam and to fully develop the flavor of the butter. This quick blast of steam gives the puff pastry its initial rise. Then the temperature is lowered to a medium oven (300° to 350°F/148° to 175°C) to bake and dry it.

Perfect puff pastry is baked all the way through, evenly browned, and well risen. It should be light and flaky and have a delicate texture.

If your dough becomes too elastic as you work, wrap it well in plastic wrap and let it rest in the refrigerator for half an hour. You can tell the dough is elastic when it snaps back after each roll with the rolling pin.

To keep the gluten development to a minimum and to keep the butter in the dough from melting, follow these rules: Use your fingers instead of your hands as much as possible. The less you touch and work the dough, the better. If the dough begins to get sticky, place it in the refrigerator until the butter hardens.

In this recipe, butter is added in two different forms. Melted butter distributes fat evenly throughout the dough. Fat breaks down gluten, keeping the dough tender. Frozen butter, however, does not distribute evenly; it creates pockets in the dough. Steam is produced when the moisture in the butter comes in contact with the heat of the oven. The pockets expand, causing the puff pastry to rise. If you added only melted butter, no pockets would form to cause a rise. If you added only frozen butter, uneven fat distribution would result in tough dough.

Classic Génoise

TWO 12 × 18-INCH SHEETS OR TWO 8-INCH ROUND CAKES

G énoise is a spongy cake layer often soaked with syrup. I always use this recipe to make wedding cakes because of its melt-in-your-mouth quality.

There is no chemical leavening in this recipe. The génoise depends on air trapped in the beaten eggs for its leavening, so take the time to beat the eggs well. For this reason, be sure to preheat the oven and prepare your baking sheet or cake pan in advance, as the batter must be baked as soon as it is ready or it will deflate.

8 large eggs			
3 large egg yolks			
Granulated sugar	*1 cup*	*7 ounces*	*200 grams*
Honey	*2½ tablespoons*	*1.7 ounces*	*50 grams*
Unbleached, unbromated pastry flour (see below), sifted	*2 cups*	*8.8 ounces*	*250 grams*

Place a 1-quart saucepan half-filled with water over high heat and bring it to a simmer. Make a double boiler by setting a large mixing bowl over the simmering water. Place the whole eggs, egg yolks, sugar, and honey in the mixing bowl and make an egg foam by whisking the mixture to 113°F (45°C) on a candy thermometer, 7 to 10 minutes. The egg foam passes through various stages, becoming foamy and then smooth, and finally it will thicken. When it is thick, it will be hot to the touch, tripled in volume, and light in color, and the sugar will have completely dissolved. If you dip the whisk into the mixture and pull it out, the batter should fall back into the bowl in a thick ribbon.

Remove the mixing bowl from the heat and whip the batter with an electric mixer on medium-high speed until it cools, increases in volume, stiffens slightly, and becomes pale yellow, 7 to 10 minutes. Take the time to whip it well; if the mixture is underwhipped, the baked génoise will be dense. Very, very carefully, fold in the flour with a rubber spatula until it is no longer visible, making sure to fold to the bottom of the bowl. Do not overmix, or the batter will deflate.

I bake the génoise on a baking sheet 99 percent of the time because I can then cut it to any size I want. Spread the batter on two parchment paper–covered baking sheets and bake in a preheated 400°F (200°C) oven until lightly and evenly browned and springy to the touch, about 10 minutes. If using cake pans, fill two buttered and parchment paper–lined 8-inch round cake pans three-quarters full. Bake at 350°F (175°C) until well risen and golden brown, about 30 minutes. Génoise is baked at a higher temperature and for a shorter period of time on a baking sheet rather than in a cake pan to allow it to retain moisture; if overbaked, it will be dry and crunchy.

Let the génoise cool slightly. Unmold and finish cooling on a wire rack to allow the air to circulate evenly around the cake. The baked génoise can be stored in the freezer for two to three weeks if well wrapped in plastic wrap. Return it to room temperature before using it.

Variation: You can easily make this recipe into a Chocolate Génoise by substituting unsweetened cocoa powder for 10 to 20 percent of the weight (a scant ¼ cup to a full ⅓ cup/0.8 to 1.6 ounces/25 to 50 grams) of the flour. Weigh the cocoa powder before you sift it.

Génoise can also be made with butter. In this recipe, you can substitute unsalted butter (5½ tablespoons; 2.7 ounces; 75 grams) for the 3 large egg yolks. Melt and cool the butter, then fold it in after the flour is added to the batter.

For génoise, I like to use a pastry flour that is unbleached and unbromated, like that made by King Arthur. The bleaching process cooks out the starch and toughens the gluten, which will keep the génoise from rising as nicely. Unbromated flour does not contain potassium bromate, a potentially carcinogenic chemical sometimes added to flour to adjust its protein level or encourage it to quickly mature or oxidize.

Biscuit

iscuit is a cake layer often used in pastry. While the recipe is pretty simple, it can be used to make the most elaborate desserts.

Everybody makes biscuit differently. The traditional way is to combine half of the sugar with the egg whites and half with the egg yolks. I think it is safer to combine all the sugar with the egg whites (meringue) and then to fold in the egg yolks, followed by the flour. Using this method, the batter won't collapse as easily. Some prefer to use lots of egg whites for a very light cake, while others prefer to use butter or additional egg yolks for a denser, moister, tastier cake.

I think I have found a good balance with this recipe.

6 large egg whites			
Granulated sugar	**¾ cup**	**5.25 ounces**	**150 grams**
8 large egg yolks, slightly beaten			
Pastry flour, sifted	**1 cup + 2½ tablespoons**	**5.2 ounces**	**150 grams**
Powdered sugar for dusting			

Place the egg whites in a large mixing bowl and whip with an electric mixer on medium speed until foamy. Make a French meringue by adding the granulated sugar 1 tablespoon at a time. Increase the mixer speed to medium-high and whip to stiff but not dry peaks, about 7 minutes. Very gently fold in the egg yolks with a rubber spatula until they are partially incorporated. Then gently fold in the sifted flour. It is important to fold as gently as possible to avoid deflating the batter.

The biscuit can be spread on parchment paper–covered baking sheets in any shape required for the dessert you are making. Always sprinkle the top with powdered sugar to form a nice crust once baked.

The biscuit is baked in a preheated oven at a high temperature (400° to 450°F/ 200° to 232°C) for a short amount of time, 6 to 10 minutes. It should be golden brown and slightly springy to the touch. Remove the biscuit from the oven and immediately unmold onto a cooling rack; otherwise, the heat from the pan will continue to bake it. Remove the parchment paper when the biscuit is cool.

If it is not to be used immediately, wrap the biscuit in plastic wrap and store in the refrigerator for up to two days or in the freezer for two to three weeks.

When you separate eggs, crack the eggs on your work surface. If you crack them on the edge of the bowl, the broken shell may pierce the yolk, which can cause a bit of yolk to go into the egg whites. If this happens, the meringue will not reach its full volume because of the fat in the egg yolks.

Meringue Cake Layers

TWO 8-INCH ROUND CAKE LAYERS OR TWELVE 2½-INCH INDIVIDUAL MERINGUES

I use this baked meringue in place of a génoise or biscuit to add a crispy texture to a cake or dessert. This is also a great recipe to use when creating a low-fat dessert because it contains no fat. It works well with all types of fillings.

I love this recipe because you can make it in one bowl in no time. The only challenge is to bake the meringue without letting it take on too much color.

5 large egg whites			
Granulated sugar	**¾ cup**	**5.25 ounces**	**150 grams**
Powdered sugar, sifted, plus extra for dusting	**1⅓ cups**	**5.5 ounces**	**150 grams**

Place the egg whites in a large mixing bowl and whip with an electric mixer on medium speed until foamy. Make a French meringue by adding the granulated sugar 1 tablespoon at a time. Increase the mixer speed to medium-high and whip to stiff but not dry peaks, about 7 minutes. Delicately fold in the powdered sugar with a rubber spatula. It is important to fold as gently as possible to avoid deflating the meringue.

continued

Place the meringue in a pastry bag and pipe it into the shape called for in the recipe you are using.

The process of baking meringue is a cross between baking it and drying it. Always sprinkle the top with powdered sugar before baking to form a nice crust. Preheat the oven to 200°F (93°C). Bake the meringue for about 1 hour if the shape is up to 1 inch thick, 1½ hours if thicker. If the meringue starts to take on color, your oven is too hot; reduce the oven temperature 50°F (10°C) and continue baking. A well-baked meringue is light in color, moist, and slightly chewy on the inside with a firm, crunchy crust.

Once baked, remove the meringue from the oven and let cool completely. The baked meringue may be used immediately or stored for two to three weeks at room temperature in an airtight container.

The whipping process transforms the egg whites from a clear liquid to an opaque white color with a mousselike consistency. Stiff peaks are formed when the egg whites are opaque and glossy and hold their shape without falling. To test this, dip the beaters into the beaten egg whites and pull them straight up. Overwhipped egg whites lose volume and look grainy and separated, like scrambled eggs. If egg whites are overwhipped, they cannot be evenly distributed throughout a batter.

Fruit Sauce 1

1¼ CUPS (12 OUNCES; 350 GRAMS)

This is a great recipe to use if you have access to a gourmet store that carries fruit purees. You can buy many different kinds and keep them in the freezer. This recipe is quick and easy to create. I make my sauces in advance and keep them on hand to jazz up any dessert.

The amount of sugar in the puree varies depending on the type of fruit used and the manufacturer. Usually the manufacturer adds sugar equal to 10 percent of the weight of the puree. The sugar retains the natural flavor of the fruit. Powdered sugar is used in this recipe instead of granulated sugar because it is easier to dissolve. It also contains cornstarch, which thickens the sauce.

Frozen fruit puree, defrosted	**1¼ cups**	**10.5 ounces**	**300 grams**
Powdered sugar	**⅓ cup + 1½ tablespoons**	**1.5 ounces**	**50 grams**

Pour the puree into a deep mixing bowl or tall container. If the puree is not completely smooth, stir it with an immersion blender or whisk. Add the sugar 2 tablespoons at a time, incorporating it well after each addition and making sure all lumps are dissolved. Watch the consistency and frequently taste for sweetness. The desired sauce is equally sweet and tangy, and smooth. You may not need to use all of the sugar or you may need a little bit more. If too little sugar is added, the sauce will be runny and tart. To fix this, add more sugar. If too much sugar is added, the sauce will be overly thick and sweet, and it will taste starchy because of the cornstarch in the sugar. To fix this, add more puree. The sauce is the ideal consistency when it holds its shape when dripped onto a plate.

This fruit sauce is very convenient to use. Store it in a squeeze bottle and drizzle it over the dessert or decorate the plate. It will keep in the refrigerator for two to three days if stored in an airtight container.

Fruit Sauce 2

1¼ CUPS (12 OUNCES; 350 GRAMS)

I love this recipe because it allows me to be creative and economical at the same time. When I have fresh fruit that is past its prime, it is usually still good for making sauce. It is hard to make a bad fruit combination and sometimes I make some pretty amazing discoveries! The only real consideration is the color of the finished sauce.

To make this sauce, it is best to use a blender, food processor, or immersion blender. You will also need a chinois or fine-mesh sieve. Use ripe, flavorful fruit, or your sauce will have no taste. Fruits that make especially good sauces are the berries and really colorful fruits like mango and papaya. I use powdered sugar here because it dissolves easily and the cornstarch it contains thickens the sauce.

Fresh fruit	About 3 cups	10.5 ounces	300 grams
Powdered sugar	⅓ cup + 1½ tablespoons	1.5 ounces	50 grams

Peel, core, seed, or pit the fruit as appropriate and chop into medium-size pieces. Puree the fruit until completely smooth. Add the sugar 2 tablespoons at a time, incorporating it well after each addition and making sure any lumps are dissolved. Watch the consistency and frequently taste for sweetness. The desired sauce is equally sweet and tangy, and smooth. You may not use all of the sugar, or you may need to add a little bit more. If too little sugar is added, the sauce will be runny and tart. To fix this, add more sugar. If too much sugar is added, the sauce will be overly thick and sweet, and it will taste starchy. To fix this, add more puree. The sauce is the ideal consistency when it holds its shape when dribbled onto a plate.

Strain the sweetened puree through a chinois or fine-mesh sieve into a clean bowl. This will separate the pulp from the fruit puree and remove any small seeds. Stir the puree until completely smooth. It will keep in the refrigerator in a small airtight container or zippered-top plastic bag for up to three days or in the freezer for up to two months.

When using fruits like raspberries, blueberries, or bananas, add a few drops of lemon juice to enhance the flavor and to prevent oxidation (browning).

Chocolate Sauce

2⅔ CUPS (23.5 OUNCES; 675 GRAMS)

E veryone loves chocolate sauce and it is easy to please with this recipe. Taste is its most important aspect, so it is imperative to use the best-quality bittersweet chocolate. I usually use a European bittersweet chocolate like Callebaut from Belgium. A lesser-quality chocolate will produce a sauce with inferior flavor.

The deep chocolate flavor of this sauce will satisfy even the toughest chocoholic. It is great to make in batches to give away as gifts, and it makes a wonderful hot fudge sauce that hardens to a chewy texture when poured over ice cream. Make this sauce a staple in your refrigerator.

Whole milk	*Generous 1 cup*	*8.8 ounces*	*250 grams*
Bittersweet chocolate, chopped		*10.5 ounces*	*300 grams*
Heavy cream	*Generous ½ cup*	*4.4 ounces*	*125 grams*
Unsalted butter	*2 tablespoons*	*1 ounce*	*30 grams*
Granulated sugar	*¼ cup + 2 tablespoons*	*2.5 ounces*	*75 grams*

Pour the milk into a 2-quart heavy-bottomed saucepan, place over medium-high heat, and bring to a boil. When the milk boils, remove it from the heat and make a ganache by adding the chopped chocolate. Whisk well, stirring into the edge of the saucepan to combine. The ganache should be homogenous and smooth. Set the ganache aside.

In a 1-quart heavy-bottomed saucepan, combine the heavy cream, butter, and sugar. Place the saucepan over medium-high heat and bring to a boil, stirring occasionally. The butter should be completely melted and the sugar completely dissolved. Once the mixture has come to a boil, pour the cream into the warm ganache.

Place the sauce over medium-high heat and bring to a boil, stirring constantly with a whisk. As the chocolate sauce cooks, it will begin to thicken slightly. When it reaches a boil, remove it from the heat and pour it into a clean, dry bowl. Cover by placing plastic wrap directly on top of the sauce to prevent a skin from forming. Let the chocolate sauce cool to room temperature before storing in the refrigerator. When cold, the chocolate sauce will become thick enough to be scooped with a spoon.

continued

One of the wonderful qualities of this sauce is that it can be reheated whenever needed. If using a microwave, simply place the chocolate sauce in a microwaveable bowl and heat it at medium-high power in 30-second intervals until it becomes liquid. On the stovetop, place it in a heavy-bottomed saucepan over medium heat and stir occasionally until it becomes liquid. If you store it in a squeeze bottle, you can easily drizzle it over a dessert or decorate a plate. It will keep in the refrigerator for up to three weeks. It can also be frozen for up to two months if stored in an airtight container, to be kept on hand for a last-minute dinner party. Thaw in the refrigerator and heat as described above until liquid.

Linda's Red Raspberry Jam

SEVEN 8-OUNCE JARS

y sister-in-law Linda's raspberry jam is legendary. If you have ever been given a jar, you know why. This recipe was passed to Linda and Kris by their grandmother. Linda tells me "Gram" used to take the girls berry picking every summer. The ritual meant getting up early on a July day, driving to the berry farm to pick the fruit, and returning home by noon to make the jam. Of all the jams and jellies Linda creates, this is the one I love and use the most. Now, when I visit her in the summer, she shares with me the time-honored tradition of making red raspberry jam.

Fresh raspberries	**5 cups**	**25.6 ounces**	**684 grams**
Powdered pectin	**1 box**	**1.75 ounces**	**49 grams**
Granulated sugar	**6 ¾ cups**	**47.8 ounces**	**1350 grams**
Unsalted butter	**1½ tablespoons**	**0.75 ounce**	**21 grams**

Carefully wash the berries and pat dry. Set aside. Wash and rinse seven 8-ounce glass canning jars. Keep the jars warm until ready to fill by leaving them in a sink filled with hot water. Fill a small saucepan with water and place over medium heat. Place the washed and rinsed canning lids and metal bands in the pan and bring to a simmer. Remove from the heat and set aside, leaving the lids and bands in the hot water until ready to use.

Place enough of the berries in an 8- to 10-quart heavy-bottomed enamel or stainless steel pot or kettle to cover the bottom. It is important to use a large pot so the jam will have enough room to rise in the pot when it boils. Use a potato masher to gently crush the berries. Add another layer of berries and crush them; repeat until all of the berries are in the pot. Add the pectin and bring to a full boil over high heat, stirring constantly with a wooden spoon. Add the sugar and butter and stir thoroughly. Bring the mixture to a full, rolling boil. (A rolling boil is one that cannot be stirred down.) At this stage, boil hard for 1 full minute, stirring constantly. Remove from the heat. Use a large spoon to skim and discard the foam that has formed.

Remove a hot jar, lid and band from the hot water. Use a sterilized jar funnel to fill the jar with the hot jam to $1/4$ inch from the top. Carefully clean the rim of the jar with a clean damp cloth. Place the lid and band on the jar and twist the band just until the lid is firmly secured—do not twist tightly at this stage. Fill each of the remaining jars in the same way. Set aside.

Sealing the jars using a water bath is optional. Be sure to read the back of the box of pectin for canning instructions. Modern techniques instruct you to simply invert the jars and when cool, turn them upright and they'll seal. Linda uses a water bath because it was the way she learned from her Gram.

To make a water bath: Use either the pot you used for the jam (clean it first) or a water bath canner. Fill the pot with about 6 inches of water and place over high heat until the water boils. It will be easiest if you set the jars in a canning rack and place the rack in the boiling water. If you do not have a canning rack, you will need to use a jar lifter to carefully place the jars upright on the bottom of the pot. The water should cover the jars by at least 1 inch. Cover the pot and allow the water to boil for 10 minutes. Remove from the heat. Carefully remove the jars from the water. Linda usually sets the jars on top of a folded dish towel on the counter. As the jars cool, a tight vacuum seal is formed. You will hear the lids make a dull "ping" noise and see that each lid has indented slightly. If you have a jar that was not filled at least $1/4$ inch from the top or if the rim of a jar was not completely clean, it may not seal. In that case, store the jar in the refrigerator and use within two months. The sealed canned jam can be stored at room temperature in a cool, dark place for up to one year. Refrigerate it once opened.

Angel Hair

ngel hair is a versatile decoration that adds drama or whimsy to any dessert. It is so easy to make that I usually assign the task to the newest person on my team. Aside from his culinary background and wonderful personality, I hired Simon because he was tall enough to reach the top shelves where the sugar is stored. I gave him the instructions for making angel hair and left the kitchen to check on a private party. When I came back, there were strands of sugar everywhere! Apparently, I forgot to tell him to use short strokes.

Remember, you are working with hot sugar, so be sure to have a bowl of cold water ready in case you get any sugar on your skin. This recipe will produce clear or pale yellow angel hair, depending on how long you cook the sugar. After it is removed from the heat, you can add food coloring to it to make the hot sugar any color you desire. It is best to make angel hair on a dry day, as humidity will "melt" the sugar.

Granulated sugar	**2½ cups**	**17.5 ounces**	**500 grams**
Water	**Scant ½ cup**	**3.5 ounces**	**100 grams**
Light corn syrup	**Scant ⅔ cup**	**7 ounces**	**200 grams**

Place the sugar, water, and corn syrup in a 2-quart heavy-bottomed saucepan over medium-high heat. Insert a candy thermometer and cook until it reaches 311°F (155°C). At that point it is cooked to the hard crack stage (page 16). Remove from the heat and pour into a medium-size heatproof glass bowl; if you leave the sugar in the saucepan, the sugar will continue to cook and turn dark brown. A glass bowl will hold the temperature of the sugar. I put a towel under the bowl to keep the bowl from tipping over and to protect my hands from the heat of the glass.

Place the bowl and towel on your work surface. Hold a wooden dowel horizontally in front of you, about 1 foot above a work surface covered with a sheet of parchment paper. With your other hand, dip a fork into the hot sugar, hold it above the bowl until the sugar flows in an even stream, and then rapidly wave the fork back and forth about 6 inches above the dowel. As the sugar falls freely from the fork, it will stretch into thin strands. When the dowel is completely covered, gently remove the angel hair and set aside. Repeat until you have used all of the sugar or have made the desired amount of angel hair. Use immediately.

Pastries and Puff Pastries

◆ ◆ ◆

MY *FIRST POSITION AS an apprentice in a small pastry shop in France was working with dough. To me, dough is very sensual. You can feel that it is alive as you knead it with your hands. It has a natural connection to the earth. When fermenting, it even smells like the earth. You can imagine how excited I am to have a new kitchen at the restaurant with one whole room for making dough.*

The recipes in this chapter are based on two different kinds of dough: one leavened with steam and the other with yeast. There are many things to learn about flour and how it reacts with moisture and yeast. You may find the information on pages 11–13 and pages 17–18 helpful. When you work with dough, you have to be prepared to adapt the amount of liquid called for in the recipe because flour reacts to the temperature and the humidity of the air. For example, you may need to decrease the amount of liquid added to the dough on a hot, humid day. In this chapter, I talk a lot about gluten. To understand the role that it plays, see page 12.

Napoleons

8 SERVINGS

This is one of the most popular French desserts in the United States. The French call it *mille-feuilles,* which means "a thousand leaves." I don't know why it is called a Napoleon unless it was named for Napoleon Bonaparte. Perhaps he was always holding his stomach because he ate too many Napoleons! I love the contrasting textures of flaky, crispy pastry and cool, creamy filling. Like Napoleon, I've been suspected of eating a few too many myself!

I like to decorate the plate with fresh fruit. My favorites are sliced strawberries, raspberries, blueberries, and diced mango and papaya. I also decorate with mango and raspberry sauces (pages 43 and 44) for color and taste.

1 recipe Quick Puff Pastry (page 35)

1 recipe Pastry Cream (page 26), flavored

Light corn syrup	³/₄ cup	8.5 ounces	255 grams
Water	Scant ¼ cup	1.75 ounces	50 grams
Powdered sugar	¼ cup	1 ounce	32 grams

Sliced fresh fruit (optional)

Prepare the puff pastry and let it rest for 1 hour in the refrigerator. While it rests, prepare the pastry cream. Let the pastry cream cool and store it in the refrigerator until

ready to use. Flavor the cold pastry cream as desired. I like to use raspberry vodka, Grand Marnier, or grated orange zest.

Preheat the oven to 350°F (175°C). Roll out the puff pastry to a 12 × 32-inch rectangle about ⅛ inch thick. Cut the rectangle in half and place each half on a parchment paper–covered baking sheet. Bake the puff pastry until it begins to take on color, about 10 minutes. The puff pastry may rise unevenly in sections; if that happens, release the air by gently piercing the dough with the tip of a paring knife.

continued

Mix together the corn syrup and water. Remove the puff pastry from the oven and brush the top of each rectangle with the corn syrup mixture. Cover each with a sheet of parchment paper and flip them. Peel off the parchment paper that is now on top. Brush this side with the corn syrup mixture. The corn syrup mixture adds sweetness, enhances the color as it caramelizes, and makes the puff pastry crunchier. Return the puff pastry to the oven and bake until evenly golden brown inside and out, about another 20 minutes. The baked puff pastry should be evenly risen, flaky, and tender. If you keep an eye on it while it is baking, you can pierce any additional air bubbles as they form. Remove the baking sheet from the oven and cool on a wire rack.

When the puff pastry has cooled, use a serrated knife to cut it into 4-inch squares. You will need three squares for each Napoleon. Set aside the eight most evenly risen squares to be used as the tops of the Napoleons. With a fine-mesh sieve, liberally sprinkle only these tops with the powdered sugar.

To assemble the Napoleons: Fill a pastry bag fitted with a ¾-inch star tip with the flavored pastry cream. Pipe a small dollop of pastry cream in the center of each plate. This will keep the Napoleons from sliding. Center a puff pastry square over each dollop of pastry cream. Pipe three rows of pastry cream onto each square. At this point, you can add a layer of fresh fruit. Top with a second layer of puff pastry. Apply another three rows of pastry cream, but this time pipe in the opposite direction. If you added fresh fruit in the first layer, your dessert will look more consistent if you repeat it here. Place the sugared puff pastry squares on top and serve immediately.

Variation: Make one big Napoleon instead of individual desserts. Bake three equal-sized pieces of puff pastry in any shape desired. The assembly instructions are the same. Be sure to use a serrated knife to cut it.

I use an electric pasta machine to roll out my puff pastry because it rolls it evenly without overworking the dough. If you don't have an electric pasta machine, lay a ⅛-inch-thick yardstick on either side of the dough. Allow the rolling pin to rest on the yardsticks as you roll out the dough. This will ensure that the dough is rolled to the proper thickness.

Pithiviers

*I*f you invite me to your house for dinner, this is probably the dessert I will bring. I get around town on my Rollerblades. When invited to dinner, I put a frozen Pithiviers in my backpack and I'm out the door. My friends are usually pretty disappointed when they see the flat, unbaked disk of dough. I smile and tell them to be patient. As the Pithiviers bakes, its mouthwatering aroma interrupts the conversation. By the time we finish dinner, the Pithiviers is done. What comes out of the oven is a beautiful golden brown dessert that is eight times its original height. My friends cannot believe the transformation!

For the Pithiviers

⅓ recipe Quick Puff Pastry (page 35)

½ recipe Almond Cream (page 28)

For the egg wash

2 large egg yolks			
1 large egg			
Whole milk	¼ cup	2 ounces	50 grams

For the glaze

Light corn syrup	Generous ¼ cup	2.8 ounces	85 grams
Water	1½ tablespoons	0.75 ounce	20 grams

Prepare the puff pastry and let it rest for 1 hour in the refrigerator. While the puff pastry rests, prepare the almond cream, place it in a pastry bag with a large opening (no tip), and set aside.

Prepare the Pithiviers: Cut the puff pastry dough in half and roll each half into an 8½-inch circle about ⅛ inch thick. Place one of the circles on a parchment paper–covered baking sheet. Pipe a 5-inch-diameter mound of almond cream in the center of the circle. The mound should be about 1 inch high.

continued

Prepare the egg wash: Whisk together the egg yolks, whole egg, and milk in a small bowl until well combined. Lightly brush the 1½-inch rim of the pastry circle with the egg wash. Place the second circle of puff pastry over the first. Gently press against the sides of the almond cream mound to remove any trapped air. Seal the edges of the two layers by pressing the top edge into the bottom edge. This will keep the almond cream from running out as it bakes. Use a sharp knife to give the circle a fluted edge. It should look like a flower when finished. Use a sharp knife to cut a ½-inch slit in the top layer at the center of the almond cream mound. This will allow steam to escape during baking.

This dessert usually has a classic pattern scored into its top. If you would like to try it, use a sharp knife to score a curved line that begins at the top of the mound and ends at the bottom of the mound. Repeat this line every ½ inch around the circumference of the mound, but be careful not to cut through the top layer and into the almond cream. Let the Pithiviers rest in the refrigerator for 1 hour before baking. (At this point, you can wrap the Pithiviers well in plastic wrap and freeze for up to 2 weeks. Let it thaw in the refrigerator, or in your backpack, before baking.)

Preheat the oven to 350°F (175°C). Bake the Pithiviers until it begins to brown slightly, about 20 minutes.

Meanwhile, prepare the glaze: Stir together the corn syrup and water. Remove the Pithiviers from the oven and brush it well with the corn syrup mixture. This adds sweetness, enhances the color, and gives it a crispy crust. Continue to bake until well risen and evenly browned, about another 20 minutes. The baked Pithiviers should be flaky and tender, and the almond cream center still moist. Remove the baking sheet from the oven and let cool on a wire rack. The Pithiviers is best when served while it is still slightly warm. Use a serrated knife to slice it.

I can't tell you how long the baked Pithiviers can be stored, because I never have any leftovers!

Bomboloni

4 ½ DOZEN BOMBOLONI

This is one of Mr. Maccioni's favorite recipes. He loves bomboloni, so he sent me to Italy to learn how to make them. As far as I know, Le Cirque was one of the first restaurants to make this dessert in the United States. I like to serve them filled with pastry cream or with my sister-in-law Linda's fresh raspberry jam. The pastry cream or jam should be made before you start.

I strongly suggest that you use a stand mixer for this recipe. I cannot guarantee that the motor of a hand-held mixer will hold up to the strength of this dough.

Fresh compressed yeast	**Scant ¼ cup (loosely packed)**	**1 ounce**	**25 grams**
Cold water	**Scant ¼ cup**	**1.75 ounces**	**50 grams**
Bread flour, plus extra if needed	**3½ cups**	**17.6 ounces**	**500 grams**
4 large eggs			
Granulated sugar, plus extra for coating	**⅓ cup**	**2.2 ounces**	**60 grams**
Salt	**1½ teaspoons**	**0.3 ounce**	**9 grams**
Unsalted butter, cubed	**¾ cup + 2 tablespoons**	**7 ounces**	**200 grams**
Vegetable or canola oil for deep-frying			
Double recipe Pastry Cream (page 26; optional)			
1 recipe Linda's Red Raspberry Jam (page 46; optional)			

In a small bowl, dissolve the yeast in the cold water. Place the flour, eggs, sugar, and salt in the bowl of a stand mixer fitted with the paddle attachment and beat on medium speed until the ingredients are dispersed, about 5 seconds. Add the dissolved yeast and beat on medium-high speed until the dough is well combined and holds together, about 2 minutes. Add the cubed butter and mix until the dough no longer sticks to the side of the mixing bowl, another 5 to 7 minutes. If the dough is overly sticky, you may need to add about 1 tablespoon more flour. (It is usually necessary to scrape down the side of the

bowl with a rubber spatula to encourage the dough to form a ball and come away from the side.) Remove the paddle and pat the dough into a ball at the bottom of the bowl. Cover the mixing bowl with plastic wrap and let the dough rest at room temperature for about 20 minutes. The dough will rise slightly.

Remove the dough from the mixing bowl and punch it down to remove the air. Spread it out on a lightly floured baking sheet with your fingers and flatten the dough until it is about ¾ inch thick. Cover with plastic wrap and let it rest in the refrigerator for a minimum of 2 hours, or overnight. It will proof slightly (page 70).

Remove the dough from the refrigerator and place on a lightly floured work surface. Flatten it slightly with your hands so it is about ¾ inch thick again. Cut the dough into circles with a 1½-inch-diameter plain cutter, keeping the cuts as close together as possible. Pat any leftover dough into a rectangle and cut more circles out of it. (At this stage, the bomboloni can be frozen for up to one week if well wrapped in plastic wrap. Allow to defrost in the refrigerator before continuing.)

Lightly dust a cloth-covered (I use a clean dish towel) baking sheet with flour and place the bomboloni on it, spacing them 2 inches apart. Loosely cover the baking sheet with plastic wrap; this keeps the bomboloni from developing a skin while proofing and traps the heat generated from fermentation, which helps them to rise. Allow the bomboloni to proof at room temperature for about 2 hours. When fully proofed, they will have doubled in size and appear light and full of air.

About 15 minutes before the bomboloni have finished proofing, in an electric deep fryer or in a 4-quart heavy-bottomed saucepan over medium-high heat, heat the oil to 330°F (165°C). If using a saucepan, you will need to fill it about halfway with oil and check the temperature with a candy thermometer. It is important to maintain this temperature, so you may need to turn down the heat or remove the pan from the burner briefly once the oil reaches it. If the oil is too hot, the outside of the bomboloni will burn before the inside cooks. If the oil is too cool, the bomboloni will absorb too much oil as they fry. Fry only five to seven bomboloni at one time; any more than that and the oil temperature will dip down too much, and they will not fry evenly or well.

Fry the bomboloni until they are golden brown, 3 to 5 minutes. Turn them once to fry evenly on each side (I turn them with chopsticks). As they fry, they will increase in size. Remove the bomboloni from the hot oil with a large slotted spoon and set on paper towels or a dish towel to drain the excess oil.

While the bomboloni are still warm, roll them in a bowl filled with granulated sugar until they are evenly coated. They can be served plain or filled.

The easiest way to fill the bomboloni is with a pastry bag fitted with a ¼-inch plain tip. Fill the pastry bag with pastry cream or jam. Use a sharp paring knife to make a small hole in the bottom of each bomboloni. Place the tip of the pastry bag in the hole and squeeze until the bomboloni feels heavy. It is easier to fill the bomboloni while they are still warm and the dough is a little softer.

Bomboloni should be served within 2 hours of frying. Do not place them in the refrigerator, or the fried dough will condense and become heavy.

In this recipe, it is very important to use bread flour, as low-protein flours do not produce enough gluten. The dough will deflate if the flour does not have enough gluten to hold the developing yeast (page 12).

Heat created from the friction between the dough and the mixer causes the temperature of the dough to rise. If the temperature rises too much, the butter will melt and the yeast cells will be killed. When you use a food processor to make the dough, you are more likely to over-mix and produce heat, melting the butter.

Baba au Rhum

ONE 10-INCH BABA OR FOURTEEN 3-INCH BABAS

I first learned how to make this dessert during my apprenticeship. Originally the pastry shop sold Babas about once a week. One time, I made a mistake and added three times as much rum as the recipe required. After that, my boss asked me to make Babas every other day. I don't know which was more popular, the Babas or the rum!

Don't be confused: When this is made in a hollow mold (like a Bundt pan), it is really called a Savarin, but I call it a Baba. I strongly suggest that you use a stand mixer for this recipe. The dough is too strong for most hand-held mixers and could cause damage to the motor.

For the Baba

Unsalted butter, melted and cooled	**4¹/₂ tablespoons**	**2.25 ounces**	**63 grams**
Fresh compressed yeast	**1³/₄ tablespoons (loosely packed)**	**0.5 ounce**	**13 grams**
Cold water	**2 tablespoons**	**1 ounce**	**30 grams**
Bread flour	**1³/₄ cups**	**8.8 ounces**	**250 grams**
4 large eggs			
Granulated sugar	**2 tablespoons**	**0.8 ounce**	**23 grams**
Salt	**¹/₂ teaspoon**	**0.1 ounce**	**3 grams**

For the soaking syrup

1 vanilla bean			
Water	**3³/₄ cups + 2 tablespoons**	**31.75 ounces**	**895 grams**
Granulated sugar	**2¹/₂ cups**	**17.5 ounces**	**500 grams**
Grated zest of 2 lemons			
Grated zest of 2 oranges			

For the garnish

Dark rum	**¹/₂ cup**	**3.5 ounces**	**100 grams**
Heavy cream, whipped to stiff peaks	**Generous 2 cups**	**17 ounces**	**500 grams**
Assorted sliced fresh fruit (optional)			

continued

Prepare the Baba: The first step is to melt the butter in a small saucepan over low heat. Allow the butter to cool to room temperature. It will appear milky and should be pourable and warm to the touch.

In a small bowl, dissolve the yeast in the cold water. Place the flour, eggs, sugar, and salt in the bowl of a stand mixer fitted with the paddle attachment and beat on medium speed just until the ingredients are dispersed, about 5 seconds. Add the dissolved yeast and beat on medium-high speed until the dough is well combined and holds together, about 2 minutes. Add the cooled butter and mix until the dough no longer sticks to the sides of the mixing bowl, another 7 to 10 minutes. The dough will be very sticky at this stage. Remove the paddle attachment. Cover the mixing bowl with plastic wrap and let it rest at room temperature for about 20 minutes. This will allow the gluten to rest and start the fermentation (page 70). If the dough is allowed to rest for more than 20 minutes, the texture of the dough will break down and the baked Baba will fall apart when soaked in the syrup.

While the dough is resting, butter and lightly flour the mold or molds; if you use a new mold, you will need to use more flour because old molds usually retain some fat. Individual molds looks like very large thimbles, about 2 to 3 inches high. (They are known as baba or *timbale* molds in French.) When using individual molds, fill them one third full with the dough. In either case, cover loosely with plastic wrap to trap the heat generated during fermentation. This will help the dough to proof. (At this stage, you can put the mold(s) in the refrigerator for a few hours, or overnight, until you are ready to proceed.)

When the dough has risen to within 1/4 inch of the top of the mold(s), remove the plastic wrap. (If the rising dough touches the plastic wrap, it will stick to it and the dough will deflate when you attempt to remove the wrap.) Let the uncovered dough rise to the top of the mold(s). The whole proofing process will take 40 to 60 minutes. The dough will take longer to rise in a cooler kitchen than a warmer one. After the dough rises, you should put it in the oven within an hour, or it will collapse.

Preheat the oven to 375°F (190°C). Bake the large Baba until it has risen to about one and a half times its size and the top is golden brown, 30 to 40 minutes. If it browns too much during baking, lower the temperature of the oven by 50°F (10°C). If you are making individual-size Babas, the baking time is 10 to 15 minutes. Remove the Baba(s) from the oven, unmold onto a wire rack, and let cool for about half an hour. (At this stage, you can store the Baba or Babas in an airtight container in the refrigerator for three to four days.)

Prepare the soaking syrup: Use a sharp knife to slice the vanilla bean in half lengthwise. Separate the seeds from the skin by scraping the blade along the inside of the bean. Combine the water, sugar, citrus zests, and the entire vanilla bean—seeds and skin—in a 1-quart heavy-bottomed saucepan and bring to a boil. Remove the syrup from the heat and let it cool for half an hour.

Place the large Baba on a wire rack over a baking sheet. The baking sheet will catch the excess syrup. When the syrup is warm, not hot, to the touch, ladle it over the Baba, allowing the Baba to soak up as much as it will absorb. It will eventually absorb most of the syrup, so recycle whatever has drained onto your baking sheet. If you have made individual Babas, you can use tongs to submerge them directly in the syrup. In this case, let them soak for about 3 minutes, then drain them on a rack over a baking sheet. (At this stage, you can store the soaked Baba or Babas in the refrigerator for one day.)

Sprinkle the top of the Baba(s) with rum to taste. I like to pour the rum directly on top of the Baba(s) instead of adding it to the sugar syrup, as this keeps the alcohol from evaporating and gives a stronger rum taste. Let the excess syrup drain for about 10 minutes and place the Baba(s) on a platter.

To garnish the Baba: Place the whipped cream in a pastry bag fitted with a ¾-inch star tip. Pipe the whipped cream into the center of the Baba ring. Individual Babas should be sliced three-quarters of the way through the middle, slicing from top to bottom. Fill the center with whipped cream. Sometimes I decorate the top with sliced fresh fruit too. Traditionally a Baba is served cold. I prefer it at room temperature for maximum flavor.

When you work with fresh yeast, be careful when you add it to a mixing bowl. Don't place the salt directly on top of it, or it will kill the yeast.

Croissants and Pain au Chocolat

20 CROISSANTS OR 16 *PAIN AU CHOCOLAT*

I used to save my allowance to buy a croissant every morning on my way to school. I usually arrived at the pastry shop just as the baker pulled them from the oven. When it was time to do my apprenticeship, I chose that same pastry shop, hoping I would be allowed to eat fresh croissants every day!

I never use a hand-held electric mixer for this recipe because the motor will not hold up to the strength of the dough. This recipe involves six quick steps and a lot of waiting time. When I want croissants for Sunday brunch, I do the first three steps on Saturday afternoon. On Sunday morning, I get up three hours before I want to serve them and complete the last three steps. You can make both croissants and *pain au chocolat* with this dough.

For the dough

Unsalted butter	3 tablespoons	1.5 ounces	40 grams
Fresh compressed yeast	Scant ¼ cup (loosely packed)	1 ounce	25 grams
Cold water	Generous ½ cup	4.5 ounces	125 grams
Bread flour, plus extra if needed	3⅓ cups	17.6 ounces	500 grams
Salt	2 teaspoons	0.4 ounce	12 grams
Granulated sugar	⅓ cup	2.3 ounces	65 grams
Whole milk	Generous ½ cup	4.5 ounces	125 grams
Room temperature unsalted butter	1 cup + 2 tablespoons	9 ounces	250 grams

For *pain au chocolat*

Bittersweet chocolate, chopped		9 ounces	250 grams

For the egg wash

2 large egg yolks

1 large egg

Whole milk	Scant ¼ cup	1.8 ounces	50 grams

continued

Prepare the dough: Melt the 3 tablespoons butter in a small saucepan over low heat. Allow the butter to cool to room temperature. It will appear milky and should be pourable and warm to the touch.

In a small bowl, dissolve the yeast in the cold water. Place the flour, salt, sugar, milk, and melted butter in the bowl of a stand mixer fitted with the paddle attachment. Set the mixer on medium speed and mix just until the ingredients are dispersed, about 5 seconds. Add the dissolved yeast and beat on medium-high speed until the dough is well combined and no longer sticks to the sides of the bowl, about 1 minute. If the dough is too soft, add more flour 1 tablespoon at a time until it is firmer. (The dough is too soft if it cannot hold its shape.) If the dough is too firm, add cold water 1 tablespoon at a time until it has softened. (The dough is too firm when it is difficult to mix.) Remove the dough from the mixing bowl. If the dough is slightly sticky and ropy, knead it with your hands for about 30 seconds, until it is smooth. Pat it into a ball. Place the dough on a lightly floured baking sheet, cover with plastic wrap, and let it proof at room temperature for about 30 minutes. This will start the fermentation process (see below).

Place the dough on a lightly floured work surface and roll it out to an 8 × 15-inch rectangle about ¼ inch thick. Wrap the rectangle in plastic wrap and refrigerate for 2 hours. The cold retards the rising process, which allows for a slow fermentation; a slow fermentation helps develop the flavor of the dough.

Remove the dough from the refrigerator, unwrap it, and place it with a long side facing you on a lightly floured work surface. Spread the softened butter evenly over the right two thirds of the dough. I like to use a large offset spatula to do this. Incorporate the butter by folding the (butterless) left third of the dough over the center, then fold the right third of the dough to the left. Now the dough should resemble a folded letter. Roll it out into a 10 × 30-inch rectangle about ⅛ inch thick. Give the dough a book fold, or double fold, by folding each short end to the middle so they meet but do not overlap. Then fold one half over the other half and, if necessary, rotate the dough so that the seam is on your right. (This process is called a book fold because the folded dough resembles a book and a double fold because the dough is folded onto itself two times.) Wrap the folded dough in plastic wrap and let it rest in

Spread the softened butter over two thirds of the rolled-out dough.

Fold the left (butterless) third of the dough to the center (to start the single fold).

Fold the right third of the dough to the left (to finish the single fold). Now the dough should resemble a folded letter.

Fold the short ends of the dough to the middle until they meet (to start the double fold).

The folded dough should meet in the center but not overlap.

Fold one half over the other half (to complete the double fold). The folded dough should resemble a book.

the refrigerator for a minimum of 2 hours. (At this stage I usually let the dough rest overnight and finish it in the morning.)

The following procedure is the final step before you form the croissants or *pain au chocolat*. Remove the dough from the refrigerator, unwrap it, and place on a lightly floured work surface. Roll it into a 10 × 30-inch rectangle and turn it so a long side faces you. Give the dough a single fold by folding the left third of the dough over the center, then fold the right third of the dough to the left. Now the dough should resemble a folded letter. Wrap in plastic wrap and let it rest in the refrigerator for 30 minutes.

continued

For Croissants

Cut out triangles with a 2½-inch base and 10-inch sides.

Lay each triangle on the work surface with the tip facing you.

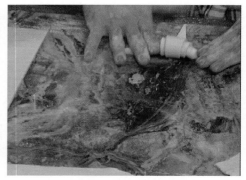

Use your fingers to roll the triangle from the base to the tip.

For *Pain au Chocolat*

Cut the dough into 3½ x 4½-inch rectangles. Place about ½ tablespoon of the chopped chocolate in the upper third of each rectangle. Fold that third over the chocolate.

Place about another ½ tablespoon of chocolate along the seam of the folded dough. Fold the bottom third of the dough over the chocolate.

Proofed croissants and pain au chocolat versus unproofed

Remove the dough from the refrigerator and place it on the lightly floured work surface. Roll out the dough into a 10 × 36-inch rectangle about ¼ inch thick. Keep the thickness even and the edges straight. This will make it easier to cut the croissants or *pain au chocolat.*

For croissants: Use a sharp chef's knife to cut out triangles with a 2½-inch base and 10-inch sides. Lay each triangle on the lightly floured work surface with the tip facing you. Gently pull the tip toward you; this light stretch adds layers to the finished croissant without adding density. Use your fingers to roll each triangle up from the base to the tip. (At this stage, they can be frozen for up to one week if well wrapped in plastic wrap. Thaw on a parchment paper–covered baking sheet overnight in the refrigerator before proceeding.)

Place the croissants on a parchment paper–covered baking sheet. The croissants will get bigger as they proof and bake, so space them about 2 inches apart. Loosely cover the baking sheet with plastic wrap. This keeps the croissants from developing a skin while proofing and traps the heat released during fermentation, which helps them to rise. Allow the croissants to proof at room temperature until they have doubled in size and appear light and full of air; this can take anywhere from 1½ to 3 hours, depending on the temperature of the room and of the dough.

For *pain au chocolat*: With a sharp chef's knife, cut the dough into 3½ × 4½-inch rectangles. Lay each rectangle on a lightly floured work surface, with a longer side facing you, and place about ½ tablespoon of the chopped chocolate in the upper third of each one. Fold that third of the dough over the chocolate. Place about another ½ tablespoon of chocolate along one seam of the folded dough. Fold the bottom third of the dough over the chocolate. (At this stage, they can be frozen for up to one week if well wrapped in plastic wrap. Thaw on a parchment paper–covered baking sheet overnight in the refrigerator before proceeding.)

Turn over the *pain au chocolat* so the seams face down. This will keep them from opening as they bake. Place them on a parchment paper–covered baking sheet; they will get bigger as they proof and bake, so space them about 2 inches apart. Loosely cover the baking sheet with plastic wrap and allow the *pain au chocolat* to proof at room temperature until they have doubled in size and appear light and full of air, 1½ to 3 hours, depending on the temperature of the room and of the dough.

Preheat the oven to 400°F (200°C). Make the egg wash by whisking together the egg yolks, whole egg, and milk in a small bowl until well combined. With a pastry brush, very gently coat the croissants or *pain au chocolat* completely with egg wash. Bake until golden brown, about 10 minutes. I love to eat both of these fresh out of the oven. If you have any leftovers, they can be stored in the freezer if well wrapped in plastic wrap for up to two weeks. Thaw at room temperature and warm in the oven before serving.

continued

Fermentation is a process that happens in any dough containing yeast. It begins as soon as the ingredients are mixed together, and continues until the dough reaches an internal temperature of 138° to 140°F (58° to 60°C) during baking, at which point the yeast dies. The ideal proofing environment is 80° to 98°F (27° to 36°C) with 80 to 85 percent humidity.

Both the carbon dioxide released during proofing and the steam produced during baking create air bubbles, which expand and push at the layers of the dough, giving the dough its rise. If the dough is too firm, it does not allow the air bubbles to expand. If the dough is too soft, it cannot hold the air bubbles. The type of flour used can contribute to the consistency of the dough. Bread flour, or high-protein flour, is needed to develop a strong enough structure to withstand the expansion of the layers. If cake or pastry flour is used, the dough will tear before it develops. Don't confuse a strong structure with an elastic dough. You can make a tender dough with a strong structure as long as you let the dough rest long enough to allow the gluten to relax.

Cookies and Petits Fours

◆ ◆ ◆

WHEN I FIRST MOVED to this country, I could not believe the amount of space the grocery stores dedicate to cookies. The diet food section is tiny, but cookies take up a whole aisle! While I was working in California, the American obsession with cookies became even more apparent to me and I decided to cash in on the concept. Part of my job was to make cookies for the afternoon meeting breaks at the hotel where I worked. Every day, I made big batches of jumbo cookies. With my limited English skills, it was difficult to make friends, so I decided to let my cookies do the talking. At 2:45, I telephoned Kris and her coworkers from the sales office to say, "Cookies are ready!" At 3:00,

I called the young ladies from the executive office to repeat the invitation. At 3:15, it was time for the front office staff. Well, everything went fine until the day Kris arrived late!

Make cookies . . . lots of cookies. They taste great and you never know where they might lead you!

Biscotti

ABOUT 5½ DOZEN BISCOTTI

The owner of Le Cirque, Sirio Maccioni, is from a small town in Italy called Montecatini. When he invited me to visit one summer, I pictured myself lying by his pool. Instead, I met a chef from his old neighborhood and spent the day learning how to make biscotti.

Traditionally, the Italians bake biscotti two times to produce a hard cookie that they like to dip in sweet wine. I adapted the recipe so the cookies are not quite so hard and also cut the baking time in half. I use cold butter so I can roll and bake them right away.

These fragrant, flavorful cookies are great by themselves or dunked in coffee. Since I'm from Provence, I prefer to dip mine in pastis.

For the biscotti

Whole unblanched almonds	**¾ cup**	**4 ounces**	**100 grams**
Whole pistachios	**⅓ cup**	**1.6 ounces**	**50 grams**
Cold unsalted butter, cubed	**7 tablespoons**	**3.5 ounces**	**100 grams**
Granulated sugar	**¾ cup**	**5.25 ounces**	**150 grams**
All-purpose flour	**2 cups**	**8.8 ounces**	**250 grams**
Anise seeds	**1 tablespoon**	**0.3 ounce**	**8 grams**
Baking powder	**1 teaspoon**	**0.2 ounce**	**6 grams**
Grated zest of 1 lemon			
Pinch of salt			
2 large eggs			

For the egg wash

1 large egg white, beaten

Prepare the biscotti: Preheat the oven to 300°F (150°C). Spread the almonds and pistachios evenly on a baking sheet and place in the oven. Toast for about 30 minutes, until they are golden brown. You will be able to smell the nuts when they are ready. A good test is to break a nut in half and check to see if it is light brown on the inside. Toasting the nuts brings out their natural flavor. Remove them from the oven and allow to cool completely on the baking sheet on a wire rack.

Place the remaining ingredients in a large mixing bowl and beat with an electric mixer on medium speed until well combined, about 5 minutes; the mixture will hold together in a soft dough. Add the cooled toasted nuts and mix until they are evenly incorporated, about 1 minute. If you are using a hand-held mixer, you may want to knead in the nuts by hand to avoid burning out the motor of the mixer.

Remove the dough from the mixing bowl and place on a very lightly floured work surface. If the dough is sticky and hard to work with, it is too soft. To fix this, flatten it into a disk, cover with plastic wrap, and place it in the refrigerator for a minimum of 1 hour. (When the butter in the dough gets cold, the dough will stiffen.) Remove from the refrigerator and proceed.

Preheat the oven to 350°F (175°C). Divide the dough into three equal pieces. Use the palms of your hands to roll each piece on the lightly floured work surface into a rope 1 to 1½ inches in diameter. Each rope should be even and fit on your baking sheet lengthwise. If the dough sticks to your hands or to the work surface as you are rolling it, dust it lightly with flour. Roll firmly to remove any trapped air bubbles. (At this stage, you can wrap the dough well in plastic wrap and freeze for up to two weeks. Bring it back to room temperature before baking.)

Place two of the biscotti ropes on a parchment paper–covered baking sheet. You will only have room for two because they spread as they bake. With a pastry brush, lightly brush each rope with the egg white; this will add shine to the baked biscotti. Bake until golden brown, about 30 minutes. Remove from the oven and let cool slightly on the baking sheet.

Use a serrated knife to slice the biscotti on a diagonal into ½-inch-thick cookies. If you do this while the biscotti are still warm, they will not crumble. The biscotti will harden as they cool. If they are still soft when you slice them, place the slices on a baking sheet and bake at 300°F (150°C) for another 10 to 15 minutes. Repeat the baking and cooling procedure with the remaining biscotti rope.

Store in an airtight container at room temperature for two to three weeks.

Variation: Dip the biscotti halfway on a diagonal into tempered bittersweet chocolate (page 9). Wipe the excess chocolate from the tip and place the biscotti on a sheet of parchment paper to allow the chocolate to set.

Langues de Chat

ABOUT 9 DOZEN SANDWICHED COOKIES

I first learned how to make these cookies when I started my apprenticeship in the South of France twenty-two years ago. I still have not figured out why they are called *langues de chat,* or cat's tongues.

These cookies are traditionally served with jam in the middle but I also like them plain. They make an elegant finish to any meal when dipped in chocolate and displayed on a plate.

Room temperature unsalted butter	*½ cup*	*4 ounces*	*113 grams*
Powdered sugar	*1 cup + 2 tablespoons*	*4.6 ounces*	*130 grams*
1 vanilla bean			
4 large egg whites			
Pastry flour	*1 cup*	*4.5 ounces*	*130 grams*
Linda's Red Raspberry Jam (page 46; optional)	*1 cup*	*10.8 ounces*	*300 grams*
Bittersweet chocolate, tempered (page 9; optional)		*12.3 ounces*	*350 grams*

Place the butter and sugar in a medium-size mixing bowl and beat with an electric mixer on medium-high speed until creamy. Use a sharp knife to slice the vanilla bean in half lengthwise. Separate the seeds from the skin by scraping the blade of the knife along the inside of the bean. Add the vanilla seeds to the butter mixture and continue mixing until it lightens in color and gains volume.

Add half of the egg whites and mix until combined. Add half of the flour and mix

until the flour is no longer visible. Add the remaining egg whites, again mixing until well combined. Mix in the remaining flour just until it is incorporated and the dough is smooth. I add the egg whites and flour in two additions for a more homogenous mixture. If your dough separates while you are adding the egg whites, don't worry. It should come back together smoothly with the final addition of flour. The separation happens when there are not enough dry ingredients to hold the liquid ingredients together. After the final addition of flour, do not overmix, or the dough will become tough and elastic (see page 12 for an explanation of gluten). Place the dough in a pastry bag fitted with a ¼-inch plain tip. Let the dough rest at room temperature for about 1 hour.

Preheat the oven to 350°F (175°C). Pipe 2½-inch-long diagonal lines of dough onto a nonstick or buttered and lightly floured baking sheet. Try to use even pressure when piping to ensure each cookie has an even thickness. Leave about 1 inch between the cookies to allow for spreading. Bake until they begin to take on color, 6 to 8 minutes. Only the edges should brown very slightly; the rest of the cookie should remain light. Remove the baking sheet from the oven. The cookies will be less likely to break if you let them sit for about 2 minutes before transferring them to a wire rack to cool completely.

When the cookies are cool, spread the jam between two of them and sandwich them together. For a more elegant finish, dip them halfway on the diagonal into the tempered bittersweet chocolate. Gently wipe the excess chocolate from the end of each cookie before placing them on parchment paper. The chocolate should set in a few minutes if the kitchen is not too hot.

The cookies can be stored in an airtight container at room temperature for up to three days.

Langues de chat batter can be frozen for up to one week. Freeze it in a pastry bag fitted with a ¼-inch plain tip and thaw in the refrigerator before using. If you let it sit at room temperature for about 20 minutes, it will be easier to pipe the batter. Then you are ready to go!

Dame Blanche

ABOUT 26 SANDWICHED COOKIES

One of my earliest memories is making these cookies with my mom. It was an all-day affair, since she made the jam from scratch. Now I see my mom only once a year. To let her know she is always on my mind, I make a big batch of these and send them to her on Mother's Day. My dad really loves that!

The texture of these cookies is like shortbread and the jam adds sweetness and moisture. Displayed on a platter, they make a simple and elegant finish to any meal.

For the dough

Cold unsalted butter, cubed	**¾ cup + 2 tablespoons**	**7 ounces**	**200 grams**
Almond flour	**½ cup**	**1.7 ounces**	**50 grams**
Powdered sugar	**¾ cup + 2 tablespoons**	**3.5 ounces**	**100 grams**
2 large eggs			
1 vanilla bean			
Pastry flour	**1 cup**	**4.4 ounces**	**125 grams**
All-purpose flour	**1 cup**	**4.4 ounces**	**125 grams**
Pinch of salt			

To finish the cookies

Linda's Red Raspberry Jam (page 46)	**½ cup**	**5.4 ounces**	**153 grams**
Powdered sugar	**¼ cup**	**1 ounce**	**32 grams**

Prepare the dough: Place the butter, almond flour, sugar, and eggs in a large mixing bowl. Mix with an electric mixer on medium speed until the mixture looks like scrambled eggs. Use a sharp knife to slice the vanilla bean in half lengthwise. Separate the seeds from the skin by scraping the blade of the knife along the inside of the bean. Add the vanilla bean seeds, pastry flour, all-purpose flour, and salt and mix on medium speed just until everything is incorporated, about 1 minute. If you overwork the

dough, it will become tough and elastic. Remove the dough from the bowl and pat it into a rectangle. Wrap it in plastic wrap and place in the refrigerator for 30 minutes to allow the dough to stiffen. (You can make the dough a day in advance and let it rest overnight.)

Preheat the oven to 350°F (175°C). Remove the dough from the refrigerator, place on a lightly floured work surface, and roll out into a $1/8$-inch-thick rectangle. If the dough sticks to the work surface or rolling pin, lightly dust each with flour. The thinner you roll it, the stickier it is likely to become. I like to use a $2^{1}/_2$-inch-wide heart-shaped cookie cutter to form the cookies, but you can use any shape and size you like; a fluted cutter makes a more decorative cookie. Cut as many cookies from the dough as you can and place them about 1 inch apart on a parchment paper–covered baking sheet. Pat together any leftover dough, gently roll it out, and use it for more cookies.

Use the top of a 1-inch plain decorating tip to cut the centers from half of the cookies on the baking sheet. Bake the cookies until they are light brown, about 10 minutes. Remove the baking sheet from the oven, place on a wire rack, and let cool completely.

To finish the cookies: Spread the raspberry jam to $1/4$ inch from the edge of each whole cookie and set aside. Place the powdered sugar in a fine-mesh sieve and liberally sprinkle the surfaces of the cut-out cookies. Now all you have to do is sandwich the cut-out tops and the bottoms together. These cookies will keep for four to five days if stored in an airtight container at room temperature.

Decorative Shortbread Cookies

ABOUT 20 CHECKERBOARD COOKIES AND 40 SPIRAL COOKIES

*A*ll my friends ask me how I make these cookies. They look complicated but the technique is pretty simple. I give the explanation of both checkerboard and spiral techniques because I think the combination looks great on a plate. The light orange and chocolate flavors go well with afternoon tea.

For the plain dough

½ *vanilla bean*			
Cold unsalted butter, cubed	¾ **cup + 2 tablespoons**	**7 ounces**	**200 grams**
Powdered sugar	**1 cup + 1½ tablespoons**	**4.4 ounces**	**125 grams**
4 large egg yolks			
Grated zest of ½ orange			
Pinch of baking powder			
Pinch of salt			
All-purpose flour	**2 cups**	**10.6 ounces**	**300 grams**

For the chocolate dough

Cold unsalted butter, cubed	¾ **cup + 2 tablespoons**	**7 ounces**	**200 grams**
½ *vanilla bean*			
Powdered sugar	**1 cup + 1½ tablespoons**	**4.4 ounces**	**125 grams**
4 large egg yolks			
Grated zest of ½ orange			
Pinch of baking powder			
Pinch of salt			
All-purpose flour	1⅔ **cups**	**8.4 ounces**	**240 grams**
Unsweetened Dutch-processed cocoa powder	½ **cup**	**2.1 ounces**	**60 grams**

continued

Prepare the plain dough: Use a sharp knife to slice the vanilla bean in half again, this time lengthwise. Separate the seeds from the skin by scraping the blade of the knife along the inside of the bean. Place the butter, sugar, egg yolks, vanilla bean seeds, and orange zest in a medium-size mixing bowl and beat with an electric mixer on low speed until the ingredients are combined, about 1 minute. Combine the baking powder, salt, and flour and add to the butter mixture all at once. Beat on low speed just until combined, about 1 minute. Do not overmix the dough, or it will become tough (see page 12 for an explanation of gluten). Remove the dough from the bowl. Form it into a 4 × 9-inch rectangle, wrap in plastic wrap, and place in the refrigerator.

Prepare the chocolate dough: Repeat the procedure described above, combining the cocoa powder with the flour and adding it to the butter mixture.

Let each dough rest in the refrigerator for at least 1 hour. I prefer to make the doughs a day in advance and let them rest overnight. This allows the doughs to chill thoroughly and the gluten to relax. Overnight all of the flavors (orange, vanilla, chocolate, butter) mature and the flour and butter absorb the flavor of the cocoa; the next day, the chocolate dough will be darker in color.

Preheat the oven to 400°F (200°C).

To make the checkerboard pattern: Remove the doughs from the refrigerator and divide each piece in half. Place one piece of each color on a work surface and put the other two back in the refrigerator. The dough will be hard when it comes out of the refrigerator and you will need to give it a few quick raps with a rolling pin to make it easier to roll. Lightly flour each side of each piece of dough and roll each into a 5 × 10-inch rectangle about ¼ inch thick. If either dough breaks, just push it back together. Lightly brush the surface of one rectangle with water. Lay the other rectangle on top of it.

Cut four 1 × 10-inch strips from the stacked dough. Set the scraps of dough aside. Lay two strips of alternating colors next to each other. Add a second layer, placing a plain strip on top of the chocolate strip and a chocolate strip on top of the plain strip. Repeat with the remaining strips; work fast so the dough does not get too soft. Mix the dough scraps together to obtain a marbled effect and roll them into a 7 × 10-inch square. Cut the square in half. Brush each half with a thin coat of water (this will help it stick to the checkerboard). Place one checkerboard lengthwise in the center of each of the marbled rectangle halves and wrap the dough around each checkerboard

Start with equal pieces of each dough.

Lightly brush the rolled out dough with water.

Lay the doughs on top of each other.

Cut 1 x 10-inch strips from the stacked dough.

Lay the alternating strips of dough next to each other to create a checkerboard pattern that is 2 strips wide by 2 strips high.

Place the checkerboard lengthwise in the center of the marbled square and wrap the dough around it.

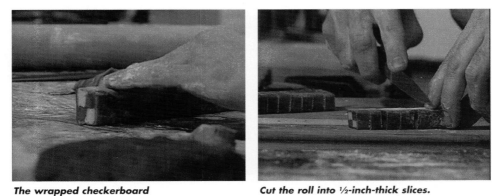
The wrapped checkerboard

Cut the roll into ½-inch-thick slices.

to form a roll. Cut the rolls into ½-inch-thick slices and place them cut side down on a parchment paper–covered baking sheet, about ½ inch apart. Bake until lightly browned, about 15 minutes. Cool on a wire rack.

To make the spiral pattern: Remove the remaining doughs from the refrigerator. They will be hard, so give them a few quick raps with a rolling pin to make them easier to roll. Lightly flour each side of each piece of dough. Roll each piece into a 7 × 16-inch rectangle about ⅛ inch thick. Place one rectangle on top of the other and roll out to an 8 × 20-inch rectangle. Brush the rectangle with a thin coat of water to help the dough stick to itself. Starting at a long side, roll the dough into a cylinder 1½ to 1¾ inches in diameter. Cut the cylinder into ½-inch-thick slices. Lay the cookies cut side down on a parchment paper–covered baking sheet, about ½ inch apart. Bake until lightly browned, about 15 minutes. Cool on a wire rack.

Store the cookies in an airtight container at room temperature for up to 5 days.

Before you roll out dough, pat it into the shape you eventually want it to be. That way, as you roll it, it will be easier to keep that shape. That is why I form the dough into a rectangle before I let it rest in the refrigerator.

To make spiral cookies, roll the stacked dough into a cylinder that is 20 inches long and 1½ to 1¾ inches in diameter.

Finish rolling the cylinder, keeping it as even as possible.

Cut the cylinder into ½-inch-thick slices.

Place the cookies on a parchment paper–covered baking sheet about ½ inch apart.

Old-fashioned Macaroons

ABOUT 55 SANDWICHED COOKIES

There are many macaroon recipes but I think this one is the easiest to make and to remember: One part sugar, one part almond paste, and as many egg whites as needed to bring the mixture to a consistency that can be piped. With those ratios in mind, you can make as much or as little of the batter as you like.

We make a lot of macaroons at Le Cirque. My sous-chef and I try to make it fun by racing to see who can pipe them onto a baking sheet the fastest. The loser has to wash the dishes. I'm not sure if I win all the time because Ken is a good sport or because I am his boss.

Almond paste	**1½ cups** (firmly packed)	**14 ounces**	**400 grams**
Granulated sugar, plus extra for sprinkling	**2 cups**	**14 ounces**	**400 grams**
4 to 5 large egg whites			

Preheat the oven to 375°F (180°C). Place the almond paste and sugar in a large mixing bowl and beat with an electric mixer on medium-high speed until the almond paste is softened and the sugar well incorporated, about 5 minutes.

Add the egg whites a little bit at a time, incorporating fully after each addition. Egg whites are difficult to pour in small amounts, so hold a rubber spatula against the rim of the bowl and use it to "cut" the egg whites as they are poured. If you add the egg whites all at once, the mixture will be lumpy because the difference in consistency between the egg whites and the almond paste mixture is too great. Use a rubber spatula to scrape down the sides of the bowl as needed. You may or may not need all of the egg whites, depending on the moistness and age of your almond paste. Stop mixing when the mixture reaches a consistency soft enough to pipe (like toothpaste).

Place the batter in a pastry bag fitted with a ½-inch plain tip. Pipe 1-inch mounds onto a parchment paper–covered baking sheet. It will be easier if you hold the pastry bag at a slight angle and allow the tip to touch the parchment as you start to pipe. Once you have formed the mound, stop squeezing and lift the tip straight up, leaving a small tail on the top of each mound. Space the macaroons about 1 inch apart to allow for spreading. Pipe carefully: Your macaroons will look nicest when they are sandwiched together if they are all the same size.

Immediately before placing them in the oven, liberally sprinkle granulated sugar over the macaroons. This will give them a nice crust that will keep the inside moist and chewy. Bake until golden brown, 8 to 10 minutes. The top of each macaroon should be very finely cracked, a characteristic for which they are known. If overbaked, the macaroons will be dry and crunchy.

Remove the baking sheet from the oven and immediately pour ¼ cup of water onto the baking sheet *under* the parchment paper. Be careful: If you get any water on the macaroons, they will be soggy. You will need to tilt the baking sheet to spread the water evenly. Let it sit for 2 minutes. The water will loosen the macaroons from the paper. Remove the macaroons from the paper two at a time and stick them together, matching the flat sides. Do not put them back on the hot, wet baking sheet or they will become soggy.

The macaroons can be stored in an airtight container at room temperature for up to three days or well wrapped in the freezer for up to one week. Unwrap them before bringing back to room temperature, or the condensation will make them soggy.

Palmiers

hen I was a child, this was one of my favorite cookies. I love its crunchiness and the taste of the caramelized sugar. Once you've mastered the technique, these are very easy to make; you can even make them from leftover scraps of puff pastry.

When I first moved to the United States, understanding English was difficult at best, and when I moved to Atlanta, I really had trouble adjusting to the accent. These cookies were like my ambassador of good will. I used to take these special treats to Mrs. Rich at the local bank. I would put on my best smile and hand her my check and a plate of cookies. She was always so helpful—who is to say whether she really loved her job or just liked my cookies.

½ recipe Quick Puff Pastry (page 35)			
Granulated sugar	**1 cup**	**7 ounces**	**200 grams**

Prepare a half batch of quick puff pastry. After the fourth and final fold, wrap the puff pastry in plastic wrap and let it rest in the refrigerator for 1 hour.

Remove the puff pastry from the refrigerator. On a work surface covered with ½ cup of the sugar, roll out the dough into a 10 × 30-inch ⅛- to ¹⁄₁₆-inch-thick rectangle with a long side facing you. Liberally sprinkle the top with the remaining ½ cup sugar. Fold each long side 1½ inches toward the center. Your dough is now about 7 inches wide. Repeat the folding process one more time so the dough is about 4 inches wide; the folds should meet in the center. Then fold the top over the bottom so that you are left with a strip about 2 inches wide. Wrap the dough in plastic wrap. (At this stage, the dough can be stored in the freezer for up to two weeks. Thaw in the refrigerator before using.) Let the dough rest in the refrigerator for 2 hours. It must be cold, or it will not slice well.

Preheat the oven to 400°F (200°C). Palmiers are baked at a high heat to caramelize the sugar. Use a sharp knife to slice the dough into ¼-inch-thick slices and place them cut side down on a parchment paper–covered baking sheet. Space the slices 2 inches apart and the rows 1 inch apart to allow room for expansion.

Bake the Palmiers until they start to take on color, 10 to 15 minutes. Remove from the oven and use a fork or pair of tongs to turn over each one. Bake until they are evenly caramelized, another 10 to 15 minutes. Remove the baking sheet from the oven and place on a wire rack. Allow the Palmiers to cool before you remove them from the baking sheet, or the hot caramelized sugar will burn your fingers. Store the baked Palmiers in an airtight container at room temperature for up to three days.

On a work surface covered with granulated sugar, roll out the dough to an 8 x 20-inch rectangle ¼ inch thick.

Fold each long side toward the center.

Repeat on each side until the folds meet in the center.

Fold the top over the bottom so that you are left with a strip about 2 inches wide.

After slicing them, space the cookies 2 inches apart in rows 1 inch apart.

Arlettes

ABOUT 150 ARLETTES

This is a classic French recipe. It is the same type of cookie as the Palmier (page 86) but the technique is slightly different. Whenever you have leftover scraps of puff pastry, you can use them to make these cookies.

The thin, light, crunchy texture of the Arlette makes it the perfect cookie to serve with ice cream.

½ recipe Quick Puff Pastry (page 35)			
Powdered sugar	**1½ cups**	**6.3 ounces**	**175 grams**

Prepare a half batch of quick puff pastry up to and including the fourth and final fold. Allow the folded dough to rest in the refrigerator for 1 hour.

Cut the dough in half, place one half on a lightly floured work surface, and return the remaining dough to the refrigerator. (I like to work with only half the dough at a time to keep it from getting too soft.) Roll out the dough into an 11 × 17-inch rectangle about ¹⁄₁₆ inch thick, with a long side facing you. Starting at the long side, roll the dough tightly into a cylinder. Brush the edge with a thin coat of water and seal the cylinder by gently pressing the damp edge against the side of the rolled

Roll out the dough to an 11 x 17-inch rectangle ⅛ inch thick. Starting at the long end, roll the dough tightly into a cylinder.

Slice the roll to ¼-inch-thick slices.

Roll out each slice into an oval shape in powdered sugar.

dough. Place it in the freezer until it stiffens enough to slice easily, about 15 minutes.

Remove the cold dough from the freezer and trim the ends of the cylinder to make the edges clean. Slice the roll with a sharp knife into 1/4-inch-thick slices. Place the slices on a work surface well dusted with the sugar and coat both sides of each slice with about 1/2 teaspoon of sugar. The sugar will caramelize in the oven to give these cookies their distinct flavor.

Roll out each slice into an oval shape in the sugar. The gluten (page 12) in the dough will cause it to be elastic, so as you roll out each Arlette, the oval will continually snap back to a smaller size. To overcome this, you will need to roll out the cookies in stages, allowing them to rest briefly between each stage. If they start to stick to the work surface, lightly dust with more sugar. When you reach a 4-inch oval shape, place the Arlette on a parchment paper–covered baking sheet. The Arlettes don't spread too

much in baking, so you can place them close together. Repeat these steps with the remaining half of the dough. Let the Arlettes sit at room temperature for 20 minutes to rest the gluten again.

Preheat the oven to 400°F (200°C). Bake the Arlettes until evenly browned, caramelized, and shiny, about 10 minutes. Remove the baking sheets from the oven and cool on a wire rack.

Arlettes can be stored in an airtight container at room temperature for up to three days, but I think they are best eaten the day they are made.

Candied Grapefruit Peels

ABOUT 180 PIECES

I f you eat a lot of grapefruit and have ever wondered what to do with the peels, this is the recipe for you. I usually wait until I have the peels of at least four grapefruit. It is easy to make a large batch of these and keep them in the refrigerator. They make great petits fours and can be given away as gifts. I especially like the contrast of sweet and citrus after dinner.

The candied peels can be served three ways, depending on personal taste: rolled in granulated sugar, partially dipped in dark chocolate, or au natural.

I prefer to use grapefruit for this recipe, but you can also use orange, lemon, or lime peels.

4 grapefruit			
Granulated sugar	**2¹/₂ cups**	**17.5 ounces**	**500 grams**
For the final presentation			
Granulated sugar (optional)	**1 cup**	**7 ounces**	**200 grams**
Bittersweet chocolate, tempered (page 9; optional)		**26.3 ounces**	**750 grams**

Use a sharp knife to cut each grapefruit into quarters. Remove the fruit from the peel, leaving the white membrane or pith attached to the peel. Save the fruit for another use. Slice each quarter peel on a diagonal into strips about ¹/₂ inch wide. If you cut them evenly, they will look nicer when displayed.

Place the sliced grapefruit peels in a nonreactive 4-quart heavy-bottomed saucepan and add enough water to cover the peels by about 1 inch. Place over high heat and bring to a rolling boil. (A rolling boil is one that cannot be stirred down.) Remove from the heat and drain. Return only the peels to the saucepan, cover again with fresh water, and repeat the boiling and draining process three more times. It is really important to change the water, because it retains the bitterness of the peel.

After the fourth boil, return the drained peels to the saucepan. Add the sugar and enough water to cover the peels by 1 inch. Place over low heat and let simmer for

2 hours. During this time, the sugar will sweeten and preserve the natural flavor of the peels. After 2 hours, they will be soft and translucent and the syrup will be thick. Let the peels cool in the syrup and keep them stored in the syrup, refrigerated, in an airtight container until you are ready to serve. They will keep this way for up to three weeks.

When ready to use, allow the peels to drain on a wire rack for a few hours to remove the excess syrup. I put my rack over a baking sheet so the syrup does not drip all over the table. Once the peels are fully drained, you have three options for serving: First, you can serve them as they are. Second, you can place the peels in a medium-size bowl filled with granulated sugar and roll the peels around in the sugar until they are well coated.

Third, you can dip the sugared peels in a bowl of tempered chocolate. Personally, I love the contrast between the bittersweet chocolate and the acidity of grapefruit. Dip two thirds of each sugared peel into the tempered chocolate. Gently wipe the excess chocolate from the end of each peel before placing on parchment paper. The chocolate should set in a few minutes if the kitchen is not too hot.

Whatever variation you choose, present the peels on a plate, in a small bowl, or, as I do at the restaurant, in petits fours cups.

Once the peels have been sugared and dipped in chocolate, they can be stored in an airtight container at room temperature for up to three days.

Chocolate Cornflakes

ABOUT 6 DOZEN PIECES

I always try to bring contrast to every dessert. I discovered cornflakes ten years ago and, being a pastry chef, wondered what would happen if I covered them with chocolate. I loved it so much that now I take cornflakes home to France and make this recipe for my friends. They wonder about the things I am learning in America, but there are never any leftovers.

Crispness is important, so use a fresh box of cornflakes. You will need to have tempered chocolate ready before you begin. Use the best-quality bittersweet chocolate that you can find. I prefer to use Callebaut chocolate from Belgium.

Cornflakes	4 cups	6 ounces	170 grams
Bittersweet chocolate, tempered (page 9)		16 ounces	454 grams

Pour the cornflakes into a large mixing bowl, then pour about half of the tempered chocolate over them. Use a rubber spatula and mix until they are coated evenly. The tempered chocolate will immediately begin to set. Once the chocolate has set, repeat with the remaining chocolate to give a second coat.

Quickly scoop the chocolate cornflakes into small mounds onto a parchment paper–covered baking sheet. I find it easiest to use one spoon to scoop and another spoon to scrape the scooped mixture onto the baking sheet. It is important to work quickly because the mixture is easier to scoop before the chocolate hardens.

If your kitchen is very hot, you can place the baking sheet in the refrigerator for about 5 minutes to allow the chocolate to harden. Do not leave the cornflakes in the refrigerator for more than 10 minutes; if they get too cold, condensation will form on them when they are removed from the refrigerator because of the difference in temperature between the cold chocolate and the warm air. This will cause the chocolate to turn white. While this doesn't affect the taste, it does ruin the appearance.

Store the chocolate cornflakes in an airtight container in a cool, dry area. They will keep for two weeks, if you can resist eating them.

Chocolate Cornflakes and Chocolate-Covered Almonds

Chocolate-Covered Almonds

ABOUT 5 DOZEN PIECES

One of my fondest memories of growing up in Provence is picking fresh almonds from the tree in our backyard. I used to roast the raw almonds on the top of my parents' wood stove. The smell of the toasting nuts when I make this recipe always reminds me of home.

I use blanched slivered almonds because the skins have already been removed and I prefer the smaller pieces. Blanched almond halves will also work. Tempered chocolate (white or milk) is used as a final sweet coat. You will need to have it ready before you begin.

Slivered, blanched almonds, toasted (page 73) and cooled	4 cups	16 ounces	454 grams
White or milk chocolate, tempered (page 9)		12 ounces	340 grams

Pour the almonds into a large mixing bowl. Pour about half of the tempered chocolate over the almonds and use a rubber spatula to mix until the almonds are evenly coated. The tempered chocolate will immediately begin to set. Once the chocolate has set, repeat with the remaining chocolate to give a second coat. This time, do not wait for the chocolate to set.

Quickly scoop the chocolate almonds into small mounds onto a parchment paper–covered baking sheet. I find it easier to use one spoon to scoop and another spoon to scrape the scooped mixture onto the baking sheet. It is important to work quickly because the almonds are easier to scoop before the chocolate hardens.

If your kitchen is very hot, you can place the baking sheet in the refrigerator for about 5 minutes to allow the chocolate to harden. Do not leave them in the refrigerator for more than 10 minutes. If they get too cold, condensation will form on them when they are removed from the refrigerator because of the difference in temperature between the cold chocolate and the warm air. This will cause them to turn white if you've used milk chocolate.

The chocolate-coated almonds will keep for two weeks if stored in an airtight container in a cool, dry area.

Variation: You can also coat the almonds in corn syrup before toasting them to add a little extra sweetness. To do this, place the almonds and about a cup of corn syrup in a 2-quart heavy-bottomed saucepan over low heat to liquify the corn syrup. You want to heat the mixture only until the corn syrup is thin enough to coat the almonds evenly; this will take 3 to 4 minutes. Remove the saucepan from the heat. Using a large slotted spoon, allow the excess corn syrup to drain as you scoop the almonds onto a parchment paper–covered baking sheet. Be sure to spread them out in an even layer so they will toast evenly in the oven.

Bake at 350°F (175°C) until the almonds are evenly caramelized, 15 to 20 minutes. Keep a close eye on them, as the sugar will burn very soon after it caramelizes. Remove the baking sheet from the oven and place on a wire rack. When the nuts are completely cooled, break apart any almonds that are clustered together. The almonds must be completely cool, because any heat will melt the tempered chocolate.

Caramelized Nuts

5½ CUPS (28 OUNCES; 800 GRAMS)

*I*f you have ever seen a street merchant roasting nuts, you will understand what this recipe is all about. I use almonds, but you can use any nut or a combination of your favorites. It is easiest to use a heavy copper pot that is rounded on the bottom like a bowl. The copper conducts heat evenly and the round bottom lets you tilt the pot to just the right angle for stirring. If you don't have one, a heavy-bottomed saucepan will work just fine as long as you take extra care to stir into the edge.

You can double this recipe, but I suggest you try it a couple of times before you do so, until you've gotten the hang of it. There are four variations to this recipe, each one building on the next. You can serve the nuts simply caramelized, covered in tempered chocolate, or covered with chocolate and rolled in powdered sugar, or cocoa powder.

Granulated sugar	*2 cups*	*14 ounces*	*400 grams*
Water	*1 cup*	*8.2 ounces*	*230 grams*
Whole unblanched almonds	*3½ cups*	*17.6 ounces*	*500 grams*
Bittersweet chocolate, tempered (page 9; optional)		*21 ounces*	*600 grams*
Powdered sugar or unsweetened Dutch-processed cocoa powder (optional)	*1¾ cups*	*7 ounces*	*200 grams*

Place the granulated sugar and water in a large copper pot or 4-quart heavy-bottomed saucepan and bring the mixture to a boil over medium-high heat. Add the almonds and stir to coat them evenly in the sugar syrup. Your goal is to cook the almonds until the sugar crystallizes and caramelizes. Let me explain what happens as you keep stirring! When water is added, the sugar crystals dissolve. As the syrup boils, it becomes thicker as the water evaporates and big soaplike bubbles begin to form. Soon, all the moisture evaporates and the mixture becomes sandy. The sandiness is the sugar recrystallizing. It only takes the reformation of one sugar crystal to recrystallize the others. Keep stirring! Next, you see the sugar closest to the heat change from sandy to a clear liquid. The melted sugar clings to the almonds. When the sugar changes from clear to

Add the almonds to the boiling mixture and stir to coat evenly in the syrup.

Almonds well coated in sugar syrup

The syrup becomes thicker as the water evaporates and big, soaplike bubbles begin to form.

Soon all of the moisture will have evaporated, and the mixture becomes sandy.

You will see the sugar closest to the heat change from sandy to a clear liquid and begin to cling to the almonds.

When the sugar changes from clear to golden brown, the nuts are caramelized.

golden brown, the nuts are caramelized. Once this happens, pay close attention; the time it takes to pass from caramelized to burned is only a matter of seconds, especially when making smaller batches. You know the nuts are finished when most of the sandy sugar is gone.

The first few times you make these, I suggest you try the following: When the sugar closest to the heat changes from sandy to liquid, remove the pan from the burner and continue to stir. The residual heat in the sugar and nuts will continue to cook the mixture while you stir it. Lower the heat to medium-low and continue to stir the nuts while moving the saucepan on and off the heat at 10-second intervals. This will give you more control as it cooks. When the nuts begin to caramelize, remove them from the heat and finish stirring.

continued

The nuts are finished when most of the sandy sugar is gone.

Slowly add the tempered chocolate in thirds, folding thoroughly and allowing it to set each time before adding more.

Add the powdered sugar and fold until the nuts are well coated.

Add the cocoa powder and fold until the nuts are well coated.

Use a wooden spoon to spread the caramelized nuts onto a parchment paper–covered baking sheet. Do not touch the nuts as they are extremely hot. Let the nuts cool completely. If your freezer will accommodate the baking sheet, you can place the nuts in the freezer for about 30 minutes to speed up the cooling process.

When the nuts are completely cooled, break apart any nut clusters that may have formed. At this stage, you can choose to serve the nuts as they are.

If you choose to coat the nuts in chocolate, place the cooled nuts in a large mixing bowl. Slowly add one third of the tempered chocolate and immediately fold the nuts until they are thoroughly coated and the chocolate has set. If you do not fold immediately, the chocolate will set and the nuts will stick together. Add another third of the chocolate and fold thoroughly until set. Add the remaining third and fold thor-

oughly, being sure all the nuts are well coated. Separate any clusters of nuts that have formed. If you plan to serve the nuts as they are, let the chocolate set completely. If you decide to move on to the next step, do not wait for the chocolate to set completely.

Add the powdered sugar or cocoa powder and stir until all of the nuts are well coated. If you'd like to coat half of the nuts in powdered sugar and the other half in cocoa powder, you can use the same bowl if you start with the powdered sugar. Before serving, place the nuts in a sieve to remove any excess sugar or cocoa powder. The nuts will keep in an airtight container at room temperature for up to two weeks.

Mendiants

Mendiant is a small chocolate disk topped with pieces of candied fruits and nuts. I like to use pistachios, almonds, walnut halves, pieces of candied pineapple, and pieces of candied papaya. You can vary this recipe to accommodate your own design. These elegant chocolate candies are quite beautiful when made with toasted nuts caramelized in corn syrup. I like to display them side by side on a silver tray. It's best to make only ten to fifteen at a time, or the chocolate will set before you have a chance to add the nuts and candied fruit.

You will need tempered chocolate in this recipe, so have it ready before you begin. You will also need several cornets (parchment paper cones) to pipe the chocolate; see page 19 for directions on how to make them, and have them ready.

Assorted nuts, chopped	**1 cup**	**5.2 ounces**	**150 grams**
Light corn syrup	**¼ cup**	**3.5 ounces**	**100 grams**
Bittersweet chocolate, tempered (page 9)		**10.5 ounces**	**300 grams**
Assorted candied fruit, diced	**⅓ cup**	**2.6 ounces**	**70 grams**

Preheat the oven to 350°F (175°C). Place the chopped nuts and corn syrup in a 2-quart heavy-bottomed saucepan and place over low heat to liquefy the corn syrup. You want to heat the mixture only until the corn syrup is thin enough to coat the nuts evenly; this will take 3 to 4 minutes. Remove the saucepan from the heat. Using a large slotted spoon, allow the excess corn syrup to drain as you scoop the coated nuts onto a parchment paper–covered baking sheet. Be sure to spread them in an even layer so they will toast evenly in the oven.

Bake until they are evenly caramelized, 15 to 20 minutes. To test for doneness, you can also break a nut in half and check to see if it is light brown on the inside. Keep an eye on the nuts, because the sugar will burn very soon after it caramelizes. Remove the baking sheet from the oven and place on a wire rack. When the nuts are completely cooled, break apart any that are clustered together.

continued

Fill a cornet half-full with the tempered bittersweet chocolate. Pipe a chocolate circle 1½ inches in diameter onto a parchment paper–covered baking sheet. If you do not have a cornet, you can use a spoon; drop a spoonful of the chocolate onto the parchment paper and spread it into a 1½-inch-diameter circle with the back of the spoon. In either case, keep the thickness of the circle as even as possible. Make about 10 circles. Then create your own design as you top each circle with the toasted nuts and candied fruit. Work quickly, or the chocolate will set before you've accomplished this. If the nuts and fruit do not stick to the chocolate, lightly dip them in the bowl of tempered chocolate and "glue" them to the top of the disk. When you finish these, repeat the process until you have used all of the tempered chocolate, nuts, and candied fruit.

Set the Mendiants aside to harden until ready to serve. I think they look better displayed side by side rather than piled on top of each other. Store the Mendiants in an airtight container at room temperature for up to one week.

I Love Chocolate

◆ ◆ ◆

I **LOVE TO WORK WITH** *chocolate because it is so versatile.
It can be molded, sculpted, melted, chilled, piped, or spread, to name a
few techniques. It goes well with almost anything. I like to play with the taste and
texture, creating different combinations at a variety of temperatures. I almost
always work with bittersweet chocolate because I prefer its strong flavor.
Whatever you do, always try to buy the best-quality chocolate you can find.*

*During my vacation last year, I had the opportunity to visit the Callebaut choco-
late factory in Belgium. I spent the day touring their classrooms and laboratories.
I sampled what seemed like hundreds of combinations of chocolate made from
different varieties of cocoa beans. When I visited the manufacturing plant, I was*

amazed to learn that they sell most of their chocolate in liquid form. They pump it into tankers by the ton and transport it around the world. When I have my dream home, I am going to build in a holding tank. I hope they will deliver!

Chocolate Soup

8 SERVINGS

The clients at Le Cirque love chocolate desserts, so I am always trying to come up with new ones. One year, Kris and I went to Disney World. She insisted I try a frozen chocolate-covered banana and, quite frankly, I questioned the concept. Well, I loved it! I didn't think Sirio would be too pleased if I served bananas on a stick at his restaurant, so here is the version I adapted for the dessert menu. I like to top the warm soup with meringue to add another layer of texture and enhance the visual appeal.

For the caramelized bananas

4 large bananas, peeled and diced			
Dark rum	¼ cup	1.6 ounces	50 grams
Granulated sugar	½ cup	3.5 ounces	100 grams
Unsalted butter (optional)	1 tablespoon	0.5 ounce	14 grams

For the soup

Whole milk	4 cups	34 ounces	970 grams
Bittersweet chocolate, chopped		10.5 ounces	300 grams

To finish the soup

7 large egg whites			
Powdered sugar	1¾ cups	7 ounces	200 grams

Prepare the caramelized bananas: Place the diced bananas in a medium-size mixing bowl with the rum and toss to coat. Let macerate at room temperature while you prepare the caramel.

Heat a heavy-bottomed frying pan over medium-high heat. If it starts to smoke, it is too hot and you need to run it under cool water, dry it, and start again. When it is warm sprinkle the sugar into the pan. Try to keep the sugar in an even layer to allow it all to caramelize at the same time. As soon as you see the sugar begin to melt, start moving the pan over the burner to keep the sugar from burning. Tilt the pan from side to side so that the melted sugar runs over the unmelted sugar. Cook until all of the sugar is a light golden brown. I usually add a tablespoon of butter at this stage because it makes the caramel smoother. Add the bananas and rum and spread evenly in the pan. When cooking with alcohol, there is always the chance of it catching on fire, so be very careful when adding the rum. Continue to cook until almost all of the liquid has evaporated and the bananas are soft but not mushy; they should still hold their shape. Remove from the heat and pour the caramelized bananas onto a plate. Cover with plastic wrap and let cool for about 20 minutes. Covering the hot bananas with plastic wrap keeps the caramel from drying as it cools.

Prepare the chocolate soup: Pour the milk into a 2-quart heavy-bottomed saucepan and bring to a boil over medium-high heat. Add the chopped chocolate and stir until well combined and the chocolate has melted. Bring the mixture to a boil again, stirring occasionally. Remove the pan from the heat and set aside while you prepare the soup bowls.

For this recipe, the bowls I use hold 4½ ounces. You can use any oven-safe bowls. Place one large spoonful of the caramelized bananas in the bottom of each soup bowl. The bananas will give texture to the soup, so be generous. Cover the bananas with the hot soup, filling each bowl three-quarters full. Set the soup bowls on a baking sheet and place in the refrigerator until chilled, about 2 hours. The soup will set and thicken, allowing it to support the meringue; chill it well before topping it.

To finish the soup: Place the egg whites in a medium-size mixing bowl and whip with an electric mixer on medium speed until foamy. Increase the mixer speed to medium-high and make a French meringue by adding the powdered sugar 1 tablespoon at a time and whipping the whites to stiff but not dry peaks.

Place the meringue in a large pastry bag fitted with a ¾-inch star tip. Remove the soup from the refrigerator and pipe the meringue onto the tops in a decorative pattern. Place the soup bowls in a deep roasting pan or baking dish and fill it with warm water to come one third of the way up the side of the bowls. Let stand for about 30 minutes to warm the soup. If you do this before you serve dinner, the soup should be ready to be gratinéed by the time you have finished eating.

Preheat the oven to 450°F (232°C). Remove the soup bowls from the warm water bath and place them on a baking sheet. Place in the oven just until the meringue begins to brown, 3 to 5 minutes. The soup should not get hot. Remove from the oven and serve immediately.

When you cut chocolate, start at one corner and always cut it on an angle. Don't try to cut big pieces, because it is too difficult. If you cut on an angle, it will be easier and safer. This way, you do not have to cut so much surface at one time.

Chocolate Soufflé

Soufflés are a staple on the dessert menu at Le Cirque. I make them with a ganache base and a French meringue to give the soufflé the strength to hold until baked. This way, I can prepare them in advance and bake them to order, which is very convenient. One day, Paul Bocuse walked past the soufflé station at Le Cirque and was amazed to see all of our soufflés sitting on the counter. He thought they were already baked and could not believe they had not deflated. Actually, you can pipe the mixture into the molds and let it sit for up to an hour before baking them. This defies everything you have ever been told about soufflés. In fact, you can have a party in your kitchen while these are baking. If you do, be sure to call me!

For the soufflé base

Half-and-half	**¹⁄₃ cup**	**2.4 ounces**	**70 grams**
Bittersweet chocolate, chopped		**1.8 ounces**	**50 grams**
Unsweetened chocolate, chopped		**1.4 ounces**	**40 grams**
Unsweetened Dutch-processed cocoa powder	**¹⁄₃ cup + 1¹⁄₂ tablespoons**	**1.8 ounces**	**50 grams**
Water	**Scant ¹⁄₂ cup**	**3.5 ounces**	**100 grams**

To finish the soufflé

8 large egg whites			
Granulated sugar	**¹⁄₂ cup**	**3.5 ounces**	**100 grams**

For the garnish

Powdered sugar for dusting

Heavy cream, whipped to stiff peaks (optional)

Crème Anglaise (page 24; optional)

Preheat the oven to 375°F (190°C). Soufflés are baked at a high temperature to ensure a good rise. Use a pastry brush to evenly coat the inside of a 1¹⁄₂-quart soufflé mold with softened butter. Fill the mold with granulated sugar, then pour out the excess. If you have properly buttered the mold, the sugar will stick to the side and bottom of it.

continued

The butter and sugar keep the soufflé from sticking to the side of the mold and allow it to rise evenly. The sugar also gives the soufflé a crunchy crust, which I think makes a great contrast to its soft interior.

Prepare the soufflé base: Pour the half-and-half into a 1-quart heavy-bottomed saucepan and heat over medium-high heat until bubbles begin to form around the edge of the pan. Remove from the heat and make a ganache by adding both types of chopped chocolate. Stir until well combined and all of the chocolate has melted.

Place a 1-quart saucepan half-filled with water over high heat and bring to a boil. Make a double boiler by setting a large mixing bowl over the boiling water. Place the ganache in the mixing bowl, add the cocoa powder and water, and whisk until very hot. Remove from the heat and set aside.

To finish the soufflé: Place the egg whites in a large mixing bowl and whip with an electric mixer on medium speed until foamy. Increase the mixer speed to medium-high and make a French meringue by adding the sugar 1 tablespoon at a time and whipping the whites to stiff but not dry peaks. Do not overwhip the egg whites, or they will not incorporate evenly into the ganache, and when baked, the soufflé will have chewy pieces of egg white in it. You can tell the egg whites are overwhipped if they start to separate and resemble scrambled eggs.

Use a rubber spatula to gently fold about half of the meringue into the warm chocolate mixture. Then fold the chocolate mixture into the remaining meringue, being careful not to deflate the batter. The soufflé mixture should be homogenous in color, but if you can still see streaks of meringue in the batter, that's okay.

Use a rubber spatula to gently place the soufflé mixture in the buttered and sugared mold. Fill to about 1 inch above the rim of the mold. Place the soufflé in the center of the oven and remove the top oven rack if necessary to allow enough room for it to rise. If the soufflé is too close to the top of the oven or under a rack, it will stick when it rises. If the soufflé is too close to the bottom of the oven, the bottom of the soufflé will burn before the inside is properly baked. Bake until the soufflé has risen to about one and a half times its original height and starts to brown on top, about 20 minutes. Remove from the oven and dust the top with powdered sugar. Serve immediately with a side of whipped cream or crème anglaise, if desired.

This soufflé can also be baked in individual buttered and sugared molds. Use a pastry bag with a large opening (no tip) to pipe the soufflé mixture into the molds to come about 1 inch above the rim. Bake until risen and lightly browned on top, 6 to 8 minutes.

Chocolate Fondants

14 FONDANTS

This is one of the most requested desserts at Le Cirque. Once you have tasted it, you will know why it is a chocolate lover's fantasy. Although it is often compared to a flourless chocolate cake, it really is a cross between a chocolate mousse and a chocolate soufflé. To make them even more decadent, I cover the baked Fondants with chocolate sauce and decorate them with candied orange or grapefruit peels. Since the peels and sauce take a while to make, you may want to prepare them a day in advance.

It is very important to use the best-quality chocolate for this recipe. I like to use Callebaut from Belgium. Fondants can be prepared in about thirty minutes. Make a double batch and keep half of them in the freezer for a tasty last-minute treat.

For the Fondants

Unsalted butter, cubed	1 cup + 2½ tablespoons	9.4 ounces	260 grams
Bittersweet chocolate, chopped		17.7 ounces	500 grams
Unsweetened Dutch-processed cocoa powder	⅓ cup + 1½ tablespoons	1.6 ounces	50 grams
Pinch of salt			
8 large egg whites			
Meringue powder (optional)	⅓ cup	1 ounce	25 grams
Granulated sugar	½ cup	3.5 ounces	100 grams

For the garnish

Heavy cream, whipped to stiff peaks	Scant 1 cup	8 ounces	220 grams
Candied orange or grapefruit peels (page 90)			
Chocolate Sauce (page 45)			

Preheat the oven to 400°F (200°C). Use a pastry brush to evenly coat the inside of 14 individual 3-ounce molds (I use disposable aluminum molds) with softened butter. Fill each mold with granulated sugar; then pour out the excess. If you have properly

buttered the molds, the sugar will stick to the sides and bottoms of them. The butter and sugar will keep the Fondants from sticking to the sides of the molds and allow them to rise evenly. The sugar will also give the Fondants a crunchy crust, which I think makes a great contrast to the soft interior. It will be easier to move the molds in and out of the oven if you place them on a baking sheet.

Prepare the Fondants: Melt the butter in a 2-quart heavy-bottomed saucepan over medium-high heat. Remove from the heat. Add the chopped chocolate, cocoa powder, and salt and stir until well combined and all the chocolate has melted. The cocoa powder and salt accentuate the taste of the chocolate.

continued

I Love Chocolate

Place the egg whites in a large mixing bowl and whip with an electric mixer on medium speed until foamy. If using the meringue powder, combine it with the sugar in a small bowl. The meringue powder contains a high quantity of albumin, which will add strength and allow for a stiffer meringue. Increase the mixer speed to medium-high and make a French meringue by adding the sugar mixture, or the sugar, 1 tablespoon at a time and whipping the egg whites to stiff but not dry peaks.

Gently but quickly fold the warm chocolate mixture into the meringue until combined. Be careful not to deflate the mixture, or your baked Fondants will be flat and heavy. The mixture should be homogenous in color. However, if you can still see streaks of meringue in it, that's okay.

Place the batter in a large pastry bag with a large opening (no tip). The pastry bag will be easier to handle if you fill it only half full; you will probably need to refill the bag two or three times to use all of the batter. Pipe the molds three quarters full with batter. (At this stage, the molded Fondants can be stored in the freezer for up to 2 weeks, well wrapped in plastic wrap. Thaw in the refrigerator for 2 hours before baking.)

Bake the Fondants until they have risen about ½ inch over the top of the mold, 7 to 10 minutes.

Meanwhile, place the whipped cream in a pastry bag fitted with a star tip and pipe rosettes onto each serving plate. Garnish with candied orange or grapefruit peels. Remove the Fondants from the oven and immediately invert each one over the center of a plate. Lightly tap the bottom and shake slightly to allow the Fondant to gently drop from the mold. Cover the Fondants with the chocolate sauce and serve. When you cut into the Fondant, the center should still be somewhat liquid.

Variation: Sometimes I like to make an orange sauce to accompany the Fondants. Combine 2 cups (16 ounces; 458 grams) orange juice, a scant ½ cup (2.5 ounces; 75 grams) Sure-Jell, and ¾ cup (5.3 ounces; 150 grams) granulated sugar in a nonreactive 1-quart heavy-bottomed saucepan and bring to a boil over medium heat. Cook until the mixture has reduced about one third in volume. Place in an ice bath (page 3) to cool. This will make 1½ to 2 cups sauce.

Chocolate Tartlet

10 TARTS

Chocolate tart is a classic dessert loved by children and adults alike. This one contains three components, all of which are simple and straightforward to make. I have added a layer of macaroon to the tartlets to give them texture and because I think the bitterness of the almond in the macaroon balances the sweetness of the chocolate in the tart. If you prefer, you can omit it; the tartlets will be denser but have a more intense chocolate flavor.

Double recipe Sugar Dough (page 34)

¹⁄₂ recipe Old-fashioned Macaroons batter (page 84)

For the filling

Heavy cream	1 cup	8.8 ounces	250 grams
Honey	2¹⁄₂ tablespoons	1.7 ounces	25 grams
Bittersweet chocolate, chopped		8 ounces	225 grams
Room temperature unsalted butter, cubed	6 tablespoons	3 ounces	87 grams

Butter ten individual 4-inch fluted tartlet pans. Prepare the sugar dough and remove it from the mixing bowl. (If you are using dough that has been refrigerated, you will need to give it four or five quick raps with a rolling pin to break up the cold butter.) Pat the dough into a rectangle and lightly flour each side. Roll the dough into a 17 × 22-inch rectangle between ¹⁄₈ and ¹⁄₄ inch thick. After each roll with the rolling pin, rotate the dough a quarter turn. This will keep it from sticking to your work surface and help to keep the shape of the rectangle. Dust the work surface with flour if needed, but be careful not to overflour, as this will make the dough tough. Don't press too hard on the rolling pin, or you will cut the dough in half. Work quickly to keep the butter from melting and the dough from becoming too soft. If this does happen, place the dough in the refrigerator until it is firm once again, about 15 minutes.

Use a 5-inch plain or fluted round cutter to cut out ten circles from the rectangle. Dust off any excess flour and place each circle in a tartlet pan. Use your fingers to gently press the dough into the bottom and side of each pan. Be sure you

press into the edge where the side of the pan meets the bottom. Dock the bottom of each tartlet shell with a fork to allow the steam to escape during baking and to keep the tartlet shell flat. Let the molded tartlet shells rest in the refrigerator for 1 hour before baking to allow the gluten (see page 12 for an explanation) to rest.

Preheat the oven to 350°F (175°C). Place the tartlet pans on a baking sheet and bake until lightly browned, about 10 minutes. Remove the baking sheet from the oven and place on a wire rack until the shells have completely cooled. Turn the tartlet pans upside down and lightly tap the bottom of each to allow the tartlet shells to gently drop into your hand. Set aside until ready to use. Increase the oven temperature to 375°F (190°C).

Prepare the macaroon batter and place it in a pastry bag fitted with a ½-inch tip. Pipe it into ten 3-inch spirals (rather than the 1-inch mounds specified in the recipe) onto a parchment paper–covered baking sheet. Try to keep the spirals flat as you pipe them. The macaroons need to be large enough to almost cover the bottom of the tartlet shells. If you have used slightly larger or smaller pans for the chocolate tartlets, adjust the size of the macaroons as necessary. Bake and cool the macaroons as specified on page 84, but do not sandwich the macaroons together! Set aside.

Prepare the filling: Pour the heavy cream and honey into a 1-quart heavy-bottomed saucepan and place over medium-high heat until bubbles begin to form around the edge of the pan. Place the chopped chocolate in a medium-size mixing bowl and make a ganache by covering with the hot cream: Add the cream in two additions, each time letting the mixture stand for about 30 seconds to allow the heat to spread throughout and then stirring slightly to combine. Once all the hot cream has been added, gently stir the ganache until all the chocolate has melted and the ganache is smooth. Add the butter and whisk until smooth and homogenous.

To assemble: Place one macaroon, flat side down, in the bottom of each tartlet shell. Use a ladle to spoon the ganache into each tartlet shell, completely covering the macaroon and filling the shell. Fill slowly to allow the ganache to settle. When all of the shells are filled, place them on a baking sheet and refrigerate until set, about 1½ hours. When set, remove the tartlets from the refrigerator and serve.

Sometimes a ganache can separate because of the temperature shock between the warm cream and the cool chocolate. This is most likely to happen when the ganache recipe contains more heavy cream than chocolate and the cream is added to the chocolate all at once. Separation occurs when all the fat molecules melt because of the heat of the heavy cream, causing the mixture to lose its emulsion. To prevent this, let the cream stand for several minutes after heating to cool slightly. Add the hot cream slowly, in two or three additions, to allow the fat molecules in the chocolate to absorb the cream slowly. Once an emulsion is created, it is safe to add the remaining hot cream. Stir gently after each addition to incorporate fully. An emulsified ganache is shiny, thick, and smooth.

If the ganache does separate (it will look grainy and dull) after all the hot cream has been added, it can usually be fixed. Slowly add a small amount of cold cream to the ganache and stir gently. Adding a cold liquid will recrystallize the fat molecules and bring the mixture back together.

Peanut Butter Cups

6 PEANUT BUTTER CUPS

I discovered peanut butter when I arrived in this country at the age of twenty-eight. Not many French people like it, but I have really developed a taste for it. Naturally, I wanted to use it in a dessert. This is a fun and easy recipe. I always think of it as a good treat to make for the kids, but it is also pretty popular with adults.

I make the cups using tempered chocolate and fill them with a combination of chocolate, peanut butter, and praline paste for a well-rounded flavor.

For the chocolate cups

Bittersweet chocolate, tempered (page 9)		**10.5 ounces**	**300 grams**

For the filling

Bittersweet chocolate, chopped		**5.2 ounces**	**150 grams**
Peanut butter	**Generous 1 cup**	**9 ounces**	**250 grams**
Praline paste (page 15)	**Generous 1 cup**	**9 ounces**	**250 grams**

Prepare the chocolate cups: Place a wire rack over a baking sheet and set aside. I use 4-inch fluted nonstick tartlet pans to make the chocolate cups, but you can use any small nonstick tartlet pans you like. Make sure the pans are clean and dry before you begin.

Fill each tartlet pan with tempered chocolate. Make sure the chocolate covers the sides of the pan. Then hold the pan upside down over the bowl of tempered chocolate and allow the excess chocolate to drip back into the bowl. Wipe the top edge of the pan against the rim of the bowl to clean off the edge. Place the chocolate-coated pans upside down on the wire rack. This will allow any remaining chocolate to drain. Wait until the chocolate begins to set, 4 to 5 minutes, then use a paring knife to scrape the edge of the pans clean again to give the finished cup a nice straight edge and to make it easier to unmold the chocolate cups.

Place the tartlet pans right side up in the refrigerator for about 10 minutes. This will cause the chocolate to retract from the sides, making it easier to remove the cups. You should be able to invert each pan and have the chocolate shell fall into your hand. If not, rest your thumbs on the outside of the pan and place your first two fingers on the inside of the cup. Gently begin to lift the chocolate from the pan. Do not press or pull too hard, or you will break the chocolate. If you've used a deeper pan, you may need to apply this lifting pressure all around the inside to loosen the chocolate from the pan. Set the chocolate cups aside on a baking sheet until ready to be filled.

Prepare the filling: Place a 1-quart saucepan half-filled with water over high heat and bring to a simmer. Make a double boiler by setting a medium-size mixing bowl over the simmering water. Place the chopped chocolate in the mixing bowl and heat until it has completely melted. Stir occasionally and keep an eye on the chocolate as it melts so that it doesn't burn. Once melted, remove the mixing bowl from the heat. Stir the mixture until smooth and set aside until cool to the touch but not so cold that it begins to harden and set.

Combine the peanut butter and praline paste in a medium-size mixing bowl. Add the cooled chocolate and whisk together. This mixture will be stiff and begin to set quickly, so whisk vigorously and thoroughly to combine.

Place the peanut butter mixture in a pastry bag with a large opening (no tip). Fill each chocolate cup to about ⅛ inch from the top. Very lightly tap the filled cups against the work surface to remove any air bubbles. Let the peanut butter cups set at room temperature for about 1 hour, then serve. If you are in a hurry, you can place the peanut butter cups in the refrigerator for about 15 minutes. They can also be frozen for two weeks if well wrapped in plastic wrap. Thaw at room temperature before serving.

Variation: If you prefer, omit the praline paste. In that instance, use 2 cups (18 ounces; 500 grams) of peanut butter and 5.5 ounces (150 grams) of chocolate. To make an even lighter dessert, add about 1 cup (1 ounce; 30 grams) of Rice Krispies to the filling. Sometimes I garnish this dessert with whipped cream and fresh peanuts.

Molded Chocolate Sculpture

1 LARGE CHOCOLATE SCULPTURE

*T*he first step in making a chocolate sculpture is tempering the chocolate. Some people think that tempering is difficult or complicated and may be afraid to try it. Actually, tempering chocolate the traditional way is like working with plaster. The method is called *tabliering.* I think you will find the most difficult thing about tempering chocolate is staying clean!

I always find the molds I use in stores that sell a lot of plastic things. You can mold chocolate in almost anything, but not all molds are filled the same way. For the techniques demonstrated in this recipe, I use a plastic box, a large dome mold, a mask, and some acetate (page 2).

Keep in mind that the temperature in your kitchen will affect the speed at which the chocolate sets.

Bittersweet chocolate, tempered (page 9)	*32 ounces*	*910 grams*
White chocolate, tempered (page 9)	*16 ounces*	*454 grams*

Use a ladle to fill a plastic box with tempered chocolate.

When it is full, empty it into the bowl of chocolate. The inside of the box should be evenly coated.

It's very easy to mold a box. Use a ladle to fill a plastic box with tempered chocolate. When it is full, empty it into the bowl of chocolate. The inside of the box should be evenly coated with chocolate. Wipe the edge of the plastic box clean on the side of the bowl and place the box upside down on a wire rack placed over a baking sheet. Once the chocolate starts to harden, about 5 minutes, scrape the edge of the box clean with a paring knife. As the chocolate sets, it shrinks or retracts from the sides of the mold. A clean edge will keep it from sticking and cracking as it shrinks. You can place the mold in the refrigerator for several minutes to help the chocolate harden.

If the chocolate is properly tempered, it will release easily from the mold. To unmold, rest your thumbs on the outside, place your first two fingers on the inside of the box, and gently begin to lift the chocolate from the mold. Do not press or pull too hard, or you will break the chocolate. You will need to apply this lifting pressure to all four sides of the box to loosen the chocolate from the mold.

When I have a really large plain dome or round mold, I like to create the illusion of texture to lighten the overall effect. Marbleizing the chocolate is a simple way to do this. Start by drizzling both white and dark chocolate into the bottom of the bowl. Then dip your clean, dry fingers in the bowl of tempered dark chocolate and use them to spread the chocolate over the drizzles to create a marbled effect. Dipping

Drizzle both white and dark chocolate into the bottom of a mold.

Dip your clean, dry fingers in the bowl of tempered dark chocolate and use them to spread the chocolate over the drizzles to create a marbled effect.

Use a very clean, dry pastry brush to coat the inside of a mask.

your fingers in chocolate coats them and adds a thin layer of chocolate to the mold, which makes it easier to create the marble pattern. When the mold is marbleized, use a ladle to add just enough dark chocolate to coat the sides completely. Empty any excess into the bowl of chocolate and invert the mold over the wire rack to drain further. Once the chocolate starts to harden, about 5 minutes, scrape the edge of the mold clean with a paring knife. When the chocolate is completely set, you should be able to gently slide the shell out of the mold by pushing on one side. The mold can be placed in the refrigerator to help the chocolate to harden. If you are using a clear plastic mold, you will be able to see that the chocolate is ready to be unmolded when it automatically pulls away from the sides of the mold.

Although a face mask with eye cutouts cannot be filled with chocolate, you can still use it as a mold. Use a very clean, dry pastry brush to coat the inside of the mask. Dip the brush in the chocolate so it permeates the bristles and brings them to the temperature of the chocolate. This tempers the brush so the chocolate will not set on the bristles while you are coating the mask. Apply a total of three layers of chocolate, allowing each to set almost completely before applying the next layer. These layers will make the molded chocolate thick enough to handle without breaking easily. When each layer is almost set, use a paring knife to scrape the edges of the cutouts clean. This will make it easier to unmold the mask. Placing the coated mask in the refrigerator for a few minutes will help the chocolate to harden. If the chocolate is properly tempered, you should be able to lift it easily from the mask.

It is easy to reproduce any line drawing in chocolate. Place the drawing under a sheet of acetate. The chocolate that is against the acetate will take on a nice shine. For this reason, I like to make that side the front of the drawing. Make two cornets (page 19) and fill one with tempered dark chocolate and the other with tempered white chocolate. Use the dark chocolate to trace the outline of the drawing onto the acetate. Use both white and dark chocolate to shade the drawing as appropriate. Be sure to completely fill the inside of the drawing so you end up with a solid re-creation of the drawing. It will also be easier to unmold and handle if there are no gaps in the drawing. Place the acetate in the refrigerator for a few minutes to help the drawing to set. To unmold, simply peel the acetate from the front of the chocolate drawing.

Trace the outline of a drawing with tempered dark chocolate.

Assemble the molded sculpture in any design that pleases your eye. Use some melted chocolate to "glue" the pieces together. If you place all the pieces in the refrigerator first, the sculpture will set faster, as the cold chocolate will cause the chocolate "glue" to harden and set quickly. If you have made an Abstract Chocolate Sculpture (page 123) and have a few extra abstract pieces, incorporate them into your design here.

Shade the drawing as appropriate with tempered white and dark chocolate.

Never coat a mold with fat when you use chocolate. It does not help the chocolate to unmold. Chocolate is like plaster—it retracts when it cools. Chocolate cannot be molded onto any porous surface, like wood or a sponge. In order of preference, the best types of molds are plastic, stainless steel, and glass. Be careful with glass, because it retains temperature, whether it be heat or cold. If the glass mold is slightly warm or cold, it will untemper the chocolate before it has time to set. When molding chocolate, always remember that the chocolate takes on the temperature of the mold.

Dessert Circus

Abstract Chocolate Sculpture

1 LARGE CHOCOLATE SCULPTURE

I was on my way to Cornell University to teach a class on working with chocolate and had all my molds and tools in a plastic bag. At the airport, I set down the bag so I could look at a magazine that caught my eye. I boarded the plane with the new magazine and left all of my molds in the airport. When I arrived at Cornell, I ran around the campus trying to find anything I could use in place of them. When the class started, the students could not imagine what I was going to do with the pieces of plastic, bubble wrap, radiator cover, fluorescent light cover, paint roller, and the host of other nonpastry items I had on the counter.

There are a lot of little tricks that make working with chocolate easier. I like to work on a marble surface because the marble is cold and that helps the chocolate set up quickly. I also keep my tempered chocolate in a glass bowl because the glass retains heat and keeps the chocolate tempered for a longer time. One of the most useful things you can use when working with chocolate is acetate (page 2). Any of the following techniques can be used to make chocolate garnishes of any shape or size.

White chocolate, tempered (page 9)	*16 ounces*	*454 grams*
Bittersweet chocolate, tempered (page 9)	*32 ounces*	*910 grams*

I use a cake comb to create alternating stripes of white and dark chocolate. I made my own comb by cutting a piece of plastic from a bucket and then cutting teeth into one side, but you can buy a comb at most cake decorating supply stores.

Spread some white chocolate on a sheet of acetate in a very thin layer, about 1/16 inch. Draw the comb through the chocolate to create parallel lines. Return the excess chocolate to the bowl. When the chocolate stripes are firm but not hard, use an offset spatula to spread a 1/8-inch-thick layer of dark chocolate over the white chocolate. Let

Draw a cake comb through white chocolate to create parallel lines.

Use an offset spatula to spread an 1/8-inch-thick layer of dark chocolate over the lines.

Carefully wrap or roll the chocolate sheet around a tube.

Randomly drizzle white and dark chocolate onto bubble wrap. Use an offset spatula to spread it in an even layer to create a marbled effect.

the dark chocolate set until firm but not hard, then place a sheet of parchment paper on top of the chocolate. Pick up the plastic by a corner and carefully wrap it around a tube: I use a heavy cardboard tube from a large roll of wrapping paper. Secure the plastic with tape and place in the refrigerator.

I really love the relief design of bubble wrap. You can use wrap with either large or small bubbles or, as I sometimes do, both. Bubble wrap gives a lot of texture to the sculpture. Place a piece of the wrap, bubble side up, on your work surface. Randomly drizzle white and dark chocolate onto the plastic. Use an offset spatula to spread the chocolate in an even layer to create a marbled effect. Place the plastic in the refrigerator.

I have a wood-grain tool that I bought at the hardware store. As with paint, it creates the illusion of wood grain when used on wet chocolate. It is especially nice to use both white and dark chocolate to achieve this effect. Spread some white chocolate onto a sheet of acetate. Pull the wood-grain tool through the chocolate to create a wood-grain design. Let the chocolate set slightly, until firm but not hard. Cover the white chocolate design with dark chocolate and use a spatula to gently spread it into a layer that is about $1/8$ inch thick at one end and increases to $1/4$ inch thick at the other end. I do this because I want to stand this piece on its edge in my sculpture and it needs to be thicker on the bottom to support its own weight. Let the chocolate set until firm

Pull a wood-grain tool through white chocolate to create a wood grain design.

Cover the design with dark chocolate.

Cover plastic with a ¼-inch-thick layer of chocolate to create any desired size.

yet still pliable. To give this piece a curve, I set it inside a tall round container, thick side toward the bottom, chocolate side facing in. Place it in the refrigerator.

One of my other favorite things to use is the plastic cover of the fluorescent light fixture that is found in the ceiling of most professional kitchens. It has a great texture and I can usually find one no matter where I am teaching a class. Cover the plastic with about a ¼-inch-thick layer of chocolate, to create a piece of any desired size, and place in the refrigerator.

Follow the same procedure to create textures on acetate using any interesting shape or design that interests you. I've used a flyswatter, a hand-held fan, a whisk broom, and a paint roller (all new and clean, of course) to spread chocolate onto the acetate. Make sure your design incorporates some pieces with only dark chocolate and some with only white chocolate.

Allowing the pieces to set in the refrigerator should facilitate the removal of the plastic. To unmold all of the chocolate pieces, remove them from the refrigerator and just gently peel away the plastic. You can tell that the plastic is ready to be removed because it becomes slightly cloudy. It may already be loosened from the chocolate in some areas. Keep the unmolded pieces in the refrigerator until you are ready to put the sculpture together. If all the pieces are cold, the sculpture will set up faster.

continued

To assemble: Use the melted chocolate to "glue" the pieces together. Arrange the chocolate pieces as if you were arranging flowers of different varieties. Keep in mind that you can use a hot knife to cut pieces in half or to create different angles or shapes. Sometimes it is necessary to cut a straight edge on the bottom of a piece so it will stand upright. Let your natural artistic eye guide you in the design. You may have enough pieces to make a second smaller sculpture.

Crème

de la Crème

◆ ◆ ◆

THIS CHAPTER DEALS WITH *mousses, parfaits, Bavarian creams, and custards. Once you've mastered the techniques for making them, you can easily adjust the recipes to accommodate your own tastes.*

When making a French meringue, sugar is added slowly to egg whites and at the beginning of whipping them for two reasons: first, to allow the sugar time to dissolve, and, second, to give strength to the egg whites so they won't collapse as easily. Don't overwhip the egg whites, or they will separate and not incorporate well into a batter. You know they are overwhipped when they become dry and look like scrambled eggs. A well-whipped meringue will be shiny, glossy, and opaque and will hold its peaks.

Whipped cream has its greatest volume when it has been whipped to soft peaks. The tendency is to keep whipping until it reaches stiff peaks, but that is not necessary, as it will set up in the refrigerator. Don't forget: When you fold whipped cream into something else, you are still "whipping" it. If you need to whip cream but do not have an electric mixer, remember this *truc* (trick of the trade): Use two whisks and it will whip twice as fast; use three whisks and it will whip three times as fast. It really works!

In France, we use a lot of cream (as well as butter and eggs). There, dairy farming is on a much smaller scale. The whole family is involved and the cows are treated more like pets than cattle. One of my favorite places is in the mountains of the Ardèche region. The French call it "the lungs" of France because it is pristine and unpopulated. The villages are tiny and the farmers cooperatively graze their dairy cows. One evening, Kris and I were about to cross the road when we saw a line of cows walking toward us, apparently unaccompanied. At first, we thought the cows had escaped from someone's farm, but then we saw a guy riding his bike between the cows near the back of the herd. We asked him if he needed help and he responded, "No, I'm just seeing the cows home." As we followed the farmer, we saw the first four cows turn down a driveway and wander into someone's barn while the others kept walking. A little farther down the lane, the next three cows turned into another driveway where a woman was waiting. This continued until the last three cows went home with the man on the bike. Apparently they all knew where they lived but needed someone to open the gate of the pasture. Now when I hear someone say, ". . . till the cows come home," I know exactly what time they are talking about.

Latte Cotto

10 LATTE COTTO

I like to please my Italian boss, Sirio Maccioni, by making his favorite desserts. You may think adding balsamic vinegar to strawberries seems very strange, but trust me, it is one of the tastiest elements of this dessert.

The only tricky part of this recipe is baking the Latte Cotto to the right consistency. When it is removed from the oven, the custard should still tremble when the mold is shaken; it will finish setting in the refrigerator. It is very easy to overcook the custard, so the oven temperature is very important. You know it is overcooked if you see bubbles when you unmold and cut into it. This usually means that the oven was too hot and it cooked too quickly.

For the custard

Heavy cream	**Generous 1 cup**	**8.8 ounces**	**250 grams**
Granulated sugar	**1 cup**	**7 ounces**	**200 grams**
Grated zest of 5 lemons			
½ vanilla bean			
Whole milk	**3 cups + 2 tablespoons**	**26.5 ounces**	**750 grams**
8 large egg whites			

For the garnish

6 sheets phyllo dough (page 14)			
Unsalted butter, melted	**5 tablespoons**	**2.5 ounces**	**70 grams**
Powdered sugar	**¾ cup + 2 tablespoons**	**3.5 ounces**	**100 grams**

For the strawberries

4 large fresh strawberries, hulled			
Balsamic vinegar	**1 teaspoon**	**0.2 ounce**	**6 grams**
Granulated sugar	**2 teaspoons**	**0.3 ounce**	**10 grams**

continued

Prepare the custard: Preheat the oven to 200°F (93°C). Lightly spray ten 3-ounce round molds with baking spray. (I prefer to use baking spray rather than butter because it gives a lighter coating.)

If you are using a conventional oven, place a baking sheet in the center of the oven and fill it with about one inch of warm water. The water bath will insulate the custard from the direct heat of the oven as it bakes, eliminating some of the danger of overbaking it. Let the water heat in the oven as you prepare the custard mixture. If you are using a convection oven, the water bath is not needed.

Place the heavy cream, sugar, and lemon zest in a nonreactive 2-quart heavy-bottomed saucepan over medium-high heat. Use a sharp paring knife to slice the vanilla bean in half again lengthwise. Separate the seeds from the skin by scraping the blade of the knife along the inside of the bean. Add all of the seeds and the skin to the saucepan and bring to a boil. The cream will take on a slight yellow color from the lemon zest.

While the cream mixture is heating, place the milk and egg whites in a large mixing bowl and whisk until well combined. You should not see strings of white.

When the cream mixture reaches a boil, remove it from the heat and pour it into the milk-and-egg-white mixture. Immediately whisk thoroughly to distribute the hot liquid evenly. Strain the liquid through a fine-mesh sieve into a clean container (it will be easier if you use a container with a spout). Pour the hot liquid into the molds, filling them to 1/8 inch from the top. Some of the moisture in the custard will evaporate during baking, so make sure to fill the molds as completely as possible. It may be easier to fill the molds after you place them in the water bath. The water in the baking sheet should come halfway up the sides of the molds. Bake for about 45 minutes. The custards will continue to set in the refrigerator, so you do not want to bake them until they are firm. They are ready if the custard ripples slightly when the mold is jiggled and the very center is not as set as the outer edges; if you see the custard move loosely under the surface, continue to bake, checking for doneness every 5 minutes.

Remove the Latte Cotto from the oven, cool on a wire rack for 30 minutes, then place in the refrigerator for a minimum of 4 hours. (At this stage, the custards can be stored in the refrigerator for up to 2 days if covered with plastic wrap.)

continued

Prepare the phyllo garnish: This can be made while the Latte Cotto are in the refrigerator, but should not be baked more than 1 hour before serving. Preheat the oven to 400°F (200°C). Place 1 sheet of the phyllo on your work surface and use a pastry brush to coat it with about 1 tablespoon of the melted butter. I find it easier to brush one long strip of butter lengthwise down the center of the sheet and then fill in the sides. Make sure to brush all the way to the edges, where the phyllo is the driest. Place the powdered sugar in a fine-mesh sieve and sprinkle about 1½ tablespoons over the buttered phyllo. Top with another phyllo sheet and repeat the butter and sugar. Slice the phyllo layers in half from top to bottom and then from left to right to make four equally sized pieces. Pick up each piece and place on a parchment paper–covered baking sheet, crumpling it slightly to give it some shape and height. Repeat this process with the remaining 4 phyllo sheets. This will make 12 garnishes; you need only 10, but this allows for breakage.

Lightly dust the remaining powdered sugar over the crumpled phyllo and bake them until golden brown, about 5 minutes. Keep an eye on them as they bake so they do not burn. As the sugar caramelizes, it gives the phyllo color and taste. Remove from the oven and cool on a wire rack until ready to serve.

Prepare the strawberries: Dice the strawberries into ¼-inch cubes and place in a small bowl. Add the balsamic vinegar and granulated sugar and fold until combined. Let macerate for 15 minutes to allow the flavors to fully develop.

Immediately before serving, unmold the Latte Cotto by running the blade of a knife around the inside of each mold. Gently invert each mold over the center of a plate and let the Latte Cotto drop out. If you have baked them in decorative ceramic molds, you can serve them in the molds. Place about 1 tablespoon of the balsamic strawberries on top of each Latte Cotto and garnish with one phyllo decoration. Serve.

Variation: Decorate with assorted sliced fresh fruit and berries. I also like to serve this dessert with banana tuiles (page 243).

Crème Brûlée

*H*ere is one of the most popular desserts at Le Cirque. It has been on the menu for more than fifteen years and is one of the most copied recipes in the restaurant business.

When Chef Dieter Schorner was the pastry chef at Le Cirque more than fifteen years ago, it was his responsibility to make the Crème Brûlée. Ever since his time, great mystery has surrounded this recipe, with everyone wondering, "Is this really the original?" I think it is, but Francisco, who has been making it for the last fifteen years, just answers me with a sly smile. Over the years, I have adapted it and served it flavored with coffee, chocolate, fruit, and a host of other ingredients. I like to use lightly fluted, heavy ceramic oval molds that are about three- by five- by one-inch high.

For the topping

Light brown sugar	1 cup (firmly packed)	4.8 ounces	135 grams

For the custard

Heavy cream	4 cups	32 ounces	960 grams
1 vanilla bean			
1 large egg			
6 large egg yolks			
Granulated sugar	¾ cup + 2 tablespoons	6 ounces	175 grams

Prepare the topping: The brown sugar will be used to finish the dessert and it needs time to air-dry to remove the moisture it contains. To do this, spread the sugar on a large plate or baking sheet and let dry, uncovered, for about 3 hours. When it is properly dried, it will feel dry and sandy. Set aside.

Prepare the custard: Pour the heavy cream into a nonreactive 1½-quart heavy-bottomed saucepan and place over medium heat. While the cream is heating, slice the vanilla bean in half lengthwise, using a sharp paring knife. Separate the seeds from the skin by scraping the bean with the knife. Place the seeds and skin in the heating

cream. Scald the cream by heating it until bubbles start to form around the edge of the pan. Remove from the heat.

In a large mixing bowl, whisk together the whole egg, egg yolks, and sugar until well blended. Continue to whisk while slowly pouring the hot cream into the egg mixture and whisk until the mixture is smooth and homogenous in color. Pour the mixture through a fine-mesh sieve to remove the vanilla bean pieces and any overcooked eggs. Your next step will be made easier if you strain the mixture into a large measuring cup with a spout.

Preheat the oven to 200°F (93°C). Place the molds on a baking sheet with 1-inch-high sides. Fill the molds half-full with the custard and set the sheet in the oven (it's much easier to transfer the sheet with the molds only half-full). Now, finish filling the molds to the top. It is important to fill the molds to the top, as the custard will lose volume as it bakes. Traditionally, Crème Brûlée is baked in a hot water bath to insulate the custard from the direct heat of the oven and to keep the eggs from cooking too fast, which would cause them to separate. Using hot water from the tap, pour enough water into the baking sheet to reach halfway up the sides of the molds. If you are using a convection oven, however, a water bath is not needed because the even circulation of the air insulates the custard from the direct heat.

In either case, baking time is approximately the same, about 30 minutes. When baked correctly, the custard should tremble slightly when gently shaken. If you detect any liquid under the skin, the custard is underbaked. Put them back in the oven and shake them every 5 minutes or so until they are ready.

Remove the molds from the water bath and place on a cooling rack for 30 minutes. Then refrigerate for 2 hours (or for up to 3 days) before serving; the custards will finish setting in the refrigerator. Let the water bath cool before removing it from the oven.

To finish the Crème Brûlée: Preheat the broiler. Pass the dried brown sugar through a sieve to remove any lumps. Immediately before serving, spread a thin layer of the brown sugar over the tops of the custards. You have spread enough sugar when the custard is no longer visible, about 2 tablespoons. It is important to spread the sugar evenly; if it is too thick or too thin in places, the caramelization will not be even across the top. Place the molds on a clean baking sheet. When the broiler is hot, place the sheet about 4 inches under the broiler and broil until the sugar is caramelized. *Keep a close eye on the Crème Brûlée during broiling.* They are finished when they are light brown. Place each mold on a small dessert plate and serve immediately.

When working with sugar and egg yolks, it is important to mix them together quickly and evenly. When sugar comes in contact with egg yolks, a chemical reaction occurs, heat is produced, and the eggs begin to scramble. The scrambled egg will cause lumps in the final product.

White Chocolate Mousse

8 SERVINGS

T his mousse is a little trickier to make than the bittersweet chocolate mousse because white chocolate can seize easily. I hope you will consider making the variation suggested at the end of this recipe. I thought of it one morning as I was squeezing toothpaste onto my toothbrush. It really makes a fun presentation and I prefer the taste of the two mousses swirled together.

White chocolate is not really chocolate. It contains cocoa butter, sugar, milk powder, vanilla, and lecithin, but it does not contain cocoa solids. You will need an ice bath (page 3) so have one ready before you begin.

For the ganache

1½ gelatin sheets or ½ envelope powdered gelatin			
White chocolate, chopped		**8.8 ounces**	**250 grams**
Heavy cream	**½ cup + 2 tablespoons**	**5.25 ounces**	**150 grams**

To finish the mousse

Heavy cream	**1¼ cups**	**10.5 ounces**	**300 grams**

For the garnish (optional)

Assorted fresh fruit, sliced, and berries

Chocolate shavings (page 324)

Prepare the ganache: If using gelatin sheets, place them in a medium-size mixing bowl with enough cold water (about 2 cups) to cover. Let stand for about 5 minutes to allow the gelatin to soften and hydrate. Cold water hydrates the gelatin without letting it absorb too much liquid. Remove the gelatin from the bowl and squeeze out the excess water with your hands. If you're using powdered gelatin, sprinkle the gelatin over ¼ cup (1.75 ounces; 50 grams) of cold water. Let the gelatin bloom until it has absorbed all the water, about 1 minute.

Place the chopped chocolate in a medium-size mixing bowl. Pour the heavy cream into a 1-quart heavy-bottomed saucepan and place over medium-high heat until bubbles begin to form around the edge of the pan. Remove from the heat and make a ganache by pouring the hot cream over the chocolate. Let stand for about 30 seconds to distribute the heat throughout the bowl. Add the hydrated gelatin and gently stir the mixture with a rubber spatula. The hot cream will cause the chocolate and gelatin to melt. Slowly mixing the heavy cream and chocolate together causes the fats in them to combine to form an emulsion (page 20). Stir the ganache until it is smooth and homogenous. Place the mixing bowl in the ice bath and stir the ganache occasionally so it cools evenly. The ganache is ready when it has thickened. Test this by using a rubber spatula to draw a line through it. If the line holds for 10 to 15 seconds, it is ready. If the line fills in immediately, the ganache is too warm. Keep cooling and retest every 30 seconds. The ganache should not cool so much that it begins to harden and set. If this happens, warm it up over a saucepan of simmering water, removing it every 10 seconds and whisking gently until it is smooth and viscous.

To finish the mousse: While the ganache is cooling, pour the heavy cream into another medium-size mixing bowl and whip to soft peaks with an electric mixer on medium speed. Be careful; if you overwhip the heavy cream, it will lose volume and the mousse will not be as light and airy.

When the ganache is cool but not cold, fold in the whipped cream in two additions until combined. The ganache should not be so cold that it has begun to set and is grainy, yet is should be cool enough that it doesn't melt the whipped cream. If the mousse begins to seize while you are folding in the whipped cream, warm it up over a saucepan of simmering water, 5 seconds at a time, until it is smooth again. Do not warm it so much that the whipped cream begins to melt. Then fold in any remaining whipped cream. When all of the whipped cream has been incorporated, the mousse will be loose and pourable. Don't worry; it will set up in the refrigerator.

It is best to serve the mousse soon after it is prepared, when it has the maximum lightness and volume. I think it looks nicest if you use a large pastry bag fitted with a 1-inch star tip to pipe the mousse into your serving dish. Don't squeeze the bag too hard or the mousse will deflate as it is pushed through the tip of the bag. The mousse will keep lightly covered in the refrigerator for up to three days. The longer it stays in the refrigerator, the heavier it will become, as the chocolate contracts.

I like to garnish this with sliced fresh fruit and chocolate shavings.

continued

. . . *Crème de la Crème* . . .

Variation: Prepare a recipe each of Bittersweet Chocolate Mousse (below) and White Chocolate Mousse. Place each mousse in its own medium-size pastry bag with a ¾-inch opening (no tip). Place both bags side by side inside another larger pastry bag fitted with a 1-inch star tip. Squeeze the large bag evenly to push both mousses through the single tip at the same time, creating a two-tone mousse. Decorate with fresh fruit or chocolate garnishes and serve.

Bittersweet Chocolate Mousse

8 SERVINGS

One day at the restaurant, a waiter brought me an order for eight desserts. That, by itself, would not cause special notice, but this order was for a table with only two people. I was intrigued and immediately marched out to the dining room to meet them. They explained that they loved all kinds of sweets but especially preferred anything with chocolate. The lady, who became my dear friend Anat, asked if I would be willing to share my recipe for chocolate mousse, and this is the one I gave to her.

In this recipe, it is especially important to use the best-quality chocolate available. I prefer to use Callebaut chocolate from Belgium for its deep chocolate flavor. Sometimes I add a dash of Grand Marnier because I think its light orange flavor stands up to the strong chocolate taste.

Bittersweet chocolate, chopped		8.8 ounces	250 grams
1 large egg			
5 large egg yolks			
Granulated sugar	½ cup + 1 teaspoon	3.8 ounces	105 grams
Water	Scant ¼ cup	1.75 ounces	50 grams
Heavy cream	1⅔ cups	14 ounces	400 grams
Grand Marnier (optional)	1 tablespoon	1 ounce	30 grams
Chocolate garnishes (page 123; optional)			

continued

Place a 1-quart saucepan half-filled with water over high heat and bring it to a simmer. Make a double boiler by setting a large mixing bowl over the simmering water. Place the chopped chocolate in the bowl and heat until completely melted, stirring occasionally. Make sure no water or steam comes in contact with the chocolate, as it can cause the chocolate to seize (harden). It is important to allow the chocolate to melt completely, or you will have lumps in the finished mousse. As soon as the chocolate is melted, remove from the heat and set aside until ready to use.

Place the whole egg and egg yolks in a medium-size mixing bowl and whip with an electric mixer on medium-high speed until light in color and thick, about 7 minutes. The egg mixture will gain in volume because of the incorporation of air. Keep whipping and begin to cook the sugar.

Place the sugar and water in a 1-quart heavy-bottomed saucepan over medium-high heat. Insert a candy thermometer and cook the sugar mixture until it reaches 250°F (121°C). At this temperature, it is cooked to what is called the soft ball stage (page 16). Remove it from the heat and pour the hot sugar down the side of the mixing bowl while you continue whipping the yolks. Be careful not to pour the hot sugar directly onto the beaters, or it will splatter. Continue to whip on medium-high speed until the outside of the bowl is warm but not hot, 2 to 3 minutes.

In a separate medium-size mixing bowl, whip the heavy cream to soft peaks with an electric mixer on medium speed. At this stage, the whipped cream has the greatest volume. If you overwhip the cream, you will lose volume and the mousse will not be as light and airy as it should be. Use a rubber spatula to gently fold in the Grand Marnier, if you are using it, being careful not to deflate the cream.

Fold the egg mixture into the whipped cream. Be careful: If the egg mixture is too hot, it will melt the whipped cream; if it is too cool, it will not fold well. Use a rubber spatula and fold gently just until the two are combined. You should still see streaks of each in the mixture. Carefully pour the warm melted chocolate into the mixture. Again, if the chocolate is too warm, it will melt the whipped cream; if too cool, it will seize (harden) upon contact with the cooler mixture and you will have pieces of chocolate in your chocolate mousse. Use a rubber spatula to gently fold in the chocolate until completely incorporated. The chocolate mousse should be the same color throughout, with no streaks of chocolate.

The chocolate mousse will begin to set quickly, so place it in the serving dish immediately. I like to use a large pastry bag fitted with a 1-inch star tip to pipe the mousse into martini glasses or a beautiful bowl. You can also use a large spoon or rubber spatula. If you use a pastry bag, don't squeeze it too hard, or the mousse will deflate as it is pushed through the tip.

It is best to serve the mousse immediately, when it has its maximum lightness and volume. You can store the mousse in the refrigerator lightly covered with plastic wrap for up to 3 days. It will condense slightly as the chocolate contracts.

I like to give the mousse a little flair by adding chocolate garnishes. Decorate the mousse with the chocolate pieces just before serving.

The traditional way of filling a pastry bag is to tuck enough of the bag into the tip to create a seal. Next, hold the bag in one hand and fill it with the other. This can be awkward and messy, depending on the type of filling. An easy way to fill a pastry bag, especially with a loose mixture such as mousse, is to close the tip of the bag with a clothespin, placing it where the bag and the pastry tip meet. This seal will keep the filling from dripping through the tip as you fill the bag. Place the bag inside a tall container with the tip down. Fold the bag over the sides of the container, leaving the bag open. This will allow you to use both hands to fill the bag.

Tiramisù

*I*n Italian, *tiramisù* means "pick me up." I am not sure if this dessert is named for love or for the coffee that it contains. Traditionally, it is made with Marsala wine and ladyfingers soaked with espresso. My version is slightly different and a little bit lighter. I begin by making a *pâte à bombe,* so the hot sugar will heat the eggs to a high-enough temperature to kill any bacteria without cooking the eggs. Then I make a parfait by folding the *pâte à bombe* with some whipped cream to lighten it. The end result is a creamy, smooth dessert well flavored with espresso, Kahlúa, and rum. For a stronger flavor, I prefer to use the dark rum of the Caribbean. Go lightly on the cocoa powder so it does not catch in your throat, make a mess, or overpower the dessert. For an easy variation, use a good-quality store-bought yellow or pound cake instead of the homemade biscuit.

¹/₂ recipe Biscuit batter (page 40)

For the syrup

Strong coffee or espresso	**1¹/₄ cups**	**10 ounces**	**225 grams**
Kahlúa liqueur (optional)	**1¹/₂ tablespoons**	**0.6 ounce**	**15 grams**
Dark rum (optional)	**1¹/₂ tablespoons**	**0.5 ounce**	**15 grams**

For the parfait

Heavy cream	**2 cups + 1¹/₂ tablespoons**	**17 ounces**	**500 grams**
Mascarpone cheese	**3 cups**	**26 ounces**	**750 grams**
12 large egg yolks			
Granulated sugar	**³/₄ cup**	**5.25 ounces**	**150 grams**
Light corn syrup	**Scant ¹/₄ cup**	**2.5 ounces**	**80 grams**
Water	**Scant ¹/₂ cup**	**3.5 ounces**	**100 grams**
Coffee extract	**2 tablespoons**	**0.8 ounce**	**20 grams**

For the garnish

Unsweetened Dutch-processed cocoa powder for dusting

continued

Preheat the oven to 400°F (200°C). Prepare the biscuit batter and bake it on a parchment paper–covered baking sheet until golden brown, 6 to 10 minutes. Remember to sprinkle the top with powdered sugar before baking for a nicer crust. Remove from the oven and immediately unmold onto a wire rack.

Prepare the syrup: Pour the coffee or espresso into a small mixing bowl and allow to cool to room temperature. (If you are short on time, the coffee can be cooled over an ice bath; page 3). Once the coffee is cool, add the Kahlúa and rum, if you are using them, and stir well to combine. Pour the coffee syrup into a squeeze bottle or cover well with plastic wrap to keep the alcohol from evaporating until you are ready to use the syrup.

Prepare the parfait: Place the heavy cream in another medium-size mixing bowl and whip to soft peaks with an electric mixer on medium speed. I think it is a good idea to whip the mascarpone on low speed for about 1 minute before you fold in the whipped cream. Using a whisk, gently fold the whipped cream into the mascarpone cheese in two additions until well combined. The mascarpone is thicker and heavier than the whipped cream; if you add the whipped cream to it all at once, you may have lumps in the finished parfait. Adding part of the whipped cream first brings the consistency of the mascarpone closer to that of the whipped cream. Store the mixture in the refrigerator until ready to use.

Place the egg yolks in a medium-size mixing bowl and whip with an electric mixer on medium-high speed until thick and light in color, about 7 minutes. The egg yolks will gain in volume because of the incorporation of air. Keep whipping while you cook the sugar.

Place the sugar, corn syrup, and water in a 1-quart saucepan over medium-high heat. Insert a candy thermometer and cook to 250°F (121°C), what is known as the soft ball stage (page 16). Make a *pâte à bombe* by pouring the hot sugar down the side of the bowl as you continue whipping the yolks. Be careful not to pour it directly onto the beaters, or the hot sugar will splatter. Whip the *pâte à bombe* on medium-high speed until the outside of the bowl is warm but not hot, 3 to 5 minutes.

Remove the whipped cream mixture from the refrigerator and make the parfait by folding the *pâte à bombe* into the whipped cream until completely incorporated.

Pour about one third of the parfait into a small mixing bowl and fold in the coffee extract. Set both bowls aside.

To assemble: I like to serve Tiramisù in wineglasses. Use a plain round cutter or sharp paring knife to cut twenty disks of biscuit slightly smaller than your wineglasses. Fill each glass about one-quarter full with the unflavored parfait. Top with a biscuit disk and soak with the coffee syrup. Fill about half-full with the coffee parfait, then top each with a second biscuit disk and soak with the coffee syrup. Finally, fill to the top with the unflavored parfait. Store the Tiramisù in the refrigerator, covered with plastic wrap, until ready to serve, for a minimum of thirty minutes or up to one day.

Just before serving, remove the plastic wrap and lightly sprinkle the top with the cocoa powder.

Tiramisù can be frozen for up to two weeks if well wrapped in plastic wrap. Thaw in the refrigerator before serving.

Variation: If you prefer to make the more traditional cake version, it is necessary to add gelatin to the *pâte à bombe* so the Tiramisù will hold its shape when sliced. Add 5 gelatin sheets that have been hydrated in water and squeezed dry or 1⅔ envelopes powdered gelatin dissolved in ½ cup (3.5 ounces; 100 grams) water to the whipping egg yolks immediately after adding the hot sugar.

To assemble, cut the biscuit into thirds and alternate the layers of sponge, syrup, and parfaits as indicated in the recipe. Smooth the top with an offset spatula. Place the Tiramisù in the refrigerator until set, about thirty minutes, or for up to two days if loosely wrapped in plastic wrap. (To freeze, place in the freezer until hard, about 1 hour. Then wrap in plastic wrap and return to the freezer for up to two weeks. Thaw in the refrigerator before serving.) Sprinkle the top of the Tiramisù with cocoa powder immediately before serving. I like to decorate the plates with plain or coffee-flavored crème anglaise (page 24).

Frozen Halvah Parfaits

y mom and I share a love for halvah. It is made from sesame seeds mixed with sugar and oil and crushed to a paste. Kris and I were walking down the street our first year in Forest Hills when we passed a store that specialized in ethnic foods. My eyes were wide when I saw all of the different varieties of halvah. I told Kris, "I have to create a halvah dessert for the restaurant." I like this recipe because the parfait is eaten frozen, but you don't need an ice cream machine to make it.

For the parfait

Halvah	⅓ cup (firmly packed)	2.8 ounces	80 grams
Heavy cream	Scant 1 cup	8 ounces	228 grams
3 gelatin sheets or 1 envelope powdered gelatin			
4 large egg yolks			
Granulated sugar	¼ cup	1.75 ounces	50 grams
Light corn syrup	1 tablespoon	0.8 ounce	25 grams
Water	2 tablespoons	1 ounce	30 grams

For the tuiles

Almond flour	½ cup	1.7 ounces	50 grams
Granulated sugar	¼ cup + 2 tablespoons	2.5 ounces	75 grams
Unsalted butter, melted	2½ tablespoons	1.25 ounces	35 grams
Cold whole milk	2 tablespoons	1.3 ounces	35 grams
Bread flour	¾ teaspoon	0.1 ounce	2 grams
Sesame seeds	3 tablespoons	0.8 ounce	23 grams

Prepare the parfait: Use a fork to mash the halvah in the bottom of a small mixing bowl. You may need to use a rubber spatula to break up any small lumps by pressing the halvah against the side of the bowl.

Pour the heavy cream into a medium-size mixing bowl and whip to soft peaks with an electric mixer on medium-high speed. Add the mashed halvah and whisk gently just to incorporate. Place the halvah whipped cream in the refrigerator until ready to use.

If you're using gelatin sheets, place them in a medium-size mixing bowl with enough cold water (about 1 quart) to cover. Let stand for about 5 minutes to allow the gelatin to soften and hydrate. Cold water hydrates the gelatin without letting it absorb too much liquid. Remove the gelatin from the bowl and squeeze out the excess water with your hands. If you're using powdered gelatin, sprinkle the gelatin over about ¼ cup (1.75 ounces; 50 grams) cold water. Let the gelatin bloom until it has absorbed all the water, about 1 minute.

Place the egg yolks in another medium-size mixing bowl and whip with an electric mixer on medium-high speed until they are thick, light, and tripled in volume, about 7 minutes. Continue to whip the yolks while you cook the sugar.

Pour the sugar, corn syrup, and water into a 1-quart heavy-bottomed saucepan over medium-high heat. Insert a candy thermometer and cook until the sugar mixture reaches 250°F (121°C), what is known as the soft ball stage (page 16). Make a *pâte à bombe* by pouring the cooked sugar down the sides of the bowl as you continue to whip the eggs. Do not pour the hot sugar onto the beaters, or it will splatter. Place the hydrated gelatin in the hot sugar pan until melted. Add it to the *pâte à bombe* and continue whipping until the outside of the bowl is warm but not hot, 3 to 5 minutes.

continued

Remove the halvah whipped cream from the refrigerator. Make the parfait by folding the *pâte à bombe* into the whipped cream with a rubber spatula. Be gentle, don't use a whisk, or the whipped cream will deflate. Place the parfait in a pastry bag fitted with a ½-inch tip and pipe into eight molds. You can use any shape or size mold you like. I use plastic cone-shaped molds that hold 1½ ounces. I place each one inside a wineglass to hold them upright as they are filled. If you use cone-shaped molds, use a wooden skewer to push the parfait into the tip to remove any trapped air. Place the molds in the freezer until hardened, about 2 hours.

Prepare the tuiles: While the parfait is in the freezer, prepare the sesame tuiles. Preheat the oven to 350°F (175°C). Combine the almond flour and sugar in a medium-size mixing bowl. Mix on medium speed with an electric mixer while you slowly add the melted butter. When all the butter is incorporated, slowly add the milk, continuing to mix on medium speed. When the mixture is homogenous, add the flour and mix just until incorporated. (At this stage the batter can be kept in the refrigerator for up to 5 days tightly covered with plastic wrap. Use it directly from the refrigerator.)

Make the tuiles by placing ¼-teaspoon mounds of batter spaced 2½ inches apart on a nonstick baking sheet. With a small offset spatula, spread each mound into a 2-inch circle. The batter should be spread very thin. Sprinkle the tops with the sesame seeds and bake until golden brown, about 5 minutes. Remove from the oven and immediately remove the tuiles from the baking sheet. To give the tuiles some shape, lift them off the baking sheet with a small offset spatula and place each one inside a small glass while it is still hot. Use a small enough glass so that the sides of the tuile fold up against the sides of the glass like a flower. Allow each tuile to cool in a glass. Set aside until ready to use. The baked tuiles can be stored in an airtight container at room temperature for up to one week.

To unmold the parfaits, dip the molds in hot water for 1 to 2 seconds and invert over the center of each serving plate. Decorate the plates with the sesame tuiles.

Popcorn Fantasy

8 SERVINGS

When I first moved to this country, I was fascinated by popcorn, which is not as popular in France as it is here. Kris bought me one of those hot air poppers. I had never seen one before, didn't know how it worked, and thought I would try it. One Sunday, I put a cup of kernels in the popper and, as I watched it whirl round and round, thought, "One cup; that's not much. How much will that really make?" So I added another cup of kernels. After a few minutes, the popcorn started to pop and pop and pop. It streamed out of the popper all over the kitchen. I didn't know I was supposed to put a bowl underneath it! In a panic, I grabbed a big garbage bag and tried to catch the popcorn by hand. Just at that moment, Kris came home. Is that what you call Murphy's Law?

Don't use microwaveable popcorn. It usually contains salt, butter, and other additives that will affect the taste of this dessert.

For the caramel popcorn

Granulated sugar	¾ cup	5.25 ounces	150 grams
Light corn syrup	2 tablespoons	1.6 ounces	50 grams
Water	¼ cup	2 ounces	55 grams
Plain popcorn kernels, popped	¼ cup	2 ounces	60 grams

For the mousse

Milk chocolate, chopped		8.8 ounces	250 grams
Heavy cream	1⅔ cups	14 ounces	400 grams

For the garnish

Chocolate Sauce (page 45)

Crème Anglaise (page 24)

Prepare the caramel popcorn: Make the caramel by placing the sugar, corn syrup, and water in a 4-quart heavy-bottomed saucepan over medium-high heat and cooking until evenly golden brown. If the sugar browns unevenly, stir it gently with a wooden spoon. I use a big copper bowl, rounded on the bottom, because it makes it

easier to mix in the popcorn. Remove the saucepan from the heat. Add the popped popcorn and use a wooden spatula (a rubber spatula will melt) to fold thoroughly, bringing the caramel from the bottom to the top.

When the popcorn is evenly coated, pour it onto a parchment paper–covered baking sheet or a slab of marble. It is good to pour this onto marble because marble cools everything down very fast. Wait a few minutes before you taste it, or the hot caramel will burn your tongue. Separate the clumps by hand, but be careful because this stuff is hot! (At this stage, you've made caramel popcorn and you could offer it to your friends.)

Prepare the mousse: Place a 1-quart saucepan half-filled with water over high heat and bring it to a simmer. Make a double boiler by setting a large mixing bowl over the simmering water. Place the chopped chocolate in the bowl and heat until completely melted, stirring occasionally. It is important to melt the chocolate fully to avoid lumps in the finished mousse. Be careful not to overheat or burn the chocolate. The chocolate will be a little bit warmer than your hands when fully melted. Remove the mixing bowl from the heat and set aside.

Place the heavy cream in a medium-size mixing bowl and whip to soft peaks with an electric mixer on medium-high speed. Fold about one third of the whipped cream into the melted chocolate, just to bring the temperature of the chocolate closer to the temperature of the whipped cream. This will keep the chocolate from hardening when it comes in contact with the cooler whipped cream. Now fold the chocolate mixture into the whipped cream. Add about three fourths of the popcorn and use a rubber spatula to fold until well combined. When everything is well mixed, spoon it into eight molds. I use 3-ounce disposable aluminum molds (page 3) but you can also use a muffin tin. Fill the molds completely and use the back of the spoon to smooth the top. Place in the freezer just until the chocolate sets, about 1 hour.

To unmold, dip each mold in hot water for about 2 seconds. Invert each mold over the center of a serving plate and remove the mold. Decorate the top of the mousse with the remaining caramel popcorn. I usually make chocolate garnishes (page 123) to give the plate a little more drama. Decorate with the chocolate sauce and crème anglaise.

Variation: Replace the corn syrup with honey to give a nice taste to the popcorn.

If you overcook the caramel, the taste will be bitter. If you undercook it, it won't have enough caramel flavor.

Apricot Charlotte

Traditionally, a Charlotte is a cake with ladyfingers on the outside and Bavarian cream on the inside. There are fancy Charlotte molds available, but you can use any nice pan as long as it is wider than it is deep. For this recipe, I use a two-quart mold that is seven inches wide and four inches deep. I created a shortcut by piping the ladyfingers into one long row (like a fence) instead of individually.

1 recipe Biscuit batter (page 40)

For the simple syrup

Granulated sugar	**1 cup**	**7 ounces**	**200 grams**
Water	**¾ cup + 2 tablespoons**	**7.2 ounces**	**200 grams**
Grand Marnier	**1 tablespoon**	**1 ounce**	**30 grams**

For the Bavarian

1 vanilla bean			
Heavy cream	**1½ cups + 1 tablespoon**	**13.3 ounces**	**375 grams**
Granulated sugar	**½ cup**	**3.5 ounces**	**100 grams**
4 gelatin sheets or 1⅓ envelopes powdered gelatin			
7 to 8 fresh apricots			
Grand Marnier (optional)	**1 tablespoon**	**1 ounce**	**30 grams**

Preheat the oven to 400°F (200°C). Draw three circles by tracing around the bottom of a 6-inch pan or mold onto a sheet of parchment paper placed on a baking sheet. Then draw two 4 × 10-inch rectangles on another sheet of parchment paper placed on a second baking sheet. Turn the paper over to keep the ink from baking into the biscuit.

Prepare the biscuit batter and place it in a pastry bag fitted with a ¾-inch plain tip. Pipe two disks by starting at the center of a circle and using a spiral motion to pipe the biscuit to the edge of the circle. In the third circle, pipe a pattern that

resembles the spokes of a wheel: Pipe each spoke into a teardrop shape that is wider at the edge and ends in a point at the center. Inside each rectangle, pipe evenly shaped ladyfingers, each about ³/₄ inch wide, spaced about ¹/₄ inch apart. When baked, they will join together and the finished piece will resemble a picket fence. Remember to dust the tops of all of the biscuit pieces with powdered sugar to give them a nice crust. Bake until evenly golden brown, about 5 minutes. Remove from the oven and immediately unmold to prevent the heat of the pan from continuing to bake the biscuit. Set aside until ready to use.

Prepare the simple syrup: Place the sugar and water in a 1-quart heavy-bottomed saucepan and bring to a boil over medium heat. The sugar should completely dissolve. Remove from the heat. Prepare an ice bath (page 3) and pour the syrup into a medium-size bowl placed in it. When the syrup is cool, stir in the Grand Marnier. (If it is added when the syrup is hot, the alcohol will evaporate.)

Prepare the Bavarian: Use a sharp paring knife to slice the vanilla bean in half lengthwise. Separate the seeds from the skin by scraping the blade of the knife along the inside of the bean. Place the heavy cream, sugar, and vanilla bean seeds in a large mixing bowl and whip to soft peaks with an electric mixer on medium-high speed. Place in the refrigerator until ready to use.

If you are using gelatin sheets, place them in a medium-size bowl with enough cold water (about 1 quart) to cover. Let stand for about 5 minutes to allow the gelatin to soften and hydrate. Cold water hydrates the gelatin without letting it absorb too much liquid. Remove the gelatin from the bowl and squeeze out the excess water with your hands. If you are using powdered gelatin, sprinkle it over ¹/₄ cup (1.75 ounces; 50 grams) of cold water. Let the gelatin bloom until it has absorbed all the water, about 1 minute.

Halve and pit the apricots, then puree the fruit using an immersion blender, food processor, or blender. Strain the fruit through a fine-mesh sieve into a small bowl to remove the skin and any large pieces of fiber. Measure out 1²/₃ cups (13 ounces; 375 grams) to be used in the Bavarian; discard any remaining puree.

Place the hydrated gelatin and one fourth of the apricot puree in a nonreactive 1-quart heavy-bottomed saucepan and place over medium heat until the gelatin dissolves. Pour the gelatin mixture into the remaining cold apricot puree and immediately whisk to combine. This will eliminate any pieces of gelatin in the Bavarian. Make the Bavarian by using a rubber spatula to gently fold the apricot puree into the whipped cream, being careful not to deflate the whipped cream. At this stage, I like to fold in a tablespoon of Grand Marnier.

To assemble: Line the bottom of the pan or mold of your choice with parchment paper. Remove the parchment paper from the back of the biscuit pieces. Soak the back (flat side) of the spiral disks and the ladyfingers with the simple syrup. Line the side of the pan or mold with the ladyfingers. You may have to trim them to fit so they do not overlap. Fill the pan or mold about half-full with the Bavarian. Cover with one soaked biscuit disk. Fill the pan or mold almost to the top with the remaining Bavarian, leaving room for the second biscuit disk. Top with the second disk, flat side up, and press down gently. Place in the freezer for about 1½ hours or in the refrigerator for 4 to 6 hours, to set.

Center a plate face down over the pan or mold. In one quick motion, flip both over so the pan or mold is on top. To unmold, gently lift the pan or mold from the Charlotte. Remove the parchment paper. Place the decorative wheel of biscuit on the top and lightly press it into the Charlotte. I like to serve it immediately, but it will hold at room temperature for up to two hours. Use a hot serrated knife to slice the dessert. Heat the knife by running it under hot water before each slice; remember to wipe the excess water from the knife after it is rinsed.

To pipe the biscuit disks, hold the pastry bag at a slight angle about 1½ inches above the parchment paper. This height and angle allows the piped batter to "fall" into place while holding the full shape of the decorating tip. Start at the center of the circle and pipe the biscuit in a spiral to the edge of the outline. If the batter breaks while you are piping it, just continue where it broke. If any air bubbles appear in the disk, go back and fill them in with the extra batter left in the pastry bag.

To pipe the ladyfingers, hold the pastry bag at a slight angle and allow the tip to touch the parchment paper as you start to pipe. Squeeze gently, applying even pressure, as you pipe the desired length, then stop squeezing and lift the tip straight up, leaving a small tail on the end of each ladyfinger.

The Mask

*I*n France, we don't celebrate Halloween. In New York, the first time the neighborhood children came to the door to trick-or-treat, I was inspired by their costumes. I thought it would be fun and relatively easy to use a mask as a mold for a child's special-occasion dessert.

When you buy a mask, select one that has the outside design indented on the inside. These indentations will indicate where to place the fresh fruit used to re-create the mask's face. It should not have any cutouts for the eyes, nose, and mouth. If you have a mask with cutouts, save it to make a chocolate sculpture (page 118). The outside rim of the mask needs to lie flat on the table so that the Bavarian filling will be even. It might be necessary to trim the edge of the mask to make it flat. The mask I used for this recipe was about ten inches wide and from two to three and a half inches deep.

You will need an ice bath, so have it ready before you begin (page 3).

¹/₂ recipe Classic Génoise batter (page 38)

Assorted fresh fruit, sliced

For the Bavarian

5¹/₄ gelatin sheets or 1²/₃ envelopes powdered gelatin

Whole milk	**1¹/₂ cups + 1 tablespoon**	**13 ounces**	**375 grams**
1 vanilla bean			
Granulated sugar	**³/₄ cup**	**5.25 ounces**	**150 grams**
5 large egg yolks			
Pistachio paste	**1 tablespoon**	**0.8 ounce**	**25 grams**
Heavy cream	**2¹/₂ cups**	**21 ounces**	**600 grams**

Angel Hair, colored yellow (page 48)

Preheat the oven to 400°F (200°C). Prepare the génoise batter and bake on a parchment paper–covered baking sheet until lightly and evenly browned and springy to the touch, about 10 minutes. Cool on a wire rack and unmold, remembering to remove the parchment paper. When the génoise is completely cooled, place the mask face side

up on it and use a sharp paring knife to cut around it. Set the génoise cutout aside until ready to use.

Select a mixing bowl slightly larger than the mask and fill the bowl with crumpled plastic wrap to create a nest. Place the mask face side down in the plastic wrap. This will hold the mask steady as you fill it. Leave the mask in its nest through all of the steps until you are ready to unmold the finished dessert.

Usually, I choose a funny clown mask. First, re-create the face with fresh fruit: Place the fresh fruit slices

Re-create the face of the mask with fresh fruit.

Spread the vanilla Bavarian over the bottom and up the sides of the mask by gently pushing it into place.

Fill the inside of the mask with the pistachio Bavarian.

Cover the Bavarian with the génoise.

in the appropriate indentations. I use thinly sliced strawberries to give the clown a red nose and a red tongue, melon slices around the mouth, apricot slices for the eyebrows, whole grapes for the eyes, sliced melon for the eyelids, and blood orange segments for the cheeks. I like to balance the colors and textures of the fruit. Be sure to fill the indentations completely, or the Bavarian will show in the gaps. Be creative and have fun; the wilder it is, the more the children will like it. Place the fruit-filled mask in the refrigerator until ready to use.

Prepare the Bavarian: If you are using gelatin sheets, place them in a medium-size bowl with enough cold water (about 1½ quarts) to cover. Let stand for about 5 minutes to allow the gelatin to soften and hydrate. Cold water hydrates the gelatin without letting it absorb too much liquid. Remove the gelatin from the bowl and squeeze out the excess water with your hands. If you are using powdered gelatin, sprinkle it over ½ cup (3.5 ounces; 100 grams) of cold water. Let the gelatin bloom until it has absorbed all the water, about 2 minutes. Set aside until ready to use.

The base of this Bavarian is a crème anglaise. Half of it will be flavored with pistachio paste and the other half will be used as is. Pour the milk into a non-reactive 2-quart heavy-bottomed saucepan and place over medium-high heat. Use a sharp paring knife to slice the vanilla bean in half lengthwise. Separate the seeds from the skin by scraping the blade of the knife along the inside of the bean. Place the seeds and the vanilla bean in the heating milk and heat until bubbles form around the edge of the pan. Remove from the heat.

In a medium-size mixing bowl, whisk together the sugar and egg yolks until well incorporated and thick. Temper (page 22) the eggs by pouring about half of the hot milk into the egg mixture and whisking thoroughly to combine. Add the hydrated gelatin and pour the tempered egg mixture into the saucepan, stirring constantly. Cook over medium-high heat, continuing to stir, until the mixture is thick enough to coat the back of a rubber spatula. You can tell it is finished cooking by using the following method: In one quick motion, dip the spatula into the crème anglaise and hold it horizontally in front of you. With the tip of your finger, wipe a clean line down the center of the spatula. If the trail keeps its shape, the crème anglaise is ready to be removed from the heat. If the trail fills with liquid, cook it for another minute and repeat the test. The objective is to remove the crème anglaise from the heat just *before* it boils.

When the crème anglaise has finished cooking, remove it from the heat. Strain it through a fine-mesh sieve into two bowls, dividing it evenly. Flavor one bowl of the cream by stirring in the pistachio paste, mixing until well combined. Set both aside while you whip the heavy cream.

Pour the heavy cream into a medium-size mixing bowl and whip to soft peaks with an electric mixer on medium-high speed.

Cool the unflavored crème anglaise in the ice bath, stirring constantly with a rubber spatula, until it is thick enough to briefly hold a line drawn through the middle. Remove from the ice bath and make a vanilla Bavarian by using a rubber spatula to gently fold in half of the whipped cream. Be careful: If the whipped cream is added when the crème anglaise is too warm, the Bavarian will be liquid because the heat of the crème anglaise will melt the whipped cream. If added when the crème anglaise is too cold, the Bavarian will be lumpy. If the crème anglaise cools too much before the whipped cream is added, warm it up over a double boiler (page 3) in 10-second intervals.

Remove the mask from the refrigerator and spread the vanilla Bavarian over the bottom and up the sides by gently pushing it into place with a rubber spatula. Do not press too hard, or you will deflate the Bavarian; simply guide the mixture into place. You can also pipe the Bavarian into the mask using a pastry bag fitted with a ¾-inch plain tip. Spread it up the sides of the mask with the back of a large spoon. Whichever method you choose, be careful not to move the fruit as you add the Bavarian. Return the mask to the refrigerator while you prepare the pistachio Bavarian.

Cool the pistachio crème anglaise in the ice bath, stirring constantly with a rubber spatula, until it is thick enough to briefly hold a line drawn through the middle. Remove from the ice bath and gently fold in the remaining whipped cream.

Fill the inside of the mask with the pistachio Bavarian by gently spreading it with a small offset spatula or the back of a large spoon, or by piping it. Fill to about 1/2 inch from the top. You want to leave enough room for the cake layer. Cover the Bavarian with the precut layer of génoise. The cake layer will support the dessert when unmolded. Gently press the génoise into the Bavarian. Place in the refrigerator until set, about 4 hours.

Remove the mask from the refrigerator and from its nest. Center a plate face down over the mask. Flip over the plate and mask at the same time so the mask is on top of the plate. Use a hair dryer to gently heat the top of the mask for about 10 seconds. Pry the edges loose with your fingers to allow some air to get between the mask and the Bavarian and gently lift it off. If the mask does not release, you may need to use the hair dryer again. Be careful not to overheat the mask, or the Bavarian will melt.

Place some angel hair around the clown's head. Present the dessert to your guests before you slice it. Use a hot knife to slice the dessert. Heat the knife by running it under hot water before each slice; remember to wipe the excess water from the knife after it is rinsed.

Variation: To make this dessert lighter, add a layer of génoise between the vanilla and pistachio Bavarian cream layers.

Floating Island

T he traditional way to prepare a Floating Island is to make a meringue and poach it in hot milk. Instead of poaching the meringue, I pipe it into a mold and bake it. I also add raspberry jam to the meringue to give it more color and flavor. I make my own jam, but you can use store-bought if you stir it with a spoon to loosen it before you add it to the meringue.

If you would like to make a low-fat alternative, float the islands in any flavor of fruit sauce (I like raspberry or mango).

For the meringue

4 large egg whites			
Granulated sugar	**¹/₂ cup**	**3.5 ounces**	**100 grams**
Linda's Red Raspberry Jam (page 46)	**¹/₂ cup**	**5.7 ounces**	**162 grams**

For the coating

Bittersweet chocolate, chopped		**7 ounces**	**200 grams**
Vegetable or canola oil	**2 tablespoons**	**1.1 ounces**	**30 grams**

For the garnish

Crème Anglaise (page 24)

Chocolate Sauce (page 45)

For the caramel

Granulated sugar	**1 cup**	**7 ounces**	**200 grams**

Preheat the oven to 400°F (200°C). Place a baking sheet or pan in the oven and prepare a water bath by filling it with about 1 inch of water. Let the water heat in the oven as you prepare the egg whites. The hot water helps the meringue cook faster.

continued

Prepare the meringue: Place the egg whites in a medium-size mixing bowl and whip with an electric mixer on medium speed until foamy. Add the sugar 1 tablespoon at a time and whip on medium-high speed to stiff but not dry peaks. Adding the sugar in this manner keeps the egg whites from crumbling and allows the sugar to dissolve. Use a rubber spatula to fold in the raspberry jam a little bit at a time. The raspberry jam is heavier than the egg whites and I add it in several additions so I don't deflate the meringue. Place the raspberry meringue in a pastry bag with a large opening (no tip). I use dome molds (page 3) but you can also use a muffin tin. Spray eight molds with baking spray and pipe the meringue into the molds, filling them to the top. Use an offset spatula to smooth the tops. Set the molds in the water bath. The water should come halfway up the sides of the molds. The water bath creates steam and protects the meringue from the direct heat of the oven.

Bake the meringues until firm, 10 to 12 minutes. The meringue will feel tight, like a marshmallow. Remove the molds from the oven. For safety reasons, I usually turn off the oven and allow the water to cool before I remove the water bath from the oven.

Prepare the coating: Place a 1-quart saucepan half-filled with water over high heat and bring to a simmer. Make a double boiler by setting a large mixing bowl over the simmering water. Place the chopped chocolate and oil in the bowl and heat until the chocolate is completely melted, stirring occasionally. When fully melted, the chocolate will be a little bit warmer than your hands. Adding an unflavored oil softens the cocoa butter in the chocolate, which allows the chocolate to set in a soft coating instead of a hard shell. Don't substitute butter, because it contains water, which would cause the chocolate to seize (harden). Remove the mixing bowl from the heat and set aside until ready to use.

To coat the meringues: To unmold the meringues, I dip my fingers in cool water and use them to slide each meringue from the mold. If it sticks, gently blow down one side of the mold to break the seal. Balance the meringue on the end of an offset spatula and hold it over the bowl of chocolate. Ladle chocolate over the meringue until it is completely covered, allowing the excess to drip back into the bowl. The chocolate coating will set up faster if the meringue has cooled slightly. Set the chocolate-covered meringue on a parchment paper–covered baking sheet. Repeat these steps to cover as many of the meringues as you would like covered with chocolate. I usually leave half of them plain because I think it makes the presentation more interesting. At this stage, the meringues can be stored, uncovered, in the refrigerator for up to 4 hours.

To assemble: Pour the crème anglaise onto a large platter. Make the Floating Islands by placing the meringues in the sauce. I like to dot the crème anglaise with chocolate sauce and run a wooden skewer through the dots to create a pattern. You can also garnish with sliced fresh fruit.

Prepare the caramel: Pour the sugar into a 1-quart heavy-bottomed saucepan and place over medium-high heat. Cook it until it is a golden brown caramel, about 5 minutes. If the sugar cooks unevenly, stir it gently with a wooden spoon. Dip a spoon into the caramel and drizzle it over the plain islands. Serve.

Fruity Delights

♦ ♦ ♦

IN THE SOUTH OF FRANCE, people are very passionate about fruit. At the daily market, the vendor asks, "When will you eat this?" before he or she chooses the fruit because he or she wants to know if you will eat it today or tomorrow, and based on your answer, will select fruit at just the right stage of ripeness. Like French bread, fruit is purchased for the day, not for the week. It is harvested only when it is ready to be consumed, and small imperfections in the fruit are accepted. Of course, France is a much smaller country and the farmers deliver right to the town square every day. In the United States, fruit is sometimes shipped across the country and has to be harvested well in advance of its prime to survive the trip. Try to support your local growers and always use the best-quality ripe fresh fruit available.

I think fruit is one of a pastry chef's best friends. It makes a very natural dessert by itself but my work is to capture its essence and to try to improve what is already a stunning creation by Mother Nature. Let the seasons influence you. As they change, so does the availability of different varieties of fruit.

Roasted Pineapple

8 TO 10 SERVINGS

When I walk through the restaurant and notice someone has not ordered dessert, I have to ask him or her why. Many times, the person responds that he or she is on a diet. Since I believe every meal should end in dessert, I like to have something ready to surprise those customers. When I saw a dessert similar to this one in my friend Pierre Hermès's book for professional chefs, I thought it would be a great dessert to make at home.

Be sure to use a sweet, ripe pineapple for the best results. Look for one with no bruises or spots and whose top leaves come out easily when gently tugged. A ripe pineapple will also have a strong pineapple smell. I like to decorate the finished pineapple with its own green leaves.

1 large pineapple			
Vanilla sugar (see below)	**1 cup**	**7 ounces**	**200 grams**
5 vanilla beans			

Fill a nonreactive 6-quart heavy-bottomed saucepan with water and bring to a boil. While the water is heating, peel the pineapple. Here is my technique: Use a serrated knife and cut off ¾ inch from the top and bottom of the pineapple (save the top for garnish, if you like). Stand the pineapple upright on a cutting board and place the blade of the knife at the top of the pineapple about ¼ inch in from the skin. With the blade of the knife at a 45-degree angle, cut along the natural curve of the pineapple from top to bottom, slicing off the skin. Repeat this procedure, moving around the pineapple, until all of the skin is removed. Remove as many of the eyes as possible. You

want the pineapple to look as clean and neat as possible since it will be presented whole. Roll the peeled pineapple in the vanilla sugar until it is well coated. Stand the pineapple on end and use the handle of a wooden spoon to pierce ten holes horizontally through the pineapple, making sure they are evenly spaced from top to bottom. The core of the pineapple is too hard to pierce, so poke the holes just off center.

Use a sharp knife to slice the vanilla beans in half lengthwise. Insert one vanilla bean half into each hole in the pineapple. The final presentation will look nicer if you push the vanilla beans all the way through the pineapple so both ends are visible. Completely and thoroughly wrap the pineapple in five or six layers of plastic wrap. You want to make sure that no water can penetrate the plastic wrap. You can also use a zippered-top plastic bag, but be sure to remove all of the air from the bag before sealing it. Place the wrapped pineapple in the now-boiling water. Reduce the heat to low and allow the pineapple to simmer until it becomes slightly translucent and the color has darkened, about 1 hour. *Do not let the water return to a boil.*

continued

. . . *Fruity Delights* . . .

About 10 minutes before the pineapple is ready, preheat the oven to 350°F (175°C). When the pineapple is ready, remove it from the saucepan. Hold the pineapple over an ovenproof nonreactive 4-quart saucepan and remove the plastic wrap, allowing any juice to drip into the pan. *Be careful; it is very hot!* Place the pineapple in the saucepan and bake until soft and slightly brown, 40 to 45 minutes. Baste it with its own juices every 5 to 10 minutes; this will help keep the pineapple moist.

Remove the saucepan from the oven. The aroma of the pineapple should fill your kitchen! Place the roasted pineapple on a platter. I usually save the top of the pineapple and reattach it with wooden skewers.

I like to serve this with exotic fruit sorbets such as mango (page 271) or coconut (page 280). Vanilla ice cream (page 286) is also a nice accompaniment. Serve the pineapple while it is still warm and let the ice cream or sorbet melt into the juices. You won't have any leftovers!

To make vanilla sugar, place any cleaned, used vanilla beans on a baking sheet and set aside until dry. There is really no specific recipe for vanilla sugar. Any amount of granulated sugar will do. With less sugar, the vanilla flavor will be stronger. I usually mix one vanilla bean with about 2 cups sugar. When the vanilla beans are dry, place them in a food processor with the sugar and process on high speed until the vanilla and sugar appear to have the same texture, about 1 minute. Pass the mixture through a fine-mesh sieve to remove any large pieces.

If you don't have a food processor, you can simply place the dried vanilla beans in some granulated sugar and store in an airtight container. The sugar will take on the flavor of the vanilla. Another way to make vanilla sugar is to use the vanilla seeds. Use a sharp knife to slice the beans in half lengthwise. Separate the seeds from the skin by scraping the blade of the knife along the inside of the bean. Mix the seeds and some granulated sugar together in a bowl. I rub the vanilla seeds and sugar between my fingers to ensure that the seeds are evenly distributed.

Vanilla sugar will keep indefinitely if stored in an airtight container at room temperature.

Winter Fruit Fricassee

8 SERVINGS

This is one of my favorite "fast and easy" recipes. In a professional kitchen, it takes only about fifteen minutes to put this dessert together. I adapted the concept from the *chef de cuisine's* vegetable fricassee. Sometimes I like to serve it with raspberry or mango sorbet (pages 270–271) to give a burst of color and contrast in temperature.

For the hats

16 sheets phyllo dough (page 213)			
Unsalted butter, melted	**1¼ cups**	**10 ounces**	**280 grams**
Powdered sugar	**3 cups + 1 tablespoon**	**12.5 ounces**	**350 grams**

For the fricassee

1 vanilla bean			
Granulated sugar	**⅔ cup**	**4.8 ounces**	**136 grams**
1 apple, peeled and cut into balls with a melon baller			
1 pear, cored and sliced			
Candied orange peels (page 90)	**¼ cup**	**1.5 ounces**	**50 grams**
½ pineapple, peeled, cored, and diced			
Red grapes	**½ cup**	**3.5 ounces**	**100 grams**
6 candied chestnuts (optional)			
Walnuts, chopped	**½ cup**	**2.8 ounces**	**80 grams**
Dark rum	**¼ cup**	**1.6 ounces**	**50 grams**

Prepare the hats: Preheat the oven to 350°F (175°C). You will need eight 3-ounce soufflé molds to make the phyllo hats. Divide the molds between two baking sheets, placing them upside down on the sheets and spacing them two per row.

Place a sheet of phyllo on your work surface. Using a pastry brush, evenly coat the phyllo with a generous tablespoon of the melted butter. Place the powdered sugar in a fine-mesh sieve and evenly sprinkle sugar on top of the butter. Top with another

sheet of phyllo and repeat with more butter and powdered sugar. Using a cake pan or a lid as a guide, cut the double sheets into an 11-inch circle. Center the double phyllo circle, butter and sugar side down, over an upside-down soufflé mold and press the phyllo circle down over the bottom and sides of the mold to give the phyllo the form of the mold. Repeat these steps with the remaining sheets. Sprinkle the molded phyllo hats lightly with more powdered sugar. When the phyllo bakes, the butter and sugar will caramelize, adding flavor to the dessert.

Place the baking sheets in the oven and bake until golden brown, 7 to 10 minutes. Remove the sheets from the oven and very gently lift the phyllo hats off the soufflé molds. If you try to unmold the phyllo after the caramel has cooled, the phyllo will stick to the molds and the hats will break. Place the hats on a clean baking sheet and set aside while you prepare the fricassee. The hats are very fragile, so handle them carefully.

Prepare the fricassee: Use a sharp knife to slice the vanilla bean in half lengthwise. Separate the seeds from the skin by scraping the blade of the knife along the inside of the bean. Combine the vanilla seeds with the granulated sugar. Heat a heavy-bottomed frying pan over medium-high heat. If it starts to smoke, the pan is too hot and you need to run it under cool water, dry it, and start again. When the pan is warm, sprinkle the sugar into the pan in an even layer so it will caramelize at the same time. As soon as you see the sugar begin to melt, start moving the pan over the burner to keep the sugar from burning. Tilt the pan from side to side so that the melted sugar runs over the unmelted sugar. Cook until all of the sugar is a light golden brown. Add the apple balls and pear slices and cook until soft, 3 to 5 minutes, depending on the ripeness of the fruit. Add the remaining fruit, the nuts, and rum and cook over high heat until most of the liquid has evaporated, 3 to 5 minutes. The fruit should be golden brown. (The fruit is cooked in two stages because the harder fruit—apples and pears—takes longer to cook than the softer fruit. This way all the fruit will be evenly cooked and ready at the same time.)

To serve, center an inverted phyllo hat on each plate and fill with the warm caramelized fruit mixture.

Variation: Fill the bottom of the phyllo hats with Pastry Cream (page 26) and top with the caramelized fruit.

Roasted Strawberries with Vanilla Ice Cream

*I*n this recipe, a cake layer absorbs and retains all the juice from the strawberries, the butter, and the sugar to create a delightful dessert. I love the intense flavor the strawberries develop when roasted. You can roast other fruits, but if you use a fruit that does not contain a lot of juice, omit the cake layer, or the dessert will be too dry.

You can buy pound cake if you don't want to make a cake layer. Unless you use store-bought ice cream, you will need to prepare the vanilla ice cream. Allow enough time for the ice cream to freeze before you serve the dessert.

1 recipe Vanilla Ice Cream (page 286)			
½ recipe Classic Génoise or Biscuit batter (page 38 or 40)			
Stoli Razberi vodka (optional)	**2 tablespoons**	**0.8 ounce**	**25 grams**
Fresh strawberries, hulled	**2 pints**		
Clarified butter (page 173)	**5 tablespoons**	**2 ounces**	**60 grams**
Vanilla sugar (page 168)	**2 tablespoons**	**0.8 ounce**	**25 grams**

You will need to bake a sheet of génoise or biscuit, whichever you prefer.

Preheat the oven to 400°F (200°C). Cut the cake layer to fit the bottom of a 6 × 12-inch casserole dish and place it in the bottom of the dish. Sprinkle the vodka over the cake, if you wish. Place the strawberries hulled side down on top of the cake. Use a pastry brush to liberally coat the strawberries with the clarified butter. I like to use my spray bottle to do this; I give each strawberry about one full squirt, which is probably about 1 teaspoon. (Clarified butter works better than melted butter because it won't burn at high temperatures.) Sprinkle the vanilla sugar over the strawberries. As the strawberries roast, the vanilla sugar will intensify their flavor. Place the casserole dish in the oven and roast until the strawberries begin to get soft and the tops are lightly browned, about 10 minutes.

Remove the casserole dish from the oven. I like to serve the roasted strawberries in small bowls with the cake positioned on the bottom. I place a scoop of vanilla ice cream on top and spoon any extra juice over the ice cream. The aroma is almost as wonderful as the taste. Serve immediately!

To clarify butter, heat it in a heavy-bottomed saucepan over low heat. Use a large pan deep enough to easily hold the amount of butter you are clarifying. The butter will separate by itself as it melts. The milk fat rises to the top and the water (whey) stays on the bottom. You want to use what is in the middle. Skim off the top as the butter melts until all of the milk fat is gone. Carefully pour the middle part into a clean bowl or a spray bottle until you reach the water on the bottom. One-half cup butter will yield about ⅓ cup clarified butter.

Clarified butter will keep in the refrigerator for up to three weeks. Simply warm it up again to liquefy before using. When using clarified butter, keep it liquid by placing the filled bowl or spray bottle in a container of warm water.

Whole Roasted Peaches with Fresh Almonds and Pistachios

8 SERVINGS

When I go home to France to visit family, this is the recipe I make so I can spend time with my young nieces and nephews. We go out to the garden and choose our favorite fruits from my dad's nectarine, peach, and apricot trees. I have the nuts already prepared in small bowls. We sit around the dining room table and everyone makes his or her own creation. Some of the older kids help the younger ones. It gives me a chance to share my profession and hear all about their latest adventures.

Slivered pistachios	*½ cup*	*3.2 ounces*	*64 grams*
Slivered blanched almonds	*½ cup*	*3.2 ounces*	*64 grams*
8 peaches			
Vanilla sugar (page 168)	*1½ cups*	*10.5 ounces*	*300 grams*
Unsalted butter, melted	*½ cup*	*4 ounces*	*113 grams*
Water	*¾ cup + 2 tablespoons*	*7.2 ounces*	*200 grams*

Preheat the oven to 350°F (175°C). If you cannot find slivered pistachios, buy whole ones and sliver them yourself. To do this, use a sharp paring knife to cut the pistachios in half lengthwise. If the pistachios are large, cut them in half again lengthwise.

Randomly press the slivered pistachios and almonds into the peaches. The skin of the peach will help to hold the nuts in place. The nuts should be spaced about ⅓ inch apart. Sprinkle half of the vanilla sugar evenly over the bottom of a 9 × 13-inch baking pan. I prefer to use a heavy copper pan because the copper distributes the heat evenly. It is important to use a pan deep enough to catch the juices of the peaches as they roast. Place the peaches on top of the sugar. Liberally brush the peaches with the melted butter; I use my spray bottle to squirt the entire peach with butter. Sprinkle with the remaining sugar. This will give the peaches a nice crust when baked. Pour the water into the bottom of the pan.

Place the pan in the oven and roast for 10 to 15 minutes. The roasting time will vary according to the ripeness of the peaches. As the peaches are roasting, baste them about every 5 minutes with their juices to keep them moist and flavorful. The peaches are ready when they are slightly brown on top, the skin has loosened slightly, and they can be pierced easily with the tip of a paring knife. Their consistency will be similar to that of the fleshy part at the base of your thumb.

Remove the pan from the oven and place the peaches on a plate. Strain the peach juices through a fine-mesh sieve into a clean bowl. If you are serving adults, you can add a little Stoli Persik vodka to the juice to give the sauce a little pizzazz. Pour the sauce over the peaches and serve immediately. I think vanilla ice cream is an excellent complement to this dessert.

Crêpes with Caramelized Pears

12 FILLED CRÊPES

*T*here's a tradition in France called the *Chandeleur,* which takes place the second Tuesday in February. It involves holding a coin in one hand while flipping a crêpe in a pan with the other. If the crêpe does not break, it means good fortune, health, and happiness for the rest of the year. In many small towns in France, like my hometown, Bandol, everyone meets in the town square to participate in this tradition. I remember going with my parents when I was younger. I never did learn to flip the crêpe without breaking it!

With this recipe, you can use any fresh seasonal fruit for the filling. When I can't find nice pears, I use peaches, apples, or apricots. Remember that it is difficult to caramelize fruit that has a lot of juice (e.g., berries, citrus fruits, and melon).

For the crêpes

3 large eggs			
Granulated sugar	¼ cup	1.75 ounces	50 grams
1 vanilla bean			
All-purpose flour	½ cup	2.6 ounces	75 grams
Grated zest of ½ orange			
Grated zest of ½ lemon			
Whole milk	Scant ⅔ cup	5.4 ounces	150 grams
Heavy cream	Scant ½ cup	3.5 ounces	100 grams
Unsalted butter	1 to 2 tablespoons	0.5 to 1 ounce	14 to 28 grams

For the caramelized pears

3 pears			
1 vanilla bean			
Dark rum	2 tablespoons	1 ounce	30 grams
Granulated sugar	¼ cup	1.75 ounces	50 grams
Unsalted butter (optional)	1 tablespoon	0.5 ounce	14 grams

Prepare the crêpes: Place the eggs and sugar in a large mixing bowl and beat with an electric mixer on medium speed until thoroughly combined. Use a sharp knife to slice the vanilla bean in half lengthwise. Separate the seeds from the skin by scraping the blade of the knife along the inside of the bean. Set the empty vanilla bean aside to use when assembling the crêpes. Add the vanilla seeds, flour, citrus zests, and half of the milk to the egg mixture and beat on medium speed until well incorporated. I add the milk in two additions to keep the dry ingredients from clumping together. Add the remaining milk and the heavy cream and continue to beat until the crêpe batter is smooth and homogenous. If the batter is lumpy, use an immersion blender, or whisk it, to make it smooth.

Grease an 8-inch nonstick crêpe pan (a nonstick frying pan will also work) with about 1 teaspoon of butter and place over medium-high heat. Once it is hot, pour a small amount of crêpe batter, about 2 tablespoons, into the pan and tilt the pan to spread the batter evenly. The batter should barely cover the bottom of the pan. Cook until it browns around the edges, about 30 seconds. Use a large spatula or pancake flipper to gently lift one side of the crêpe and carefully flip it. Cook the crêpe until the other side starts to brown, about another 30 seconds. You may need to adjust the level of heat if it cooks too quickly and burns in places. The crêpe should be thin, light, and unevenly browned. Slide the crêpe onto a plate and continue to make crêpes until all of the batter is used. If the crêpes begin to stick to the bottom of the pan, lightly butter the pan again as necessary.

The finished crêpes can be stacked directly on top of each other. They can be made one to two days in advance if kept well wrapped in the refrigerator. When the crêpes are cold, they may stick together because of the butter residue on the surface of the crêpes. If you warm the stacked crêpes slightly in the microwave for 10 to 15 seconds on high power, they will separate easily.

Prepare the caramelized pears: Peel, core, and cut the pears into 1/2-inch-thick slices. Use a sharp knife to slice the vanilla bean in half lengthwise. Separate the seeds from the skin by scraping the blade of the knife along the inside of the bean. Set the empty vanilla bean aside to be used later when assembling the crêpes. Place the vanilla seeds and the pears in a small mixing bowl. Add the rum and let macerate for about 10 minutes.

Heat a large heavy-bottomed frying pan over medium-high heat. If it starts to smoke, the pan is too hot and you need to run it under cool water, dry it, and start again. When the pan is warm, sprinkle the sugar into the pan in an even layer so it will caramelize at the same time. As soon as you see the sugar begin to melt, start moving the pan over the burner to keep the sugar from burning. Tilt the pan from side to side so that the melted sugar runs over the unmelted sugar. Cook until all of the sugar is a light golden brown. I usually add a tablespoon of butter at this stage because it makes the caramel smoother. Add the pear mixture and spread it evenly in the pan. Let cook over medium-high heat until most of the liquid has evaporated and the pears are soft but not mushy. They should hold their shape but the tip of a paring knife should easily pierce them. If the pears are still hard when most of the liquid has evaporated, add a few tablespoons of water and continue cooking until the pears are done. Pour the caramelized pears onto a plate. Cover with plastic wrap and let cool for about 20 minutes. Covering the hot pears with plastic wrap keeps the caramel from drying as it cools.

To assemble the crêpes: Use a sharp paring knife to slice each of the vanilla bean halves into three strips lengthwise. If your vanilla bean halves are not wide enough to cut into three strips, just cut them in half lengthwise. These pieces will be used to tie the crêpe bundles together. It is easiest to tie the bundles together if you have long, thin vanilla bean strips.

Place one crêpe on a clean work surface. Fill the center of the crepe with about 2 tablespoons of the caramelized pears. Fold the crepe in half so that it looks like a fan. Bring the ends of the fan towards the center and tie the bundle with a vanilla bean strip. Make eleven more crêpe bundles. If you don't have enough vanilla bean strips you can just fold the crepes closed. Stand the crêpe bundles upright in the center of the plates and serve.

When I serve these in the restaurant, I place two crêpe bundles on each plate and decorate with raspberry sauce (page 44) to give the plate some color. If I have left-over caramelized fruit, I place it around the bundles. Vanilla ice cream (page 286) also goes well with this dessert, especially if served when the filling is still warm.

The filled crêpes should be served within one hour of assembly. If necessary, heat the crêpe bundles in the microwave on high power for 30 seconds or covered with aluminum foil in a preheated 350°F (175°C) oven for 5 to 10 minutes.

Traditionally, crêpe batter is made with melted butter. When you add cold milk, the butter separates and the fat floats to the top. By substituting heavy cream for the butter, I keep the fat without having to worry about the butter separating.

Individual Raspberry Soufflés

SIX 4-INCH SOUFFLÉS

I think Americans must love soufflés, because this is one of the most popular desserts at Le Cirque. There are many myths about soufflés. I have heard people say you shouldn't open the oven door or make any loud noises when they are baking. Actually, soufflés are not as fragile as you might think. Try this recipe and I believe you will be quite pleased with the results. I adapted the traditional soufflé recipe to make it easier and to ensure successful soufflés every time.

For the soufflé base

Fresh raspberries	*About 2 cups*	*8.8 ounces*	*250 grams*
Granulated sugar	*½ cup + 2 tablespoons*	*4.5 ounces*	*125 grams*
Sure-Jell	*2 tablespoons*	*0.75 ounce*	*20 grams*

For the Italian meringue

Water	*¼ cup*	*2 ounces*	*50 grams*
Granulated sugar	*½ cup + 2 tablespoons*	*4.5 ounces*	*125 grams*
8 large egg whites			

To finish the soufflés

Powdered sugar for dusting

Preheat the oven to 400°F (200°C). Soufflés are baked at a high temperature to ensure a good rise. Use a pastry brush to evenly coat the inside of six 1-cup soufflé molds with softened butter. Fill each mold with granulated sugar, then pour out any excess. If you have properly buttered the molds, the sugar will stick to the sides and bottom. The butter and sugar will keep the soufflés from sticking to the sides and will allow them to rise evenly. The sugar will also give the soufflé a crunchy crust, which I think makes a great contrast to its soft interior.

Prepare the soufflé base: Place the raspberries, sugar, and Sure-Jell in a 1-quart saucepan and whisk over medium-high heat until the mixture boils and thickens. Allow it to boil for 1 to 2 minutes, whisking continuously. Remove from the heat and set aside.

Prepare the Italian meringue: Pour the water and sugar into a 1-quart heavy-bottomed saucepan and place over medium-high heat. When bubbles start to form around the edge of the pan, insert a candy thermometer in the mixture. When the sugar reaches 245°F (118°C), begin to whip the egg whites.

Place the egg whites in a large mixing bowl and whip with an electric mixer on medium-high speed until foamy and slightly soft peaks.

The sugar is ready when it reaches 250°F (121°C), what is known as the soft ball stage (page 16). Make an Italian meringue by pouring the cooked sugar down the side of the bowl as you continue whipping the egg whites. Be very careful not to pour the hot sugar onto the beaters, or it will splatter. Continue whipping the meringue until the outside of the bowl is warm but not hot, about 5 minutes. Do not overwhip, or it will not incorporate evenly into the base and, when baked, the soufflés will have pieces of chewy egg white in the center. You can tell the egg whites are overwhipped if they start to separate and look like scrambled eggs.

Fold the warm soufflé base into the warm Italian meringue in two additions. Fold just until combined (you may still see flecks of raspberry), being careful not to deflate the mixture. It is important for both of these mixtures to be warm so they will combine together smoothly. If one mixture is significantly cooler than the other, it will form clumps when the two are folded together. The warm meringue will also add stability to the unbaked soufflé by slightly cooking the egg whites, keeping the soufflé from collapsing.

Place the soufflé mixture in a large pastry bag with a 2-inch opening (no tip). Pipe into the buttered and sugared molds. The best way to do this is to hold the pastry bag directly over each mold with the tip down. Place the tip inside the mold about 1 inch from the bottom. Using even pressure, pipe the soufflé mixture into the mold, lifting the pastry bag straight up as the mold fills. When you have piped to about 1 inch above the rim of the mold, stop squeezing and lift the tip straight up, leaving a small tail at the top of the soufflé. The piped soufflé will look like a pink chocolate kiss. If you do not have a pastry bag, you can use a rubber spatula to gently spoon the soufflé mixture into the molds. (The unbaked soufflés will hold at room temperature for one hour before baking.)

It will be easier to remove the soufflés from the oven if you place the molds on a baking sheet. Set the baking sheet in the center of the oven; do not place the baking sheet under a rack. If the soufflés are too close to the top of the oven or under a rack, they will stick to the oven or the rack when they rise. If the soufflés are too close to the bottom of the oven, the bottoms will burn before the insides are properly cooked. Bake until the soufflés double in height and start to brown on top, about 10 minutes. Remove the baking sheet from the oven and dust the tops of the soufflés with powdered sugar. Serve immediately.

If you prefer to make one large 8-inch (1½-quart) soufflé, you can gently spoon the mixture directly into the buttered and sugared mold with a rubber spatula; it is not necessary to pipe it with a pastry bag. The soufflé mixture should come to about 1 inch above the rim of the dish. Bake at 375°F (190°C) for about 20 minutes.

The soufflé base can be stored in the refrigerator in an airtight container for up to two weeks. It should be brought to a boil before it is combined with the Italian meringue.

Fresh Fruit Tart

ONE 10-INCH TART; 10 SERVINGS

Usually, when people ask me for a recipe, they take notes on a recipe card. One day, my friend Glenn invited me to dinner and asked me to teach him how to make this fresh fruit tart. He's a very successful lawyer who concentrates on details, so I didn't really think that much about it when he used his Dictaphone to record the steps. We finished the tart, put our steaks on the grill, and enjoyed a lovely evening.

A few days later, I received a large official-looking envelope. The last thing I expected to find inside was an eighteen-page legal transcript detailing every word I had said during the fresh fruit tart lesson! I hope this is as close as I ever come to being in court!

Traditionally, tarts are made with a thinner crust than what I have specified in this recipe. I like a thicker crust because it absorbs more of the flavor from the almond cream, which complements the buttery, crunchy shortbread flavor of the crust.

¹/₃ recipe **Pastry Cream (page 26), flavored**
¹/₂ recipe **Almond Cream (page 28)**
1 recipe **Sugar Dough (page 34)**
Assorted fresh fruit, sliced

Prepare the pastry cream and store tightly covered in the refrigerator until ready to use. Since the pastry cream plays a significant role in this dessert, I like to enhance its flavor with either framboise liqueur or grated orange zest.

You will also need to prepare some almond cream, which adds another dimension of flavor and texture to the tart. You will use the almond cream shortly after you make it, so there is no need to store it in the refrigerator; just set it aside until ready to use. If you have leftover almond cream already stored in the refrigerator, let it come to room temperature and then beat it with an electric mixer at medium speed until it returns to its original volume. (If you are allergic to nuts, you can omit the almond cream from this tart.)

Preheat the oven to 350°F (175°C). Butter a 10-inch fluted tart pan with a removable bottom. Prepare the sugar dough and remove it from the mixing bowl. (If

you are using refrigerated dough, you will need to give the cold dough four or five quick raps with a rolling pin to break up the cold butter.) Pat the dough into a disk and lightly flour each side. Roll the dough into a 12-inch circle that is ¼ inch thick. After each roll with the rolling pin, rotate the dough a quarter turn; this will keep it from sticking to the work surface and help to maintain the shape of the circle. Dust the work surface with flour if needed, but be careful not to overflour, as this will make the dough tough. As you roll out the dough, don't press too hard on the rolling pin, or you will cut the dough in half. Work quickly to keep the butter from melting and the dough from becoming too soft; if this happens, place the dough in the refrigerator until it is firm once again, about 15 minutes.

Transfer the dough to the pan by rolling it around the rolling pin. Hold the rolling pin over the pan and unroll the dough into the pan. Use your fingers to gently press the dough into the bottom and sides of the pan. Be sure you also press into the edge where the side of the pan meets the bottom. Remove the excess dough by rolling the rolling pin over the top of the pan to make a nice clean cut. Dock (page 20) the bottom of the tart shell with a fork to allow the steam to escape during baking and to keep the tart shell flat.

Spread about a ¼-inch-thick layer of almond cream in the tart shell. Place the tart pan on a baking sheet and bake until the almond cream and tart shell are lightly browned, about 10 minutes. The almond cream will have risen slightly and should still be moist inside. Remove the baking sheet from the oven and place on a wire rack until the baked tart shell has completely cooled.

Unmold the tart shell from the pan by pushing up the bottom and releasing the side. Slide a metal spatula or knife between the tart shell and the tart pan bottom to loosen the tart from the bottom of the pan. Slide the tart shell onto a flat plate or cake platter (if you use a plate with slightly raised sides, the tart shell will break).

Spread about a ½-inch-thick layer of pastry cream over the almond cream, filling the tart to the top edge. You can either arrange the sliced fruit in concentric circles on top to form a nice pattern or let the fruit create its own design. I like my fruit tarts to have contrast in color and flavor, so I include assorted berries, apricots, mangoes, and papayas. It is best to serve the tart within 2 hours of assembly.

It is easier to achieve even layers if you use a pastry bag to pipe the almond cream and pastry cream into the tart. For a professional finish, you can glaze the tart. Mix about 1 tablespoon water with ¼ cup apricot jam and heat in the microwave on high power or in a nonreactive 1-quart saucepan over medium heat until liquid. Brush it on with a pastry brush.

Crispy Tarts with Fresh Fruit

8 SERVINGS

I understand it was Ben Franklin who said, "Necessity is the mother of invention." Since I do everything possible to honor a request at the restaurant, sometimes a little invention is necessary. I was just pulling some baked puff pastry circles from the oven when the waiter gave me an order from one of my favorite customers. Dr. Kruger always has the fruit tart, and on this particular day we had just served the last piece. I eyed the puff pastry circles, the pastry cream, and the fresh fruit, and the concept for a new dessert was born. Here is the recipe for what has become Dr. Kruger's favorite dessert.

³⁄₄ recipe Quick Puff Pastry (page 35)			
¹⁄₂ recipe Pastry Cream (page 26), flavored			
Light corn syrup	**³⁄₄ cup**	**8.5 ounces**	**255 grams**
Water	**Scant ¹⁄₄ cup**	**1.75 ounces**	**50 grams**
Bittersweet chocolate, tempered (page 9)		**5.8 ounces**	**160 grams**
Assorted fresh fruit, sliced			
Powdered sugar for dusting			

Prepare the puff pastry up to the point where it is ready to be rolled. While the puff pastry is resting in the refrigerator after its fourth and final fold, prepare the pastry cream and flavor it according to your taste. I like to add framboise liqueur or grated orange zest. Store the pastry cream tightly covered in the refrigerator until ready to use.

Preheat the oven to 400°F (200°C). On a lightly floured work surface, roll the puff pastry into a 12 × 24-inch rectangle about ¹⁄₈ inch thick. Cut it in half and place on two parchment paper–covered baking sheets. Bake until it barely begins to take on color, about 10 minutes. The puff pastry may rise unevenly in sections. If that happens, release the air by gently piercing the dough with the tip of a paring knife. Meanwhile, mix together the corn syrup and water.

continued

Remove the puff pastry from the oven and reduce the oven temperature to 350°F (175°C). Brush the tops of the puff pastry with the corn syrup mixture. Cover with another sheet of parchment paper and flip over the puff pastry. Peel off the parchment paper that is now on top and brush this side with the corn syrup mixture. I like to use the corn syrup to add sweetness, enhance the color as it caramelizes, and make the puff pastry crunchier.

Use a sharp paring knife to cut eight 5-inch circles from the half-baked puff pastry; discard the excess dough. I cut the circles when the dough is half-baked so they will keep their shape. Place the puff pastry circles back in the oven and continue to bake until crispy and golden brown, about another 15 minutes. Remove from the oven and place on a wire rack until completely cooled.

Use a pastry brush to coat one side of each cooled circle with the tempered chocolate and set aside to allow the chocolate to set at room temperature, about 5 minutes. This layer of chocolate keeps the tarts from getting soggy.

To assemble: Spread about 2 tablespoons of the pastry cream on each tart shell on top of the chocolate coating. Cover with assorted sliced fresh fruit. I like to arrange the fruit in a sunburst pattern, fanning each type of fruit from the center of the circle toward the edge. Sprinkle the tops of the tarts with powdered sugar right before you serve them.

It's best to assemble the tarts at the last minute. If the fruit is sliced within 45 minutes of serving, it stays fresh looking and does not wilt or oxidize (brown). Sometimes I place a scoop of sorbet (page 270 or 275) in the center of the tart and garnish with Angel Hair (page 48).

Tarte Tatin

8 SERVINGS

*T*arte Tatin has always been a French classic, but I could almost rename this recipe Tarte Tatin à la Benenson. Mr. Benenson is a regular customer at Le Cirque, and he always requests this dessert. On his behalf, I have experimented with every possible combination of components to achieve the exact taste, texture, consistency, and coloring that Mr. Benenson prefers. He likes it this way. Let me know what you think!

¹/₃ recipe Quick Puff Pastry (page 35)

Light corn syrup	**Generous ¹/₄ cup**	**2.8 ounces**	**85 grams**
Water	**1¹/₂ tablespoons**	**0.75 ounce**	**20 grams**
7 to 8 Golden Delicious apples			
Room temperature unsalted butter	**3¹/₂ tablespoons**	**1.75 ounces**	**50 grams**
Granulated sugar	**¹/₂ cup**	**3.5 ounces**	**100 grams**
Crème fraîche or sour cream (optional)			

Prepare the puff pastry. When you are ready to roll it out, preheat the oven to 400°F (200°C). On a lightly floured work surface, roll out the puff pastry into a twelve-inch square about ¹/₈ inch thick. Place it on a parchment paper–covered baking sheet and bake until it barely begins to take on color, about 10 minutes. The puff pastry may rise unevenly in sections. If that happens, release the air by gently piercing the dough with the tip of a paring knife. Meanwhile, mix together the corn syrup and water in a small bowl.

Remove the puff pastry from the oven and reduce the oven temperature to 350°F (175°C). Brush the top of the puff pastry with the corn syrup mixture. Cover with another sheet of parchment paper and flip over the puff pastry. Peel off the parchment paper that is now on top and brush this side with the corn syrup mixture. I like to use the corn syrup to add sweetness, enhance the color as it caramelizes, and make the puff pastry crunchier. Use a sharp paring knife to cut an 8-inch circle from the half-baked puff pastry; discard the excess dough. I cut out the circle when it is halfway through baking so it will keep its shape. Place the puff pastry circle back in

the oven and continue to bake until crispy and golden brown, about another 15 minutes. Remove from the oven and place on a wire rack until completely cooled. Do not turn off the oven.

While the puff pastry circle is cooling, you can prepare the apples: Peel, core, and halve the apples. With a pastry brush or paper towel, spread the butter evenly over the bottom and sides of an ovenproof 9-inch-wide 1-quart heavy-bottomed saucepan. Sprinkle the sugar evenly over the bottom. Set the apples on end, packing them as tightly together as possible in the pan. It is extremely important to pack them tightly because they will shrink as they cook. If the tart is loosely packed, it will fall apart when unmolded.

Place the saucepan over medium-high heat and cook until the sugar and butter caramelize, about 20 minutes. The butter and sugar will go through a number of phases before you see the caramelization. First you have just butter and sugar. As the pan gets hotter, the apples release some of their juices. These juices mix with the butter and sugar and the mixture begins to bubble. As the moisture evaporates, the sugar turns golden brown as it caramelizes. At this stage, remove the pan from the heat.

Immediately place the pan in the oven and bake until the apples are evenly browned and soft but not mushy, about 20 minutes. They should be soft enough to pierce easily with the tip of a paring knife. Remove from the oven.

Place the baked puff pastry circle on top of the pan; it should fit just inside the rim of the pan, completely covering the apples. Cover the pan with a flat plate. Put on oven mitts and in one fast motion carefully flip everything over while holding one hand on the bottom of the pan and one hand on the bottom of the plate. If you flip it slowly, the hot caramel could drip out of pan and burn your arm. Remove the saucepan.

Traditionally, Tarte Tatin is served with a scoop of crème fraîche. In the restaurant, I serve it with a scoop of pistachio ice cream. I've heard Americans like to serve apple pie with Cheddar cheese, but I haven't tried that idea with Tarte Tatin.

I've tried this recipe with different varieties of apples. I always come back to Golden Delicious because I prefer the texture and the flavor (so does Mr. Benenson). I also think this variety contains just the right amount of acidity needed to give the tart the correct flavor. Sometimes I use Granny Smith or Roma apples. If another variety works well for you, let me know.

Grape Clafoutis

ONE 10-INCH CLAFOUTIS

The classic Clafoutis is made with cherries. I like to make mine with all different kinds of fruit. One day at the restaurant, I received a fantastic variety of grapes and thought it would be fun to make a grape Clafoutis. When Julia Child was a guest on my television show, she said she liked this version better than the traditional Clafoutis recipe because it contains less flour and the custard flavor is more intense. I was thrilled to receive such a lovely compliment.

1 recipe Sugar Dough (page 34)

For the custard

Whole milk	**¹/₂ cup**	**4 ounces**	**120 grams**
¹/₂ vanilla bean			
2 large eggs			
2 large egg yolks			
Granulated sugar	**¹/₃ cup**	**2.4 ounces**	**70 grams**
Pastry flour	**1 tablespoon**	**0.3 ounce**	**8 grams**
Crème fraîche or sour cream	**1 tablespoon**	**0.4 ounce**	**14 grams**

For the filling

Large seedless grapes	**About 2 cups**

To finish the Clafoutis

Powdered sugar for dusting

Prepare the tart shell: Preheat the oven to 350°F (175°C). Lightly butter the bottom of a 10-inch fluted tart pan, or you may have trouble unmolding the baked Clafoutis. I try not to use a tart pan with a removable bottom for this recipe just in case the tart shell cracks and spills the custard onto the baking sheet.

Prepare the sugar dough and remove it from the mixing bowl. (If you are using refrigerated dough, you will need to give the cold dough four or five quick raps with a rolling pin to break up the cold butter.) Pat the dough into a disk and lightly

flour each side. Roll the dough into a 12-inch circle between ¼ and ⅛ inch thick. After each roll with the rolling pin, rotate the dough a quarter turn. This will keep it from sticking to the work surface as well as maintain the shape of the circle. Dust the work surface with more flour if needed, but be careful not to overflour, as this will make the dough tough. When you roll out the dough, don't press too hard on the rolling pin, or you will cut the dough in half. Work quickly to keep the butter from melting and the dough from becoming too soft; if this happens, place the dough in the refrigerator until it is firm once again, about 15 minutes.

Transfer the dough to the pan by rolling it up around the rolling pin. Hold the rolling pin over the pan and unroll the dough into the pan. Use your fingers to gently press the dough into the bottom and sides of the pan. Make sure you press into the edge where the side of the pan meets the bottom. Remove the excess dough by rolling the rolling pin over the top of the pan to make a nice clean cut. Dock (page 20) the bottom of the tart shell lightly with a fork to allow the steam to escape during baking and to keep the shell flat.

Place the tart pan on a baking sheet and bake for 5 minutes. The tart dough takes longer to bake than the custard, and for that reason, the dough is partially baked before the custard is added. Remove the baking sheet from the oven and set aside until ready to use. Keep the tart pan on the baking sheet, as this will make it easier to transfer the tart shell back into the oven once it is filled.

Prepare the custard: Place the milk in a 1-quart heavy-bottomed saucepan over medium heat. Use a sharp knife to slice the vanilla bean in half lengthwise. Separate the seeds from the skin by scraping the blade of the knife along the inside of the bean. Place the seeds and skin in the heating milk. Adding the vanilla to the heating milk will allow the full flavor of the vanilla to infuse the milk and give the Clafoutis a stronger vanilla flavor. When bubbles begin to form at the edge of the pan, remove from the heat.

Place the whole eggs and egg yolks in a large mixing bowl and whisk until well mixed. Whisk in the sugar, flour, and crème fraîche. When smooth, whisk in the heated milk mixture until well combined. Strain the mixture through a fine-mesh sieve into a clean bowl (I prefer to use a large measuring cup with a spout). Straining the mixture removes the vanilla bean as well as any pieces of cooked egg or lumps of flour. Set the custard aside.

To assemble the Clafoutis: Place the grapes in the bottom of the prebaked tart shell. I like to alternate rows of color when I have different varieties of grapes. Completely fill the bottom of the tart. Pour the custard into the tart shell to fill the pan. Place the baking sheet in the oven and bake until the custard sets, about 20 minutes. You can tell if the custard is set by gently shaking the tart pan; if the custard trembles slightly, it is ready. If it is too loose, it needs to be baked longer. In that case, check it every 5 minutes until it is ready. Remove the baking sheet from the oven and allow the Clafoutis to cool.

To unmold the cooled Clafoutis, center a flat plate face down over the tart pan. If you use a plate with raised edges, the tart will break. Flip over the plate and pan at the same time so the tart pan is on top of the plate. Gently lift off the tart pan. Center a second flat plate face down over the unmolded tart. Flip over both plates at the same time so that the Clafoutis is now right side up. Remove the top plate.

Sprinkle the top with powdered sugar before serving. The baked Clafoutis will keep well wrapped in the refrigerator for up to two days.

Fraisier

ONE 9-INCH CAKE

Even though *fraises* means strawberries in French, I like to add raspberries because I think they complement the flavor. Usually I make my own raspberry jam (actually, it's my sister-in-law Linda's recipe). It is necessary to cool freshly made jam in an ice bath before you add it to the buttercream, or it will melt the buttercream. You can use a good-quality store-bought jam if you do not have the time or inclination to make the jam yourself. I don't strain out the seeds because I think they actually blend well with the buttercream.

For the simple syrup

Granulated sugar	**1¼ cups**	**8.7 ounces**	**250 grams**
Water	**1 cup + 1½ tablespoons**	**8.8 ounces**	**250 grams**
Fresh raspberries	**2⅔ cups**		
Framboise liqueur (optional)	**¼ cup**	**1.9 ounces**	**50 grams**

For the cake

1 recipe Biscuit batter (page 40)

For the buttercream

1 recipe Basic Buttercream 1 or 2 (page 31 or 32)

Linda's Red Raspberry Jam (page 46), chilled	**¾ cup**	**9.5 ounces**	**275 grams**

To finish

Fresh strawberries, hulled and sliced, plus 1 whole berry for decoration	**1½ to 2 pints**
Fresh raspberries (optional)	**About 1⅓ cups**

continued

Prepare the simple syrup: Place the sugar and water in a 1-quart heavy-bottomed saucepan and bring to a boil over medium heat. The sugar should completely dissolve. Add the raspberries and return to a boil. Whisk to break the raspberries so they release their juices and cause the syrup to turn red. Remove from the heat.

Prepare an ice bath (page 3). Strain the simple syrup through a fine-mesh sieve into a 2-quart bowl. Discard the seeds and any remaining pieces of berry. When the syrup is cool, add the framboise liqueur, if desired. (If this is added when the syrup is hot, the alcohol will evaporate.) Pour the syrup into a squeeze bottle or a small bowl and set aside until ready to use.

Prepare the cake: Preheat the oven to 400°F (200°C). Prepare the biscuit batter and place it in a pastry bag fitted with a 1/2-inch plain tip. You will need to pipe two biscuit disks. To make the biscuit disks, trace two 8-inch circles on a sheet of parchment paper. Turn the paper over so the outlines are face down on a baking sheet, so the biscuit does not absorb the ink. Start at the center and pipe the biscuit batter in a spiral to the edge of each circle. (I work counterclockwise because I am right-handed.) If the biscuit batter breaks while you are piping it, just continue where it broke. If any air bubbles appear on the disks, simply fill them in with any extra batter left in the piping bag. It takes practice to get the disks perfectly round; don't worry if yours are slightly misshapen. You can gently cut away any imperfection after they are baked. Remember to sprinkle the disks with powdered sugar for a nicer crust.

Start at the center and pipe the biscuit batter in a spiral to the edge of each drawn circle.

Finish piping the biscuit disks.

Place the baking sheet in the oven and bake until the disks are lightly browned, 6 to 10 minutes. Remove the baking sheet from the oven and immediately unmold the disks onto a wire rack, or the heat from the sheet will continue to bake them. Remove the parchment paper when the disks are cool. Set aside.

Prepare the buttercream: Flavor the buttercream by adding the cold raspberry jam to the finished buttercream and beating with an electric mixer on medium speed until

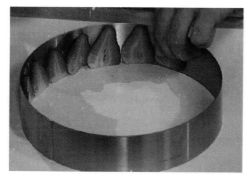

Line the sides of the cake pan with sliced strawberries, their tips pointing up.

Pipe a 1-inch-thick layer of buttercream on top of the biscuit disk and behind the sliced strawberries to hold them in place.

Finish piping the first layer of buttercream.

combined, about 1 minute. Cold jam will help give the buttercream more volume; warm or room-temperature jam will cause the buttercream to lose volume by softening the butter. Place the buttercream in a pastry bag with a large opening (no tip).

To assemble the Fraisier: I use a pan that is slightly larger than the biscuit disks so that the disks will not show through the buttercream on the side of the finished cake. Line the bottom and sides of a 9 × 2-inch cake pan with parchment paper to make it easier to unmold the cake. To do this, cut a parchment paper disk the size of the cake pan and place it on the bottom of the pan. Cut a 2-inch-wide 27-inch-long strip of parchment paper and use it to line the side of the pan.

Line the parchment paper–covered side of the pan with some of the sliced strawberries, with their tips pointing up. Try to use strawberries of equal size so your cake will look nice when unmolded. Place a biscuit disk in the bottom of the cake pan and soak it with half the simple syrup. If you don't have a squeeze bottle for the syrup, use a pastry brush, being careful not to tear the biscuit as you brush it. Pipe a 1-inch-thick layer of buttercream on top of the biscuit disk and behind the sliced strawberries to hold them in place. Use the back of a spoon to smooth the buttercream up the side of the pan. This will give the finished cake a smooth, even look. Place a layer of sliced strawberries or raspberries on top of the buttercream. Pipe a 1/4-inch-thick layer of buttercream on top of the fruit and smooth it out to the edge with an offset spatula to make a nice, even layer. Place the second biscuit disk on top and press it down slightly. Soak the biscuit with the remaining simple syrup. Cover the biscuit disk with about a 1/4-inch-thick layer of buttercream. All of these layers should have filled the cake pan; use an offset spatula to smooth the top of the cake even with the rim of the cake pan. Place in the refrigerator until set, about 2 hours.

To unmold, carefully dip the bottom of the cake pan in hot water for about 5 seconds. *Do not let the pan get hot, or the Fraisier will melt.* Cover the top of the Fraisier with plastic wrap. This will keep the top from sticking to the plate as you unmold it. Center a plate face down over the Fraisier. Flip over the plate and cake pan at the same time so the pan is on top of the plate. Lift the cake pan and remove the parchment paper from the bottom and side of the biscuit. Center a serving plate over the upside-down Fraisier and flip it over again so the Fraisier is right side up. Remove the first plate and plastic wrap.

Place the second biscuit disk over the layers of buttercream, strawberries, and buttercream.

Decorate the top of the Fraisier with more sliced strawberries. I like to start by placing strawberries, tip side out, at the outer edge of the Fraisier and then work my way toward the center in concentric circles. To decorate the center, I make about six slices in a whole strawberry cutting only three fourths of the way from the tip toward the hull and then I spread it into a fan shape.

Decorate the top with sliced strawberries. If using a cake pan, remember to unmold the Fraisier before doing this; if using a cake ring, decorate the top before unmolding it.

If you cut the Fraisier with a hot knife, you will have nice, clean slices. This cake can be stored well wrapped in the refrigerator for up to two days, but it is best when eaten the day it is prepared. Don't try to freeze the cake, as the strawberries release too much water when they thaw.

If you lightly dock (page 20) the biscuit layers before soaking, they will absorb more syrup. This makes the cake more flavorful and moist. If oversoaked, they will become too soggy and fall apart.

For a professional finish, glaze the cake. Mix about 1 tablespoon water with ¼ cup strawberry jam and heat in the microwave on high or in a nonreactive 1-quart saucepan over medium heat until liquid. Apply with a pastry brush.

Grape Terrine

ONE 1½-QUART TERRINE; 10 SERVINGS

ast year, I was visiting my friend Greg in the hospital when his dinner tray arrived. When I asked him what his dessert was, he pointed to a bright green square and made a face. I made the same face when I discovered that American hospitals do not serve wine with dinner. The next day, I experimented in the kitchen to see if I could find a happy medium. Here is my solution. When I brought it to Greg in the hospital, he gave it rave reviews.

This is a lovely dessert to serve during the summer. I like to use large seedless California grapes. You can use other varieties and mix the colors for an interesting display. It is not essential to peel the grapes but I do recommend it as the skins can affect the texture of the terrine. If the grapes are kept in the refrigerator until they are ready to be used, the terrine will set up more quickly.

7 gelatin sheets or 2⅓ envelopes powdered gelatin

Sauternes wine	*2¼ cups*	*17.6 ounces*	*500 grams*

2 large bunches large seedless grapes, peeled

If you are using gelatin sheets, place them in a medium-size bowl with enough cold water (about 2 quarts) to cover. Let stand for about 5 minutes to allow the gelatin to soften and hydrate. Cold water hydrates the gelatin without letting it absorb too much liquid. Remove the gelatin from the bowl and squeeze out the excess water with your hands. If you are using powdered gelatin, sprinkle the gelatin over ⅔ cup (5.3 ounces; 150 grams) of cold water. Let the gelatin bloom until it has absorbed all the water, about 2 minutes.

Place the hydrated gelatin and ¼ cup of the Sauternes in a nonreactive 1-quart saucepan over low heat. Remove the mixture from the heat as soon as the gelatin has dissolved. I dissolve the gelatin with a small amount of the wine to keep it from burning when it is heated and from clumping when it is added to the remaining cooler wine. If I heated more wine, all the alcohol would evaporate, and I would have to wait for the mixture to cool.

Pour the remaining 2 cups Sauternes into a medium-size mixing bowl. Add the dissolved gelatin and stir well to distribute it evenly throughout the wine. Stirring will prevent the gelatin from setting too quickly, which would result in pieces of gelatin in your mixture.

Evenly line the bottom of a 1½-quart terrine mold with about one third of the grapes. (You can also use small individual molds.) The finished terrine will look nicest if the grapes are tightly packed. Pour in one third of the Sauternes mixture. Repeat the grape and wine layers two more times. I do this in stages because it ensures that the grapes and the wine are evenly distributed throughout the terrine. Place the mold in the refrigerator until set, about 2 hours. (The molded terrine will keep in the refrigerator for up to two days.)

To unmold, carefully dip the bottom of the mold in hot water for 5 to 10 seconds. *Do not let the mold get hot, or the terrine will melt.* Tilt the mold slightly and give it a gentle shake to allow air to get between the mold and the terrine. You will know it is ready to unmold when you see the terrine loosen from the sides. If the terrine does not release from the mold, you may need to dip the mold in warm water more than once. Center a plate face down over the mold. Flip over the plate and mold at the same time so the mold is on top of the plate. Lift off the mold. Slice the terrine with a serrated knife and serve. I like to decorate the plate with grapes dipped in caramelized sugar (page 305).

Mimosa Aspic

8 SERVINGS

hen Kris and I first moved to New York, we vowed to keep our Sundays special. When she served me what I thought was orange juice in a champagne glass, I immediately thought, "Uh-oh, the dishwasher is broken." That was my introduction to the Mimosa. Naturally, I wanted to re-create this flavor and texture in a dessert. I tried a few things before I came up with this one. I think you will like it.

I make this recipe in individual 4-ounce molds but you can also use a one-and-a-half-quart mold. When I want to make a dramatic presentation, I use blood oranges.

10 to 12 tangerines			
6 gelatin sheets or 2 envelopes powdered gelatin			
Orange juice	**1 cup**	**8 ounces**	**226 grams**
Champagne	**1 cup**	**8 ounces**	**226 grams**

Use a sharp paring knife to remove the rinds and as much of the white membrane as possible from the tangerines. To do this, I usually slice off ¼ inch from the top and bottom so the tangerine sits flat on the table. Then I hold the tangerine steady with one hand and cut away the remaining rind. Hold the blade of the knife at a 45-degree angle as you follow the natural curve of the tangerine from top to bottom. Don't just peel the fruit by hand. Section the tangerine with a sharp knife by cutting between the membranes to remove the fruit. Allow the fruit segments to drain on a wire rack placed over a baking sheet until ready to use.

If you are using gelatin sheets, place them in a medium-size bowl with enough cold water (about 2 quarts) to cover. Let stand for about 5 minutes to allow the gelatin to soften and hydrate. Cold water hydrates the gelatin without letting it absorb too much liquid. Remove the gelatin from the bowl and squeeze out the excess water with your hands. If you are using powdered gelatin, sprinkle the gelatin over ½ cup (3.5 ounces; 100 grams) of cold water. Let the gelatin bloom until it has absorbed all the water, about 2 minutes.

Place the hydrated gelatin and ¼ cup of the orange juice in a nonreactive 1-quart saucepan over low heat. Remove the mixture from the heat as soon as the gelatin has dissolved. I dissolve the gelatin with a small amount of orange juice to keep the gelatin from burning when it is heated and from clumping when it is added to the remaining cooler juice. If I heated more juice, I would have to wait for all of it to cool before adding the Champagne.

continued

Fruity Delights

Pour the remaining ¾ cup orange juice into a medium-size mixing bowl. Add the dissolved gelatin and stir well to distribute it evenly throughout the orange juice. Stirring prevents the gelatin from setting too quickly, which would result in pieces of gelatin in your mixture. Add the Champagne and stir well.

Place the tangerine segments evenly over the bottom and around the side of each mold. Placing them close together helps the aspic hold its shape when unmolded. Slowly pour the mimosa mixture into each mold, making sure to cover the tangerine segments. Place the filled molds in the refrigerator until set, about 2 hours. (The molded aspic will keep in the refrigerator for up to two days.)

To unmold, carefully dip the bottom of each mold in hot water for 5 to 10 seconds. *Do not let the molds get hot, or the aspic will melt*. Tilt each mold slightly and give it a gentle shake to allow air to get between the mold and the aspic. You will know it is ready to unmold when you see the aspic loosen from the sides. If you used a large mold, you may need to dip it in warm water more than once. Center a plate face down over each mold. Flip over the plate and mold at the same time so the mold is on top of the plate. Lift the mold. I like to decorate the plate with fresh fruit.

Serve immediately. If you used a large mold, cut the aspic with a serrated knife.

Signature Desserts

♦ ♦ ♦

OVER THE YEARS, I have been asked to make a lot of things. One client wanted a statue of her body in white chocolate; another asked me to re-create all of the fabulous Madison Avenue shops. I am inspired by the things I see every day. Texture, color, shape, and size all play a role in deciding what will work in the pastry kitchen. Kris will tell you that I see desserts everywhere. Some of our friends even send ideas or pictures they've cut from magazines, or make requests from their own personal experiences. Fortunately, my job allows me to be very whimsical. My boss has been very supportive of the zany creations I have developed over the years. This chapter is dedicated to those desserts. When one of my desserts is continually requested, even after it is no longer on the menu, that is when I consider it a Signature Dessert.

I hope you will use all of the techniques and basic recipes outlined in this book. If you apply a little imagination, you can create your own Signature Desserts. If you do, send me a picture!

Apple Apple Apple

8 SERVINGS

This dessert presents apples in three different ways: apple syrup, apple sorbet, and apple chips. I usually make it in the fall when the countryside smells of apples, but it makes a refreshing summer dessert too! I prefer to use Granny Smiths because of their tart flavor and crisp texture. You will need to allow time for the sorbet to freeze and to dry the apple slices, so you may want to start the dessert early in the day.

For the sorbet

Sweetened apple juice	*2 cups*	*17 ounces*	*500 grams*
Simple Syrup (page 267)	*¼ cup*	*2.7 ounces*	*75 grams*

For the apple chips

1 large red apple

For the syrup

½ gelatin sheet or ¼ envelope powdered gelatin

Water	*Generous 1 cup*	*8.8 ounces*	*250 grams*
Granulated sugar	*½ cup*	*3.5 ounces*	*100 grams*

Juice of 1 lemon

1 large apple, preferably Granny Smith

Prepare the sorbet: Mix the apple juice with the simple syrup in a medium-size mixing bowl. Place the sorbet mixture into an ice cream machine and spin according to the specifications of that machine. The sorbet is ready when it is smooth and creamy, with a consistency similar to that of soft-serve ice cream. Remove the sorbet from the machine and place in an airtight container in the freezer until ready to use. (The sorbet can be frozen for up to two weeks.)

Prepare the apple chips: Preheat the oven to 250°F (121°C). Use a nonstick baking sheet or spray a sheet of parchment paper with baking spray and place it on a baking sheet. Peel the red apple and set the peel aside to be used in the apple syrup. (If you have an apple corer, you may choose to core the apple.) Lay the apple on its side and use a sharp chef's knife to slice it very thin, cutting through its core (I make my apple slices with a mandoline, page 3.) It's okay if some of the slices are not perfectly whole and round. Place the slices on the baking sheet and bake until golden brown and dry, about 1½ hours. Remove the apple chips from the oven and cool on a wire rack while you prepare the apple syrup.

Prepare the syrup: If you are using a gelatin sheet, place it in a medium-size bowl with enough cold water (about 1 cup) to cover. Let stand for about 5 minutes to allow the gelatin to soften and hydrate. Cold water hydrates the gelatin without letting it absorb too much liquid. Remove the gelatin from the bowl and squeeze out the excess water with your hands. If you are using powdered gelatin, sprinkle the gelatin over 2 tablespoons (1 ounce; 30 grams) cold water. Let the gelatin bloom until it has absorbed all the water, about 1 minute. Set aside.

Combine the apple peel (the peel will give color to the syrup), water, sugar, and lemon juice in a nonreactive 1-quart heavy-bottomed saucepan and bring to a boil over medium-high heat. When the mixture reaches a boil, stir in the gelatin and remove from the heat. The gelatin will thicken the syrup when it cools.

Strain the syrup through a fine-mesh sieve into a clean medium-size bowl. (At this stage the syrup can be kept in the refrigerator, tightly covered with plastic wrap, for up to one month.) Prepare an ice bath (page 3) and place the bowl in it to cool the syrup.

To assemble the dessert: Immediately before serving, pour enough syrup into each soup bowl to cover the bottom. Peel and core the remaining apple. With a sharp chef's knife, slice the apple into matchstick-size pieces and divide the pieces among the bowls. Place one large scoop or three small scoops of sorbet in the center of each bowl. Top each with four apple chips and serve.

The Fontaine

*I*n French, *fontaine* means fountain. When I created these, I imagined the chocolate oozing out, like water rushing out of a fountain. The combination of raspberries and chocolate is a popular one, the bittersweet chocolate balancing the strong flavor of the raspberries. This dessert is filled with contrasts: warm/cold, acid/sweet, crunchy/smooth. The delicate crisp phyllo dough triangles create an architectural quality, giving the dessert an elegant height.

It will be easiest if you make the ganache a few hours in advance and let it cool at room temperature. If you put it in the refrigerator to cool, it will become too hard.

For the ganache

Heavy cream	**Scant ½ cup**	**3.5 ounces**	**100 grams**
Bittersweet chocolate, finely chopped		**5 ounces**	**140 grams**

For the cake

½ recipe Chocolate Génoise batter (page 39)

For the raspberry syrup

Granulated sugar	**1 cup**	**7 ounces**	**200 grams**
Water	**¾ cup + 2 tablespoons**	**7.2 ounces**	**200 grams**
Fresh raspberries	**About 1⅓ cups**		
Framboise liqueur (optional)	**2 tablespoons**	**0.8 ounce**	**25 grams**

For assembly and phyllo garnish

Fresh raspberries	**About 2 cups**		
8 sheets phyllo dough (page 213)			
Unsalted butter, melted	**¾ cup**	**6 ounces**	**170 grams**
Powdered sugar	**1⅓ cups**	**5.2 ounces**	**150 grams**
Heavy cream, whipped to stiff peaks	**½ cup**	**4 ounces**	**115 grams**
Fresh raspberries	**About ⅔ cup**		

continued

Prepare the ganache: Heat the heavy cream in a 1-quart heavy-bottomed saucepan until bubbles begin to form around the edge of the pan. Place the chopped chocolate in a medium-size mixing bowl. Make a ganache by pouring the hot cream over the chocolate and letting it sit for 30 seconds to melt the chocolate, then slowly whisking until smooth and homogenous. Pour the ganache onto a clean baking sheet to allow it to cool. As it cools, it will begin to set and thicken.

Prepare the cake: Prepare the chocolate génoise batter and bake it on a parchment paper–covered baking sheet as directed in the recipe. Cool on a wire rack until ready to use.

Prepare the raspberry syrup: Place the sugar and water in a nonreactive 1-quart heavy-bottomed saucepan and bring to a boil over medium-high heat. The sugar should completely dissolve. Add the raspberries and return to a boil. As the mixture boils, whisk thoroughly to break up the raspberries and allow them to release their juices. This will cause the syrup to turn red. Remove from the heat. Prepare an ice bath (page 3) and strain the syrup through a fine-mesh sieve into a medium-size bowl placed in it. Discard the seeds and any pulp. When the syrup is cool, add the framboise liqueur. (If added when the syrup is hot, the alcohol will evaporate.) Store the syrup in a squeeze bottle or a bowl covered with plastic wrap until ready to use.

Top each cake circle with a layer of ganache.

To assemble the Fontaines: If you have not already done so, peel the parchment paper from the back of the cooled génoise. Use a 2-inch fluted round cutter to cut twelve small circles from the génoise. Keep the cuts as close together as possible to avoid waste. Line the circles up in rows on a parchment paper–covered baking sheet and soak evenly with the raspberry syrup.

When the ganache has cooled to the consistency of toothpaste, scrape it into a pastry bag fitted with a $1/2$-inch plain tip and top each cake circle with a layer of ganache. (I use a pastry bag because it is a clean, easy way to add the layer of ganache.) Place 6 raspberries on top of each ganache layer and press gently to anchor them in the

Place 6 raspberries on top of each ganache layer and press gently to anchor them in the chocolate.

Use a pastry brush to spread the melted butter over the entire surface of the phyllo sheet.

Liberally sprinkle the buttered phyllo sheet with powdered sugar.

Place one raspberry ganache cake in the center of each section of phyllo. Fold the phyllo over each cake.

chocolate. Place the baking sheet in the freezer for about 15 minutes to allow the ganache to harden slightly.

Lay one sheet of the phyllo on your work surface. Keep the remaining phyllo dough covered with a clean kitchen cloth to keep it from drying. Use a pastry brush to spread about 2 tablespoons of the melted butter over the entire surface of the phyllo sheet. It will be easier if you start by brushing a line of butter lengthwise down the center and then fill in by brushing top to bottom from the center toward the edges. Be sure to brush all the way to the edges, where the phyllo is the driest. Place the powdered sugar in a fine-mesh sieve and liberally sprinkle the buttered phyllo sheet with it. Cover with a second sheet of phyllo and repeat with more butter and powdered sugar. Use a sharp paring knife to cut the doubled phyllo sheets in half from top to bottom and then from left to right. Place one raspberry ganache cake in the center of each section of phyllo. Fold each side of the phyllo over each cake and tuck under the edges. Lightly brush the tops with melted butter and place on a parchment paper–covered baking sheet. Repeat these steps using four more phyllo sheets, until all of the cakes are wrapped. (At this stage, the Fontaines can be stored in the refrigerator for a few hours or in the freezer for up to two weeks if well wrapped in plastic wrap; to thaw, place in the refrigerator for an hour before baking.)

To make the phyllo garnish (you should have the garnish ready before you bake the Fontaines): Preheat the oven to 400°F (200°C). Lay one of the remaining sheets of phyllo dough on a parchment paper–covered baking sheet. Use a pastry brush to spread about 2 tablespoons of the remaining melted butter over the entire surface of the phyllo sheet, making sure to brush all the way to the edges. Using the fine-mesh sieve, liberally sprinkle the powdered sugar over the buttered phyllo. Cover with the remaining phyllo sheet and repeat with more butter and sugar. Use a sharp paring knife to cut the doubled phyllo in half lengthwise. Make diagonal cuts from the top to the bottom of each half to create thin elongated triangles (1½ inches at the base and 4 inches tall). Bake until evenly golden brown, about 5 minutes. Stay at the oven and watch these carefully, because they burn very quickly after they brown. Remove from the oven and let cool on a wire rack. (Leave the oven on.)

Use a small offset spatula or knife to loosen the triangles from the parchment paper once they have cooled. Be gentle—they are extremely fragile.

To bake the Fontaines, place them on a baking sheet and bake until the phyllo wrapping begins to brown, 7 to 10 minutes. While these are baking, you can decorate the plates. You will need six phyllo triangles for each serving. Place three triangles in a circle in the center of each plate with the tips toward the edge. Place the whipped cream in a pastry bag filled with a ¼-inch star tip. Pipe a dollop (or rosette) of whipped cream between each triangle and top each dollop with a raspberry.

Remove the Fontaines from the oven. Sprinkle with powdered sugar and center each on a plate, on top of the triangles. Stand three triangles on end to form a tower over each centered Fontaine, using the raspberries to help support the triangles. Serve immediately.

Finish folding the cake in the phyllo dough and tuck under the ends.

Lightly brush the tops with melted butter.

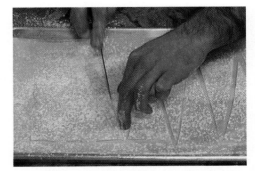

Butter and sugar two sheets of phyllo dough. Make diagonal cuts from top to bottom to create elongated triangles.

Always store phyllo dough well wrapped in the refrigerator to keep it from drying. If it dries, you will have to throw it away. If the phyllo is frozen, you will not be able to separate the layers. Let it thaw, covered, at room temperature. It comes rolled up and you will want to lay it flat. If you have any slight tears in a layer, you can still use it by "gluing" it together with butter. If you tear a layer beyond repair, just throw it away.

Paillason

This dessert's crunchy and creamy contrast makes it similar to a Napoleon. I call it a Paillason because the shredded disks remind me of the traditional shredded potato specialty *pommes paillason*. This recipe contains just three steps: You prepare the paillason cream, bake the shredded phyllo disks, and assemble the Paillason. The paillason cream is crème brûlée custard with strawberries and bananas added, and it is baked in a nine-inch cake pan. The strawberries add acidity and sweetness; the bananas give it an exotic flair.

Using shredded phyllo is a fast, easy way to give any dessert a baked base. When I first started using it, I had trouble distributing the butter evenly: too much and the phyllo gets soggy, too little and it won't hold together. One day, while spraying plants at home with a spray bottle, an idea popped into my head. I took a spray bottle to work and discovered that as long as I keep the butter warm and liquid, I can spray the exact amount of butter needed on the shredded phyllo.

If you cannot find shredded phyllo, which is sometimes called kataifi, buy regular phyllo dough and cut it into thin strips with a sharp knife.

For the paillason cream

1 recipe Crème Brûlée (page 133)

1 large banana, peeled and sliced

5 large fresh strawberries, hulled and halved

For the disks

Shredded phyllo dough (page 217)	**5 cups (loosely packed)**	**5 ounces**	**125 grams**
Clarified butter (page 173)	**½ cup**	**3.6 ounces**	**100 grams**
Powdered sugar	**½ cup**	**2.1 ounces**	**60 grams**
Sliced blanched almonds	**¾ cup**	**4 ounces**	**100 grams**

For the garnish

10 to 12 large fresh strawberries, hulled and sliced

Raspberry sauce (page 43 or 44)

Crème Anglaise (page 24)

continued

Prepare the paillason cream: Preheat the oven to 200°F (93°C). Prepare the crème brûlée mixture but do not pour it into molds. Evenly distribute the sliced banana and strawberry halves in the bottom of a 9-inch cake pan set on a baking sheet with 1-inch-high sides. Fill the cake pan with the crème brûlée mixture. Carefully set the baking sheet in the oven. Use hot water from the tap to fill the baking sheet with water. This custard is baked in a hot water bath to insulate it from the direct heat of the oven and to keep the eggs from cooking too fast, which would cause the custard to separate.

Bake until the custard trembles only slightly when the cake pan is gently shaken, about 45 minutes. If you detect any liquid under the skin, the paillason cream is under-baked. Put it back in the oven and check it every 5 minutes until it is ready.

Remove the cake pan from the oven and place it on a wire rack to cool for 30 minutes, then refrigerate for a minimum of 2 hours. It will continue to set in the refrigerator, and it is best when refrigerated overnight. For safety reasons, I usually turn off the oven and allow the water to cool before I remove the water bath from the oven.

Prepare the disks: Preheat the oven to 400°F (200°C). Use a 4-inch plain round cutter as a guide to shape the phyllo disks. Place the cutter on a parchment paper–covered baking sheet and fill it with a ⅛-inch-thick layer of shredded phyllo. You should be able to see a little bit of the parchment paper through the layer, yet it should be thick enough to hold together when baked. Pat down the shredded phyllo and remove the cutter, being careful not to change the shape of the disk. Repeat the procedure to make a total of twenty-four disks.

If you have a spray bottle, give each disk three full sprays of clarified butter, about 2 teaspoons. If you do not have a spray bottle, apply the butter with a pastry brush. Place the powdered sugar in a fine-mesh sieve and generously sprinkle each buttered disk with sugar. Sprinkle the center of each disk with 4 to 5 almond slices. (If your freezer will accommodate the baking sheet, you can store the disks in the freezer for up to two days. Thaw at room temperature and bake no more than an hour before serving, or they will become soggy.)

Bake the phyllo disks until golden brown, about 5 minutes. Baking the phyllo disks at a high temperature caramelizes the sugar and allows the butter to brown and develop a deep, rich flavor. The butter and sugar hold the baked disks together. Remove from the oven and let the disks cool completely before using.

To assemble the Paillasons: Immediately before serving, place 7 to 10 strawberries slices in a circle in the center of each plate. The pointed ends of the strawberries should face out, like a star. Leave enough room in the center to place a phyllo disk over the strawberry circle. It will be easier to remove these fragile disks from the baking sheet if you use a large spatula. Place a disk in the center of each plate and use a large spoon to place a scoop of paillason cream in the center of each disk. Cover with a second disk and another scoop of paillason cream. Top with a third disk.

Decorate the plates with the raspberry sauce and crème anglaise. I usually alternate drops of each and swirl them together with a wooden skewer.

To shred the phyllo dough yourself, simply stack six phyllo sheets and roll into a cylinder. Then slice very finely with a paring knife.

Capelines

a capeline is a lady's hat from the 1930s. I like to make it for a woman's birthday, for a wedding shower, or to celebrate the arrival of spring.

Passion fruit is very acidic, like lemons, but it also has a lot of flavor. It is not too sweet, but when you add a little bit of sugar, the taste is really dynamic.

I use dome molds (page 3), but you can use any molds with a round bottom. I also use a paint sprayer to give the finished dessert a wonderful texture. This may sound crazy, but it is a technique I use often. If you try this, make sure you buy a brand-new sprayer and use it only for chocolate. If you don't have time to prepare the cake layer, use store-bought pound cake.

For the passion crème brûlée

½ recipe Crème Brûlée (page 133)			
Passion fruit puree	1 cup	8.8 ounces	250 grams

For the cake

½ recipe Classic Génoise or Biscuit batter (page 38 or 40)

For the apricot mousse

10 fresh apricots			
3 gelatin sheets or 1 envelope powdered gelatin			
Water	2 tablespoons	1 ounce	30 grams
Granulated sugar	½ cup	3.5 ounces	100 grams
Light corn syrup	Generous 1 tablespoon	0.8 ounces	25 grams
3 large egg whites			
Heavy cream	Generous 1 cup	8.8 ounces	250 grams

To finish the Capelines

White chocolate, tempered (page 9)		14 ounces	400 grams
Sliced fresh fruit (optional)			
Edible flowers (optional)			

Prepare the passion crème brûlée: Preheat the oven to 200°F (93°C). Prepare the crème brûlée mixture but substitute the passion fruit puree for half of the amount of the heavy cream: Add the passion fruit puree to the heavy cream in the saucepan and follow the rest of the procedure as described in the recipe, but do not pour the mixture into crème brûlée molds.

Place a mini-muffin pan on a baking sheet with 1-inch-high sides. Fill the muffin pan with the passion crème brûlée and carefully set the baking sheet in the oven. (If you have any remaining passion crème brûlée, bake it as indicated in the crème brûlée recipe.) This custard is baked in a hot water bath to insulate it from the direct heat of the oven and to keep the eggs from cooking too fast, causing the custard to separate. Using hot water from the tap, fill the baking sheet with enough water to come halfway up the sides of the mini-muffin pan. Bake until the custard trembles only slightly when gently shaken, about 15 minutes. If you detect any liquid under the skin, it is under-baked. Put it back in the oven and shake every 5 minutes until it is ready. Remove the muffin pan from the water bath and cool it on a wire rack for 30 minutes. Place in the freezer for a minimum of 2 hours, or overnight; the passion crème brûlée needs to be frozen to assemble the dessert.

To unmold, dip the muffin pan in hot water for 5 seconds. Slide the frozen crème brûlée out and place on a parchment paper–covered baking sheet. If the crème brûlée does not release from the mold, it may be necessary to dip the muffin pan more than once, but be careful not to let it get hot, or the crème brûlée will begin to melt. Keep the passion crème brûlée in the freezer, well wrapped in plastic wrap, until ready to use. (The crème brûlée can be frozen for up to two weeks.)

Prepare the cake: Prepare the génoise or biscuit batter and bake on a parchment paper–covered baking sheet as directed in the recipe. Place on a wire rack until completely cooled.

Peel the parchment paper off the cake and use a 2-inch plain or fluted round cutter to cut twelve circles from the cake layer. Cut the circles as close together as possible to avoid waste. Set aside until ready to use.

Prepare the apricot mousse: Halve and pit the apricots and puree with an immersion blender, food processor, or blender. Strain the puree through a fine-mesh sieve to remove the skins and any fruit fibers. Set aside.

If you are using gelatin sheets, place them in a medium-size bowl with enough cold water (about 1 quart) to cover. Let stand for about 5 minutes to allow the gelatin to soften and hydrate. Cold water hydrates the gelatin without letting it absorb too much liquid. Remove the gelatin from the bowl and squeeze out the excess water with your hands. If you are using powdered gelatin, sprinkle the gelatin over 1/4 cup (1.75 ounces; 50 grams) cold water. Let the gelatin bloom until it has absorbed all the water, about 1 minute. Set aside.

Pour the water, sugar, and corn syrup into a 1-quart heavy-bottomed saucepan and place over medium-high heat. When bubbles start to form around the edge of the pan, insert a candy thermometer. When the sugar reaches 245°F (118°C), begin to whip the egg whites.

Place the egg whites in a large mixing bowl and whip with an electric mixer on medium-high speed until foamy and slightly soft peaks.

The sugar is ready when it reaches 250°F (121°C), what is known as the soft ball stage (page 16). Make an Italian meringue by pouring the cooked sugar down the side of the bowl as you continue whipping the egg whites. Do not pour the hot sugar onto the beaters, or it will splatter. Add the hydrated gelatin and continue whipping the meringue on medium speed until the outside of the bowl is warm but not hot, about 5 minutes; the meringue should be stiff and glossy. I add the gelatin to the meringue instead of to the fruit puree because it is an emulsifier (page 20) and will help the egg whites become even lighter.

Pour the heavy cream into a medium-size mixing bowl and whip to soft peaks with an electric mixer on medium speed. Fold half of the apricot puree into the whipped cream, then fold the other half into the Italian meringue, being careful not to deflate either mixture. Fold the meringue mixture into the whipped cream until combined.

Place the mousse in a pastry bag with a large opening (no tip). Pipe the mousse into the dome molds, filling each three fourths full. Spread the mousse to the top of the molds with the back of a large spoon. Place one frozen passion crème brûlée in the center of each mold and gently push into the mousse. Fill with the remaining apricot mousse almost to the top of the mold. Top each with a cake circle and press down slightly. Place the molds in the freezer to allow the mousse to set, about 2 hours.

Spread a ⅛-inch-thick layer of the tempered white chocolate onto a sheet of parchment paper or acetate (page 2). The acetate will give the chocolate a nice shine. Let the chocolate harden until firm but not set, about 5 minutes.

To make the brims of the hats, use a 5-inch fluted round cutter to cut twelve circles from the white chocolate sheet. Place a clean sheet of parchment paper over the chocolate sheet and flip over both. Peel off the parchment paper or acetate. Separate the chocolate cutouts and place one in the center of each plate.

To assemble: Unmold by dipping the mold in hot water for 5 seconds. Press against one side of the mousse to slide each dome out of the mold. Place one dome, cake side down, in the center of each white chocolate circle. I like to decorate with fresh fruit to give the plate some color. Sometimes I use edible flowers on the brim.

continued

Signature Desserts

Let thaw in the refrigerator for two hours before serving. The Capelines will hold in the refrigerator for up to twenty-four hours.

Variation: Place equal amounts of white chocolate and cocoa butter over a double boiler (page 3) and melt until smooth, with no lumps. Assemble the desserts on a parchment paper–covered baking sheet and place in the freezer for about 5 mintues. The surface of the dessert must be chilled so that the chocolate coating will harden on contact, giving it the desired texture.

Remove the desserts from the freezer. Place the chocolate mixture in a clean paint sprayer and use it to coat the desserts with the chocolate. Cleanup will be much easier if you use a plastic-lined cardboard box as a backdrop to the baking sheet when you spray the desserts.

The Clown

8 CLOWNS

In French, Le Cirque means The Circus. When you visit the new restaurant, you will see that it really does look like a circus. About three years after I started working at Le Cirque, Tina gave me some chef's pants that were decorated with all different kinds of desserts in bright, wild colors. The manager, Benito Savarin, was mortified the first day he saw me wearing them. So often in the kitchen, chefs wear the standard houndstooth black-and-white pants. Benito said to me, "You really look like a clown." Now, when I introduce myself, I say, "I am the clown at Le Cirque," and people who know me well say that is a good description.

I use plastic dome molds (page 3) to make the individual clowns. If you have children, let them decorate their own clowns. It is especially easy to give each clown a different hairstyle (punk, Elvis, or Bozo). Be sure your molds have round bottoms, or your clowns will have flat heads!

½ recipe Classic Génoise batter (page 38)

Granulated sugar	**1 cup**	**7 ounces**	**200 grams**
Water	**¾ cup +** **2 tablespoons**	**7.2 ounces**	**200 grams**
Fresh raspberries	**1⅓ cups**		
Framboise liqueur (optional)	**2 tablespoons**	**0.8 ounce**	**25 grams**

For the filling

1 recipe White Chocolate Mousse (page 136)

½ recipe Bittersweet Chocolate Mousse (page 139)

For the decorations

Bittersweet chocolate, tempered (page 9)		**7 ounces**	**200 grams**
White chocolate, tempered (page 9)		**5.3 ounces**	**150 grams**
Angel Hair, colored red (page 48)			
8 fresh raspberries			
4 large fresh strawberries, hulled			
Raspberry sauce (page 43 or 44)			
Mango sauce (page 43 or 44)			

Prepare the génoise batter and bake it on a parchment paper–covered baking sheet as directed in the recipe. Cool on a wire rack.

Remove the parchment paper from the back of the génoise. (A good quality store-bought yellow or pound cake can also be used.) Use a 3-inch plain or fluted round cutter to cut eight circles from the génoise, cutting as close together as possible to avoid waste. Set the circles aside until ready to use.

Prepare the raspberry syrup: Place the water and sugar in a nonreactive 1-quart heavy-bottomed saucepan and bring to a boil over medium-high heat. The sugar should completely dissolve. Add the raspberries and return the mixture to a boil. As it boils, whisk thoroughly to break up the raspberries and allow them to release their

juices. This will cause the syrup to turn red. Remove from the heat. Prepare an ice bath (page 3) and strain the syrup through a fine-mesh sieve into a medium-size bowl placed in it. Discard the seeds and any pulp. When the syrup is cool, add the framboise liqueur. (If it is added when the syrup is hot, the alcohol will evaporate.) Set aside until ready to use.

Prepare the filling: Make the white chocolate mousse and place it in a large measuring cup with a spout. Fill eight dome molds half-full and use the back of a large spoon to spread the mousse gently up the sides to the top in an even layer. The white chocolate mousse should completely cover the insides of the molds or the bittersweet chocolate will show through when unmolded. If the white chocolate mousse does not coat the insides of the molds because it is too liquid, place the filled molds in the refrigerator for 3 to 5 minutes, then try spreading the mousse again. If necessary, return them to the refrigerator and then try again. Place the molds on a baking sheet in the refrigerator while you prepare the bittersweet chocolate mousse.

Place the bittersweet chocolate mousse in a clean pastry bag with a large opening (no tip). Remove the molds from the refrigerator and fill each almost to the top with it. Dip each cake circle in the cooled raspberry syrup and top each mold with a cake circle, pressing it down slightly. Place the molds in the freezer until set, about 2 hours.

Prepare the chocolate pieces: Spread a 1/8-inch-thick layer of the tempered bittersweet chocolate onto a sheet of parchment paper or acetate (page 2). The acetate will give the chocolate a nice shine. Let the chocolate harden until firm but not set, about 5 minutes. To make the brims of the hats, use a 2-inch plain round cutter to cut eight circles from the chocolate sheet. Place a clean sheet of parchment paper over the chocolate sheet and flip over both. Peel off the parchment paper or acetate. Separate the chocolate cutouts and set them aside.

Spread a 1/8-inch-thick layer of the tempered white chocolate onto another sheet of parchment paper or acetate. Let the chocolate harden until firm but not set, about 5 minutes. To make the eyes, use a 1-inch plain round cutter and cut sixteen circles from the sheet of chocolate. Cut the circles close together to avoid waste. Place a clean sheet of parchment paper over the chocolate sheet and flip over both. Peel off the parchment paper or acetate. Separate the chocolate cutouts. Fill a cornet (page 19) half-full with tempered bittersweet chocolate and make the pupils by piping

Spread the white chocolate mousse up the sides of the mold.

Finish spreading the mousse evenly up the sides of the mold.

Fill each mold almost to the top with bittersweet chocolate mousse.

Top each mold with a cake circle and press down slightly.

a 1/2-inch circle in the center of each of the eye circles. To make the clown's eyebrows, pipe sixteen 2-inch-long zigzags on a clean sheet of parchment paper. Go back to the hat brims and pipe a 1-inch mound of chocolate in the center of each to create the top of the hat. Set aside the parchment paper and let the chocolate harden. If necessary, place the parchment paper on a baking sheet in the refrigerator to speed up the process.

Remove the dome molds from the freezer and unmold the chocolate mousse by dipping the molds in hot water for about 5 seconds. Push gently on one side of each mold and slide the mousse out with your fingers onto a parchment paper–covered baking sheet. Place the sheet in the refrigerator until ready to assemble the dessert. (At this stage, the mousse can be stored in the freezer for up to two weeks if well wrapped in plastic wrap.)

To assemble: Make the red angel hair immediately before serving. Center one dome of mousse on each plate. Place 1 raspberry, tip side out, in the front for the nose. To make the mouths, lay a large strawberry on its side and slice it into 1/4-inch-thick slices. Cut out the center of each slice. Slice as many strawberries as necessary to make eight mouths. Place one slice under each nose. Place two eyes and two eyebrows on each clown. Fashion some angel hair on the top of each clown and top each with a hat. Use the raspberry sauce to outline a collar on the plate around the clowns. Fill in with the mango sauce and serve.

The Manhattan

12 SERVINGS

I created this dessert as a tribute to my New York experience. This town is truly an amazing place, especially to me, since my hometown would fit inside Central Park! I try to capture the spirit of New York in this dessert through the tall tower of cake, the chocolate grid representing the city streets, gold leaf to show the wealth of the town, and mango sauce to depict the sea of yellow cabs. You can customize this dessert to represent your hometown by writing in the names of the streets in your neighborhood.

For the Manhattan biscuit

Almond paste	1½ cups (very firmly packed)	15 ounces	425 grams
4 large eggs			
4 large egg yolks			
4 large egg whites			
Powdered sugar, plus extra for dusting	⅓ cup	1.2 ounces	35 grams
Unsweetened Dutch-processed cocoa powder, sifted	⅓ cup + 1½ tablespoons	1.8 ounces	50 grams

For the syrup

Water	¾ cup + 2 tablespoons	7.2 ounces	200 grams
Granulated sugar	1 cup	7 ounces	200 grams
Fresh raspberries	1⅓ cups		
Framboise liqueur (optional)	2 tablespoons	0.8 ounce	25 grams

For the Manhattan cream

Whole milk	⅔ cup	5.6 ounces	160 grams
Bittersweet chocolate, finely chopped		10.5 ounces	300 grams
Unsalted butter, cubed	1¼ cups + 1½ tablespoons	10.75 ounces	300 grams

For the garnish

Bittersweet chocolate, tempered (page 9)		5.3 ounces	150 grams
White chocolate, tempered (page 9)		5.3 ounces	150 grams
Raspberry sauce (page 43 or 44; optional)			
Mango sauce (page 43 or 44; optional)			
Gold leaf (optional)			

Prepare the Manhattan biscuit: Preheat the oven to 375°F (190°C). Place the almond paste in a large mixing bowl and beat with an electric mixer on medium speed to

soften the almond paste. Gradually add the whole eggs and egg yolks, incorporating fully after each addition. Beat until the mixture gains in volume.

Place the egg whites in a medium-size mixing bowl and whip with an electric mixer on medium speed until foamy. Increase the mixer speed to medium-high and make a French meringue by adding the powdered sugar 1 tablespoon at a time and whipping the whites to stiff but not dry peaks. Gently fold the meringue into the almond paste mixture. It is important to fold as gently as possible to avoid deflating the meringue. Fold in the sifted cocoa powder just until incorporated. Do not overmix.

Use an offset spatula to spread the batter in an even layer on a parchment paper–covered baking sheet by lightly resting the edge of the spatula on the batter and pushing the excess toward the edges. If you press too hard, you will deflate the batter. Liberally sprinkle the top with powdered sugar.

Place in the oven and bake until the top springs back when pressed, 8 to 10 minutes. The edges of the cake should not have begun to pull away from the sides of the baking sheet. Remove from the oven and immediately unmold the cake layer onto a wire rack to keep the heat of the baking sheet from continuing to bake it. Let cool completely then remove the parchment paper. Set aside.

Prepare the syrup: Place the water and sugar in a nonreactive 1-quart heavy-bottomed saucepan and bring to a boil over medium-high heat. The sugar should completely dissolve. Add the raspberries and return the mixture to a boil. As it boils, whisk thoroughly to break up the raspberries and allow them to release their juices. This will cause the syrup to turn red. Remove from the heat.

Prepare an ice bath (page 3) and strain the syrup through a fine-mesh sieve into a medium-size bowl placed in it. Discard the seeds and any remaining pulp. When the syrup is cool, add the framboise liqueur. (If it is added when the syrup is hot, the alcohol will evaporate.) Store the syrup in a squeeze bottle or in a bowl covered with plastic wrap until ready to use.

Prepare the Manhattan cream: Pour the milk into a 1-quart heavy-bottomed saucepan and heat until bubbles begin to form around the edge of the pan. Place the chopped chocolate in a medium-size mixing bowl. Make a ganache by pouring the hot milk over the chocolate and letting it sit for 30 seconds to melt the chocolate, then slowly whisking until smooth and homogenous. Let the ganache cool until it is lukewarm. Add the cubed butter and mix with an electric mixer on medium speed until it is fully incorporated and the ganache is once again smooth and homogenous, 5 to 10 minutes.

To assemble the cake: Cut the cake into three 5½ × 12-inch pieces. Place the first layer of cake on a parchment paper–covered baking sheet. Soak the cake with one third of the raspberry syrup. I use a squeeze bottle because a pastry brush can tear the cake. With an offset spatula, spread one third of the Manhattan cream over the syrup-soaked cake layer. Be sure to spread the cream in an even layer all the way to the edges, since it will show when the cake is finished. Repeat the layers of cake, syrup, and Manhattan cream two times. Be sure that the last layer of Manhattan cream is very even and smooth, since this is the top of the cake. Place the cake in the refrigerator until set, about 1 hour. (At this stage, the cake can be stored in the freezer well wrapped in plastic wrap for up to two weeks.)

Prepare the garnish: The chocolate roof pieces can be made while the cake is setting in the refrigerator. Spread a ⅛-inch-thick layer of tempered bittersweet chocolate on a sheet of parchment paper. If you spread the chocolate beyond the edges of the paper, lift the chocolate-covered paper by its corners and move it to a clean space on your work surface. Let the chocolate harden slightly, 4 to 5 minutes. Cover the chocolate with another sheet of parchment paper and flip over both. Peel the paper off what is now the top. The chocolate should be firm enough to cut but not hard. You will need a total of twenty-four bittersweet chocolate triangles for the roof pieces. Use a sharp paring knife to cut 2-inch equilateral triangles, making sure to cut all the way through the chocolate. Work quickly before the chocolate becomes too hard.

Make another twenty-four equilateral triangles in the same way using the tempered white chocolate. Each Manhattan roof is made up of two bittersweet and two white chocolate triangles. Set everything aside until you are ready to assemble the dessert.

To assemble the dessert: Remove the cake from the refrigerator. Heat a sharp chef's knife by running it under hot water and wiping it dry. Cut the cake into twelve 2-inch squares.

With a cornet (page 19) half-filled with bittersweet chocolate, draw a street map to your specifications on each dinner plate. Use the cornet to write the names of the streets on the map. If you have fruit sauces on hand, you can draw stoplights and/or taxicabs with raspberry and/or mango sauce. Place one cake square in the center of each street map. Stand two bittersweet and two white chocolate triangles on top of each cake square to form a pointed roof. I decorate the tip of each roof with a piece of gold leaf. Serve.

The Chocolate Stove

12 STOVES

Gaston Lenôtre, one of the most respected pastry professionals in France, created a cake in the 1960s called L'Opéra. It is made up of three layers of cake, two layers of coffee buttercream, and one layer of chocolate ganache, and it is decorated with chocolate glaze and gold leaf. The original cake is made with almond flour. Since I like the flavor of hazelnuts, I substitute fresh hazelnut paste, which makes the cake moist.

I incorporated this elegant cake into the dessert I created for Pierre Franey's sixty-fifth birthday party. I thought a fitting tribute to such a well-known chef would be a life-size edible stove. He loved it and so did my boss. A miniature version of the stove has become a permanent item on my dessert menu at Le Cirque. When this dessert is served at the restaurant, the waiters lift the stove off the cake and set it to one side of the plate. They then pour the fruit sauce from the pots on the stove over the cake.

When making the stove, use the best-quality chocolate you can find. I like to use Callebaut chocolate from Belgium. It is easy to work with and has great flavor. You can use any hard plastic rectangular boxes, but I use a plastic mold that contains twelve boxes (see equipment photograph, page 4) to make the body of the stove. I found the mold in a hardware store. I think it is actually the bottom of a covered box for organizing nails.

continued

For the cake layers

Ingredient	Volume	Ounces	Grams
Blanched hazelnuts, toasted (page 73)	1¼ cups	6 ounces	170 grams
Powdered sugar, plus extra for dusting	1½ cups + 2 tablespoons	6.5 ounces	185 grams
Pastry flour	3 tablespoons	0.9 ounce	25 grams
7 large egg whites			
Meringue powder (optional)	3 tablespoons	0.4 ounces	10 grams

For the buttercream

Ingredient	Volume	Ounces	Grams
Pure coffee extract	1 tablespoon	0.7 ounce	20 grams
½ recipe Basic Buttercream 1 or 2 (page 31 or 32)			

For the ganache

Ingredient	Volume	Ounces	Grams
Heavy cream	⅓ cup	2.7 ounces	75 grams
Bittersweet chocolate, finely chopped		3.6 ounces	100 grams

For the glaze

Ingredient	Volume	Ounces	Grams
Bittersweet chocolate, finely chopped		7.2 ounces	200 grams
Unflavored oil of your choice	2½ tablespoons	1 ounce	30 grams

For the stoves

Ingredient	Volume	Ounces	Grams
Bittersweet chocolate, tempered (page 9)		32 ounces	910 grams
White chocolate, tempered (page 9)		10.5 ounces	300 grams

Fruit sauce of your choice (page 43 or 44)

Prepare the cake layers: Preheat the oven to 400°F (200°C). To make hazelnut paste, place the hazelnuts in a clean, dry blender or food processor and blend until liquid. The oil that is released from the hazelnuts will make the cake moist.

Combine 1 cup (4 ounces; 115 grams) of the sugar with the flour in a small bowl and set aside.

continued

Place the egg whites in a large mixing bowl and whip with an electric mixer on medium speed until foamy. Increase the mixer speed to medium-high and make a French meringue by adding the remaining 10 tablespoons (2.5 ounces; 70 grams) of sugar and the meringue powder 1 tablespoon at a time and whipping to stiff but not dry peaks. Very gently fold in the hazelnut paste. Use a rubber spatula to fold in the flour and sugar mixture just until incorporated. It is important to fold as gently as possible to avoid deflating the meringue; if the batter deflates, the baked cake will be heavy.

Cover the cake layer with half of the coffee buttercream.

Spread about two thirds of the batter onto a parchment paper–covered baking sheet. Spread the remaining batter onto one half of another parchment paper–covered baking sheet to make an 8 × 12-inch piece. It is easier to spread the batter in an even layer if you use an offset spatula. Lightly rest the edge of the spatula on the batter and gently push the excess toward the edges of the baking sheet. Liberally sprinkle the tops of the cake layers with powdered sugar.

Bake just until the cake layers begin to brown, 5 to 6 minutes. Remove from the oven and immediately unmold onto a wire rack to keep the heat of the baking sheet from continuing to bake them. Remove the parchment paper when the layers are completely cool. Set aside until ready to use.

Prepare the buttercream: Stir the coffee extract into the buttercream and whip with an electric mixer on medium-high speed until combined, about 1 minute. Set aside.

Prepare the ganache: Heat the heavy cream in a 1-quart heavy-bottomed saucepan until bubbles begin to form around the edge of the pan. Place the chopped chocolate in a medium-size mixing bowl. Make a ganache by pouring the hot cream over the chocolate and letting it sit for 30 seconds to melt the chocolate, then slowly whisking until smooth and homogenous.

To assemble the cake: Cut the large cake layer in half to form two 8 × 12-inch pieces. You should now have three equally sized pieces of cake. Place one piece of cake on a parchment paper–covered baking sheet. Cover with half of the coffee buttercream, spreading it to the edges in an even layer. Add a second layer of cake and very gently press it down. Spread all of the ganache on top of this layer. Top with the third piece of cake and gently press it down. Cover the top with the remaining coffee buttercream, spreading it to the edges in an even layer. Place in the refrigerator and allow to chill for about 30 minutes.

Spread all of the ganache on top of the second layer of cake.

Prepare the chocolate glaze: The glaze cannot be made more than 15 minutes before using. Melt the chocolate and oil over a double boiler (page 3) just until all of the chocolate is melted and the mixture is smooth and homogenous.

Remove the cake from the refrigerator. Use an offset spatula to coat the top of the cake with the chocolate glaze, spreading it smoothly and evenly. Return the cake to the refrigerator until the glaze has set, about 10 minutes.

Top with a third piece and cover with the remaining coffee buttercream.

Remove the cake from the refrigerator. Use a hot chef's knife to trim about ½ inch from each side of the cake. A hot knife will make a cleaner cut. Run the knife under hot water between each cut, dry it, and then make the slices. Slice the cake to fit within the molds you will use to make the stoves. (I cut mine into 1½ × 3½-inch rectangles.) Return the cut cake pieces to the refrigerator while you prepare the chocolate stove. (At this stage the cake can be frozen for up to two weeks if well wrapped in plastic wrap. Thaw in the refrigerator before assembling.)

Cover the top of the cake with the chocolate glaze.

To make the cutouts for the stoves: The tempered chocolate should be in a large, wide bowl. Make sure your stove molds are clean and dry. Use a ladle to fill each mold with chocolate to within ½ inch of the top. Tap the sides of the mold with the handle of a knife or spatula to remove any air bubbles. Invert the mold over the bowl of tempered chocolate and allow the excess to drip back into the bowl. Scrape the edges of each box clean with an offset spatula or chef's knife. Place a wire rack over a baking sheet and set the molds upside down on the rack until the chocolate begins to set, 4 to 5 minutes. When the chocolate is partially set, use a paring knife to scrape the edges clean again. This will give the stoves nice straight edges, make it easier to unmold them, and keep the chocolate from breaking as it contracts. Place the molds in the refrigerator for about 5 minutes. As the chocolate sets, it will retract from the sides of the boxes.

To unmold the stoves, rest your thumbs on the outside of the mold, place your first two fingers on the inside, and gently lift the chocolate from the mold. Do not press or pull too hard, or you will break the chocolate. You may need to apply this lifting pressure to all four sides of the box to loosen the chocolate from the mold. Unmold the remaining eleven boxes and set aside while you make the stove pieces.

You can use a round tablespoon measure or a mini ice-cube tray to make the pots. Fill either with tempered bittersweet chocolate, then pour out the excess. Let the chocolate harden until almost set and scrape the edges clean with a sharp paring knife. Place in the refrigerator for about 5 minutes, then unmold. Make a total of twenty-four pots.

If you use tablespoon measures, you will need to give each pot a flat base. To do this, use the tip of your finger to dab a small amount of tempered chocolate onto a parchment paper–covered baking sheet. Immediately adhere a pot to the center of the dab. Repeat with the remaining pots. Place the baking sheet in the refrigerator until the chocolate has set.

To make the chimneys, refer to the template opposite and copy this shape on a piece of cardboard. The base of the chimney should be slightly smaller than the length of the stovetop. Place a sheet of parchment paper on your work surface. Use an offset spatula to spread a ⅛-inch-thick layer of tempered white chocolate to the edges of the paper. Lift the chocolate-covered paper by its corners and move it to a clean space on your work surface. Let the chocolate harden slightly, 4 to 5 minutes. The chocolate should be firm enough to cut but not hard. Use the tip of a sharp paring knife to trace the chimney template, making sure to cut all the way through the chocolate; cut twelve chimneys. If you alternate the chimney template top to bottom, you will minimize waste. Work quickly, or the chocolate will become too hard to cut.

Use a 1-inch plain round cutter to cut out twenty-four burners from the same sheet of white chocolate. Next, use a sharp paring knife to cut twelve 1½-inch squares for the oven doors. Cut twelve stove handles. They should be as long as the stovetop and ¼ inch wide. To make the handle supports, cut twenty-four right-angle triangles with ¼-inch-long legs. Make twenty-four pot handles by cutting ⅛ × 1-inch strips. Cover the chocolate with a sheet of parchment paper and flip over both. Peel the paper from what is now the top. Separate all of the chocolate cutouts.

To assemble the stoves: Dab a bit of melted white chocolate (it does not have to be tempered) on the back of each burner and "glue" two burners to the top of each stove. Glue an oven door to the center of the front of each stove. Glue the triangular handle supports about ¼ inch in from each side of the front of the stove, just below the level of the stovetop. Rest the handle on top of the supports. Glue a chimney to the back edge of each stovetop. Glue the pot handles to the pots and set one pot on each burner.

Make a cornet (page 19) and fill it half-full with tempered bittersweet chocolate. On a 10- or 12-inch dinner plate, draw a 9-inch square grid to resemble the tiles of a kitchen floor, allowing room at the top of the plate for the stove. Fill alternating squares of the grid with fruit sauce. Remove the pieces of cake from the refrigerator. Center a piece of cake above the grid and cover it with a stove. Fill the pots with fruit sauce. Serve.

The Snowman

12 SNOWMEN

I didn't see snow until I was eight years old. It doesn't snow much in the South of France. However, once my parents took us for a ride to Aix-en-Provence, which is north of my hometown. We saw snow and we all got out of the car to touch it. It is a very big memory for me. In 1995, New York was hit by a huge snowstorm that shut down the city. Le Cirque was one of the few places open that day. The restaurant was surprisingly busy considering that all of the streets and most businesses were closed. On that day, I created The Snowman and served it as the daily dessert special. For this recipe, you will need special half-sphere, or dome, molds (page 3).

Double recipe Meringue Cake Layers batter (page 41)			
Double recipe Lemon Curd (page 29)			
Bittersweet chocolate, tempered (page 9)		**8 ounces**	**225 grams**
Angel Hair (page 48)			
Heavy cream, whipped to stiff peaks	**1²/₃ cups**	**14 ounces**	**400 grams**

Pipe a large mound of meringue into each dome mold.

Preheat the oven to 200°F (93°C). Use a pastry brush to lightly butter twenty-four dome molds and set aside.

Place the meringue batter in a pastry bag with a large opening (no tip). To make the bodies of the snowmen, pipe a large mound of meringue into each dome. Keep the tip of the bag in the meringue as you pipe to keep air pockets from forming. Use the back of a large spoon to spread the meringue in an even layer between ⅛ and ¼ inch thick around the inside of the dome. You will have too much meringue, so just scoop out the extra and return it to the mixing bowl; it is easier to remove the excess after forming the layer than it is to add more.

continued

Spread the meringue in an even layer, 1/8 inch to 1/4 inch thick, inside the dome.

To make the heads of the snowmen, pipe 1-inch round mounds onto a parchment paper–covered baking sheet.

To unmold, push on one side of the meringue shell.

To make the heads of the snowmen, add any remaining meringue to the pastry bag and pipe 1-inch round mounds onto a parchment paper–covered baking sheet. Place the filled dome molds on the baking sheet next to the heads, and place both in the oven. Bake until the meringue has dried and is firm in texture, 1 to 1½ hours. If the heads are dry before the dome molds, remove them from the oven. If the meringue starts to take on color, lower the oven temperature about 50°F (10°C) and finish baking. Remove the dome molds (and the heads, if you have not already done so) from the oven and let cool for 5 to 10 minutes.

To unmold, just push on one side of the meringue shell and it should slide right out of the mold. The meringue shells are extremely fragile, however, so be careful when you unmold them. Set aside until ready to use. (At this point, the meringue can be stored in an airtight container at room temperature for up to one week.)

While the meringue is baking, prepare the lemon curd and place it in the refrigerator for at least 1 hour to thicken and set.

To make the chocolate garnishes: Use a cornet (page 19) half-filled with tempered bittersweet chocolate to make one set of the following chocolate garnishes for each snowman: Pipe all of the garnishes onto a sheet of parchment paper. To make the fence, pipe a 3- to 4-inch-long railroad track with the outside rails spaced about 2 inches apart and the inside ties spaced about ½ inch apart. To make the broom, pipe a 4-inch-long handle and squirt a ¼-inch dab of chocolate at the end of the handle. Drag the tip of a paring knife through the dab of chocolate to create the broom bristles. Make the pipe by piping a 1-inch checkmark. To make the hat, dip a spatula into the bowl of tempered chocolate and spread a 1½-inch circle on the parchment paper.

When it has almost set, cut out a circle with a 1-inch plain round cutter and remove the inner circle. Pipe a ½-inch round mound of chocolate on top of this circle (the brim). Let all of the chocolate pieces set at room temperature, or place in the refrigerator for about 5 minutes to speed up the process.

Fill the shell with lemon curd and whipped cream.

Just before assembling, make the angel hair.

To assemble: Use a box grater to gently shave the edges of two meringue shells so the two halves will fit together smoothly. Gently shave the rounded bottom of one shell to allow it to sit on a flat surface. This will be the bottom half of the body. Place the bottom piece in the center of a serving plate. Place 2 to 3 heaping tablespoons of lemon curd inside the shell and spread it evenly with the back of a large spoon to about a ½-inch thickness. Place 1 heaping tablespoon of whipped cream on top of the lemon curd and gently spread it to the sides, filling the shell to about ¼ inch below the top edge. Fill the second shell in the same manner and place it on top of the first to make a ball. Fill the remaining shells, then finish all of the snowmen.

Fill a cornet with melted chocolate (it does not have to be tempered) and "glue" the head to the top of the body. Pipe on the eyes, nose, and buttons. Use a toothpick to make a small hole in the face for the pipe and insert it. Glue all of the remaining pieces into place. Surround the snowman with angel hair and serve. If you have fresh fruit in the refrigerator, slice it and place around the plate for color.

I make a lot of meringue shells at the restaurant and this little trick saves me a lot of time: I use a homemade scraper to spread the meringue layer evenly inside the dome molds. Following the shape and curve of the mold, I cut a piece of stiff plastic ¼ inch smaller than the inside of the mold. After piping in the meringue, I rotate the scraper inside the mold. As it spreads the meringue in an even layer, it gathers the excess in the center. This tool makes it easier to remove the extra meringue.

The Cauldron

8 CAULDRONS

ere is another idea I got while visiting the Caribbean. Kris took me to Virgin Gorda and introduced me to piña coladas. I loved the combination of coconut and pineapple. I wanted to make something special for Kris to thank her for taking me with her, so I made a Piña Colada Bavarian. Then, while I was trying to decide how to present it, I noticed the restaurant's big stockpots. They look like huge witch's cauldrons. Now, whenever I serve this dessert in the restaurant, I have a pleasant memory of our trip!

¹/₂ recipe Classic Génoise or Biscuit batter (page 38 or 40)

For the simple syrup

Granulated sugar	**1 cup**	**7 ounces**	**200 grams**
Water	**³/₄ cup + 2 tablespoons**	**7.2 ounces**	**200 grams**
Dark rum	**1 tablespoon**	**0.4 ounce**	**12.5 grams**

For the cauldrons

Bittersweet chocolate, tempered (page 9)		**12 ounces**	**340 grams**

For the piña colada Bavarian

4 sheets gelatin or 1¹/₃ envelopes powdered gelatin

Unsweetened coconut milk	**¹/₂ cup**	**3.6 ounces**	**100 grams**
Pineapple juice	**¹/₂ cup**	**3.6 ounces**	**100 grams**
Granulated sugar	**¹/₂ cup**	**3.5 ounces**	**100 grams**
Dark rum	**2 tablespoons**	**0.8 ounce**	**25 grams**
Heavy cream	**³/₄ cup + 2 tablespoons**	**7.1 ounces**	**200 grams**

4 large bananas

Water	Generous ¹/₂ cup	4.5 ounces	125 grams
Granulated sugar	¹/₂ cup + 2 tablespoons	4.5 ounces	125 grams
Pastry flour	1 cup	4.4 ounces	125 grams

For assembly

Sweetened coconut flakes	1 cup	3.5 ounces	100 grams
Angel Hair (page 48)			
Mango sauce (page 43 or 44)			
Raspberry sauce (page 43 or 44)			

Prepare the génoise or biscuit batter and bake on a parchment paper–covered baking sheet as directed in the recipe. Place on a wire rack until completely cooled. Peel off the parchment paper and use a 2-inch plain or fluted round cutter to cut eight circles from the cake layer. Cut the circles as close together as possible to avoid waste. Set aside until ready to use.

Prepare the simple syrup: Place the sugar and water in a 1-quart heavy-bottomed saucepan and bring to a boil over medium-high heat. The sugar should completely dissolve. Remove from the heat and pour the syrup into a clean medium-size bowl. Set aside to cool before adding the rum. (If you add the rum while the syrup is still hot, the alcohol will evaporate.) If you are pressed for time, you can speed up the cooling process by placing the simple syrup in an ice bath (page 3). Once the rum has been added, cover the bowl with plastic wrap until ready to use to keep the alcohol from evaporating.

Prepare the cauldrons: I use dome molds (page 3) to make the body of the cauldron. Any type of half-sphere or rounded mold will do. If you use a sheet of molds as I do, make sure the tempered chocolate is in a wide bowl. Fill eight molds with chocolate and tap the sides with the handle of an offset spatula to remove any air bubbles. Invert the molds over the bowl of chocolate and allow the excess chocolate to drip out. Scrape the top of the molds clean with the edge of the spatula and place the molds upside down on a wire rack set over a baking sheet. Let any additional excess choco-

late drip from the molds. After about 5 minutes, when the chocolate has begun to harden but is not completely set, scrape the edge of each chocolate shell clean with a sharp paring knife. This will make it easier to unmold the shells and will keep the chocolate from breaking as it contracts. It will also give each cauldron a cleaner rim. Place the molds on a baking sheet in the refrigerator until completely set, about 5 minutes.

Remove the molds from the refrigerator and unmold. With the molds I use, I can just push against one edge of the shell and slide it out of the mold. Depending on your mold, you may need to lift the chocolate from the mold. Set the chocolate cauldrons aside.

While the chocolate cauldrons are setting in the refrigerator, you can make the lids, legs, and spoons. Spread a 1/8-inch-thick layer of tempered bittersweet chocolate onto a sheet of parchment paper. Let the chocolate harden slightly until firm but not set, about 5 minutes. To make the lids, use a 3-inch plain round cutter to cut eight circles from the chocolate. To make the legs, cut out three 1/2-inch equilateral triangles from the chocolate for each cauldron, making a total of twenty-four triangles.

To make the spoons, fill a cornet (page 19) half-full with tempered chocolate. On a clean sheet of parchment paper, pipe eight 3-inch-long lines 1/8 inch thick, each ending with a small dollop of chocolate. Go back to the lids and pipe a small dollop of chocolate in the center of each to create a handle. Place all of the cauldron pieces in the refrigerator until completely set, about 5 minutes.

Use tempered chocolate to "glue" the legs to the cauldrons. Place the cauldrons upside down on a sheet of parchment paper to allow the legs to adhere.

Prepare the piña colada Bavarian: Make the Bavarian last because it needs to be piped into the chocolate cauldrons before it begins to set. If you are using gelatin sheets, place them in a medium-size bowl with enough cold water (about 1 quart) to cover. Let stand for about 5 minutes to allow the gelatin to soften and hydrate. Cold water hydrates the gelatin without letting it absorb too much liquid. Remove the gelatin from the bowl and squeeze out the excess water with your hands. If you are using powdered gelatin, sprinkle the gelatin over 1/3 cup (2.7 ounces; 75 grams) cold water. Let the gelatin bloom until it has absorbed all the water, about 1 1/2 minutes. Set aside.

continued

Pour the coconut milk, pineapple juice, and sugar into a medium-size mixing bowl and whisk until well combined. Pour about ½ cup of this mixture into a 1-quart heavy-bottomed saucepan, add the hydrated gelatin, and place over medium heat until the gelatin has completely dissolved. Pour the gelatin mixture into the remaining juice mixture and whisk well to combine. Add the rum and set aside.

Pour the heavy cream into a medium-size mixing bowl and whip to soft peaks with an electric mixer on medium speed. Place in the refrigerator while you cool down the juice mixture.

Prepare an ice bath (page 3). Place the bowl with the juice mixture in the ice bath. Cool the juice mixture, stirring constantly with a rubber spatula, until it is thick and viscous. Remove the bowl from the ice bath and make a Bavarian by using a rubber spatula to gently fold the whipped cream into the juice mixture.

Place the Bavarian in a pastry bag with a large opening (no tip). Carefully pipe the Bavarian into the cauldrons, filling each half-full. Dip the cake circles into the simple syrup and place one circle in each cauldron. Fill the cauldrons to the top with the Bavarian. Place the filled cauldrons on a baking sheet in the refrigerator for about an hour to allow them to set slightly. (At this stage the filled cauldrons can be stored in the freezer for up to two weeks if wrapped in plastic wrap.)

Prepare the banana tuiles: Preheat the oven to 425°F (218°C). The tuiles can be made while the Bavarian is setting. Peel the bananas and puree with the water, sugar, and flour using an immersion blender, food processor, or blender. Use a spatula to spread a very thin layer of this mixture on a nonstick baking sheet. Run the tip of the spatula through the batter to create two 9 × 12-inch tuiles. Bake until they start to take on a light brown color, less than 5 minutes. Lift each baked tuile by one corner and allow only the bottom quarter to rest on the work surface. You may have to hold each tuile for 10 to 15 seconds in a position that will allow it to stand on its own; it will cool very quickly. Like a snowflake, every tuile will be different. Make a total of eight tuiles.

To toast the coconut: Reduce the oven temperature to 400°F (200°C). Spread the coconut on a baking sheet and place in the oven for about 3 minutes. Remove from the oven and stir to keep the sugar in the coconut from burning. Return to the oven and toast until golden brown, about 3 more minutes. Remove the baking sheet from the oven and cool on a wire rack.

To assemble the cauldrons: Prepare the angel hair right before you are ready to serve the cauldrons. The angel hair will represent the smoke swirling from the cauldron.

When you are ready to serve the cauldrons, decorate the center of each plate with a circle of mango sauce and a circle of raspberry sauce. Use a wooden skewer to swirl them together to resemble flames. Place one cauldron in the center of each plate and sprinkle the tops with about a tablespoon of the toasted coconut. Top with angel hair and set the lids at an angle on the tops. Place a spoon inside each cauldron, add a tuile for garnish, and serve.

Instead of filling and emptying the molds to make the cauldrons, you can use a clean, dry pastry brush to spread the chocolate inside each mold. Paint one layer, allow it to set, and then add another layer. Place the molds in the refrigerator to allow the chocolate to set completely, about 5 minutes. Unmold as indicated in the recipe.

Banana Moon Cakes

16 SERVINGS

ris and I have a favorite place up in the mountains in France that we visit every summer. It is a tiny village with about three hundred residents, one store, a church, a stop sign, and a post office. For many of the people who live there, modern conveniences like electricity are a luxury. When we sit outside at night, it is pitch black, but the stars in the sky are absolutely brilliant. When the moon is out, it shines so brightly that it feels as if you could touch it if you only stood on the roof. I was inspired to create this dessert by the summer moon of that small village.

½ recipe Chocolate Génoise batter (page 39)

For the simple syrup

Granulated sugar	**1 cup**	**7 ounces**	**200 grams**
Water	**¾ cup + 2 tablespoons**	**7.2 ounces**	**200 grams**
Dark rum	**2 tablespoons**	**0.8 ounce**	**25 grams**

For the caramelized banana

1 large banana

Dark rum	**1 tablespoon**	**0.4 ounce**	**12.5 grams**
Granulated sugar	**¼ cup**	**1.75 ounces**	**50 grams**
Unsalted butter (optional)	**½ tablespoon**	**0.25 ounce**	**7 grams**

For the mousse

3 sheets gelatin or 1 envelope powdered gelatin

Water	**¼ cup**	**2 ounces**	**55 grams**
Granulated sugar	**½ cup**	**3.5 ounces**	**100 grams**
Light corn syrup	**Generous 2 tablespoons**	**1.6 ounces**	**50 grams**

3 large egg whites

3 large bananas

Juice of ½ lemon

Heavy cream	**Generous 1 cup**	**8.8 ounces**	**250 grams**

Bittersweet chocolate, tempered (page 9)	*12 ounces*	*340 grams*
White chocolate, tempered (page 9)	*4 ounces*	*113 grams*
Chocolate Sauce (page 45)		
Crème Anglaise (page 24)		

Prepare the chocolate génoise batter and bake on a parchment paper–covered baking sheet as directed in the recipe. Cool on a wire rack until ready to use. (You can also use a good-quality store-bought chocolate cake if you would prefer not to make the cake layer yourself.)

Prepare the simple syrup: Place the sugar and water in a 1-quart heavy-bottomed saucepan and bring to a boil over medium-high heat. The sugar should completely dissolve. Remove from the heat and pour the syrup into a clean medium-size bowl. Set aside to cool before adding the rum. (If you add the rum while the syrup is still hot, the alcohol will evaporate.) If you are pressed for time, you can speed up the cooling process by placing the simple syrup in an ice bath (page 3). Once the rum has been added, cover the bowl with plastic wrap until ready to use to keep the alcohol from evaporating.

Prepare the caramelized banana: Peel the banana and dice it into 1/4-inch cubes. Place the cubes in a small mixing bowl with the rum and about one third of the sugar and let macerate for 10 minutes.

Heat a medium-size heavy-bottomed frying pan over medium-high heat. If it starts to smoke, the pan is too hot and you need to run it under cool water, dry it, and start again. When the pan is warm, sprinkle the remaining sugar into it. Try to keep the sugar in an even layer to allow it all to caramelize at the same time. As soon as you see the sugar begin to melt, start moving the pan over the burner to keep the sugar from burning. Tilt the pan from side to side so that the melted sugar runs over the unmelted sugar. Cook until all of the sugar is a light golden brown. I usually add half a tablespoon of butter at this stage because it makes the caramel smoother. Add the banana mixture and spread it evenly in the pan. Cook over medium-high heat until most of the liquid has evaporated and the bananas are soft but not mushy. If the bananas are still firm when most of the liquid has evaporated, add a few tablespoons of water and continue cooking until they are done. Remove from the heat and pour the caramelized banana

onto a plate. Cover with plastic wrap and let cool completely. Covering the hot banana with plastic wrap keeps the caramel from drying as it cools.

Prepare the mousse: If you are using gelatin sheets, place them in a medium-size bowl with enough cold water (about 1 quart) to cover. Let stand for about 5 minutes to allow the gelatin to soften and hydrate. Cold water hydrates the gelatin without letting it absorb too much liquid. Remove the gelatin from the bowl and squeeze out the excess water with your hands. If you are using powdered gelatin, sprinkle the gelatin over ¼ cup (1.75 ounces; 50 grams) cold water. Let the gelatin bloom until it has absorbed all the water, about 1 minute. Set aside.

Pour the water, sugar, and corn syrup into a 1-quart heavy-bottomed saucepan and place over medium-high heat. When bubbles start to form around the edge of the pan, insert a candy thermometer. When the sugar reaches 245°F (118°C), begin to whip the egg whites.

Place the egg whites in a large mixing bowl and whip with an electric mixer on medium-high speed until foamy and slightly soft peaks.

The sugar is ready when it reaches 250°F (121°C), what is known as the soft ball stage (page 16). Make an Italian meringue by pouring the cooked sugar down the side of the bowl as you continue whipping the egg whites. Do not pour the hot sugar onto the beaters, or it will splatter. Add the hydrated gelatin and continue whipping the meringue on medium speed until the outside of the bowl is warm but not hot, about 5 minutes. The meringue should be stiff and glossy.

Peel and puree the bananas with the lemon juice using an immersion blender, food processor, or blender. Set aside.

Pour the heavy cream into a medium-size mixing bowl and whip to soft peaks with an electric mixer on medium-high speed. With a rubber spatula, fold half of the banana puree into the whipped cream. Fold the remaining banana puree into the meringue until incorporated. Then fold all of the banana whipped cream into the meringue in two additions, being careful not to deflate the mixture.

Pour one third of the banana mousse into a smaller bowl. Gently fold the cooled caramelized bananas into the remaining mousse. You now have a banana mousse and a caramelized banana mousse.

continued

To assemble the cake: Remove the parchment paper from the back of the cooled génoise and cut the génoise in half. Place one half on a parchment paper–covered baking sheet. Spread the caramelized banana mousse over the génoise, making sure to spread all the way to the edges of the cake layer. Top with the second half of génoise and press down gently. Make sure the top of the cake is level. Spread the banana mousse over the top of the génoise and smooth with an offset spatula. Your finished cake will look nicest if this layer is spread evenly. Place the assembled cake in the refrigerator until set, about 1 hour.

Prepare the chocolate moon cutouts: Spread a ⅛-inch-thick layer of tempered bittersweet chocolate on a sheet of parchment paper. Let the chocolate harden until firm but not completely set, about 5 minutes. Use a 4-inch plain round cutter to cut crescent moons: To do this, start at the upper left-hand corner of the chocolate sheet and press the top half of the cutter into the chocolate, making sure to cut all the way through it. Lift the cutter, move it down 1 inch, and repeat the cut, creating a crescent-moon shape. Repeat until you have a total of thirty-two half-moons. Place a sheet of parchment paper over the chocolate sheet and flip over both. Peel off the first piece of parchment paper and remove the cutouts.

Repeat the procedure with the tempered white chocolate to make sixteen white crescent moons. Set the cutout moons aside until you are ready to assemble the cake.

Remove the cake from the refrigerator. Heat the cutter you used to make the crescent moons by running it under hot water. With a dry cutter, mark sixteen crescent moons on top of the cake, spaced 1 inch apart. Use a hot sharp paring knife to cut the crescent moons, being sure to cut all the way through the cake. Heat and dry the knife every few slices to ensure clean cuts. (At this stage, the cake will keep in the refrigerator, well wrapped in plastic wrap, for up to two days and in the freezer for up to two weeks. If frozen, thaw in the refrigerator before proceeding.)

To assemble the dessert: Place one crescent-moon cake in the center of each plate. Decorate each cake with one white and two bittersweet chocolate crescent moons. Decorate the plates with the chocolate sauce and crème anglaise. Serve immediately.

Variation: You can make Bittersweet Chocolate Mousse (page 139) and substitute it for one layer of banana mousse. You can also omit the cake altogether and pipe bittersweet chocolate mousse and banana mousse into beautiful glasses.

The Ladybug

I love these little insects. They are thought to bring good luck. I make the syrup a day in advance to give the raspberries time to macerate. On the show, I made this dessert in a large round ten-inch plastic mold. I prefer individual servings and use small dome molds (page 3). I think these make a nicer presentation served individually.

¹/₂ recipe Classic Génoise or Biscuit batter (page 38 or 40)

For the macerated raspberries

Water	*Generous 1 cup*	*8.8 ounces*	*250 grams*
Granulated sugar	*¹/₂ cup*	*3.5 ounces*	*100 grams*
Fresh raspberries	*about 1¹/₃ cups*		
Stoli Razberi vodka	*2 tablespoons*	*0.8 ounce*	*25 grams*

For the raspberry mousse

Fresh raspberries	*about 2 cups*		
3 gelatin sheets or 1 envelope powdered gelatin			
Water	*¹/₄ cup*	*2 ounces*	*55 grams*
Granulated sugar	*¹/₂ cup*	*3.5 ounces*	*100 grams*
Light corn syrup	*Generous 2 tablespoons*	*1.6 ounces*	*50 grams*
3 large egg whites			
Heavy cream	*Generous 1 cup*	*8.8 ounces*	*250 grams*

For the garnish

Bittersweet chocolate, tempered (page 9)		*16 ounces*	*454 grams*
Sour cream	*2 tablespoons*	*0.8 ounce*	*28 grams*

For assembly

Raspberry sauce (page 43 or 44)

Mango sauce (page 43 or 44)

continued

Prepare the génoise or biscuit batter and bake on a parchment paper–covered baking sheet as specified in the recipe. Place on a wire rack until completely cooled. Peel off the parchment paper and use a 2-inch plain or fluted round cutter to cut twelve circles from the cake layer. Cut the circles as close together as possible to avoid waste. Set aside until ready to use. (Good-quality store-bought yellow or pound cake can also be used.)

Prepare the macerated raspberries: Pour the water and sugar into a nonreactive 1-quart heavy-bottomed saucepan and bring to a boil over medium heat. Add the raspberries and bring to a boil again. Do not stir once the raspberries have been added; they should remain as intact as possible. Remove from the heat and pour into a clean small bowl. Let cool completely before adding the raspberry vodka. (If the vodka is added when the syrup is hot, the alcohol will evaporate.) Store the raspberries and syrup in the refrigerator, tightly covered with plastic wrap, until ready to use.

Prepare the raspberry mousse: Puree the raspberries with an immersion blender, food processor, or blender and set aside.

If you are using gelatin sheets, place them in a medium-size bowl with enough cold water (about 1 quart) to cover. Let stand for about 5 minutes to allow the gelatin to soften and hydrate. Cold water hydrates the gelatin without letting it absorb too much liquid. Remove the gelatin from the bowl and squeeze out the excess water with your hands. If you are using powdered gelatin, sprinkle the gelatin over ¼ cup (1.75 ounces; 50 grams) cold water. Let the gelatin bloom until it has absorbed all the water, about 1 minute. Set aside.

Pour the water, sugar, and corn syrup into a 1-quart heavy-bottomed saucepan and place over medium-high heat. When bubbles start to form around the edge of the pan, insert a candy thermometer. When the sugar reaches 245°F (118°C), begin to whip the egg whites.

Place the egg whites in a medium-size mixing bowl and whip with an electric mixer on medium-high speed until foamy and soft peaks.

The sugar is ready when it reaches 250°F (121°C), what is known as the soft ball stage (page 16). Make an Italian meringue by pouring the cooked sugar down the side of the bowl as you continue whipping the egg whites. Do not pour the hot sugar onto the beaters, or it will splatter. Add the hydrated gelatin and continue to whip the meringue on medium speed until the outside of the bowl is warm but not hot, about 5 minutes. The meringue should be stiff and glossy.

Pour the heavy cream into a large mixing bowl and whip to soft peaks with an electric mixer on medium speed. Fold half of the raspberry puree into the whipped cream and the other half into the Italian meringue, being careful not to deflate either mixture. Fold the meringue into the whipped cream until combined.

Place the mousse in a pastry bag with a large opening (no tip). Pipe the mousse into twelve dome molds, filling them halfway. Spread the mousse up the sides of the molds to the rim with the back of a large spoon. Place a spoonful of the macerated raspberries in the center of each mold. Fill almost to the top of the mold with the remaining raspberry mousse. Top each with a cake circle and press down slightly. Place the molds in the freezer to allow the mousse to set, about 2 hours.

Prepare the chocolate garnishes: You will need one head and two antennae for each ladybug, plus spots for the backs. To make the heads, fill a round tablespoon measure full of tempered bittersweet chocolate. Empty the tablespoon into the bowl of tempered chocolate, allowing the excess to drip back into the bowl. Place the tablespoon upside down over a wire rack placed over a baking sheet. Once the chocolate is set, about 5 minutes, slide the chocolate shell from the tablespoon. Repeat five times for a total of six shells. With a hot knife, slice each shell in half. These halves will be the heads.

To make the antennae, fill a cornet (page 19) half-full with the bittersweet chocolate. On a clean sheet of parchment paper, pipe twenty-four 4-inch-long lines about 1/8 inch thick, ending with a dollop of chocolate at the tip. You may want to make extras since they break easily.

Spread a 1/8-inch-thick layer of bittersweet chocolate onto another sheet of parchment paper. Let the chocolate harden until firm but not completely set, about 5 minutes. Using the tip of a 1/2-inch decorating tip, cut circles from the sheet of chocolate. You will need eight to ten spots for each ladybug. Place another sheet of parchment paper on top of the chocolate sheet and flip over both. Remove the first sheet of parchment paper and separate the chocolate circles. Set them aside until ready to use.

To assemble the ladybugs: Remove the mousse from the refrigerator. Unmold by quickly dipping the bottom of each mold in hot water for about 5 seconds. Push on one side of the mousse to slide it from the mold. Place one ladybug body, cake side down, in the center of each plate.

Gently press the cut side of a head into one side of each ladybug. With a cornet half-filled with bittersweet chocolate, draw a line down the center of each ladybug. Randomly stick the chocolate spots onto the bodies of the ladybugs. Insert two antennae into the mousse directly behind each head. Fill a cornet half-full with the sour cream and use this to pipe dots for eyes onto each ladybug.

Use the raspberry and mango sauces to decorate the plates so it looks as if each ladybug is sitting on a flower. Serve immediately.

The Piano

12 PIANOS

*I*n the South of France, the area between Nice and St. Tropez is known as the Esterel. The soil is very red and the coast is wild and beautiful. The raspberry jam in this recipe is used to simulate the red soil.

I form the tops of the grand pianos on acetate (page 2) because I like the shine the chocolate takes from the plastic. I use a plastic scraper (page 6) to make the keyboard. You can make your own tool by cutting teeth into a plastic scraper.

For the cake layers

Blanched hazelnuts, toasted (page 73)	¾ cup	4.4 ounces	125 grams
4 large eggs			
Powdered sugar, plus extra for dusting	1⅔ cups	6.1 ounces	175 grams
5 large egg whites			
Unsalted butter, melted	2 tablespoons	1 ounce	30 grams
Pastry flour, sifted	¼ cup	1.1 ounces	35 grams
Linda's Red Raspberry Jam (page 46)	¼ cup	2.6 ounces	75 grams

For the ganache

Heavy cream	½ cup + 2 tablespoons	5.25 ounces	150 grams
Bittersweet chocolate, finely chopped		7 ounces	200 grams

For the garnish

Bittersweet chocolate, tempered (page 9)		16 ounces	454 grams
White chocolate, tempered (page 9)		4 ounces	113 grams
Chocolate Sauce (page 45)			
Raspberry sauce (page 43 or 44)			
Crème Anglaise (page 24)			

continued

Prepare the cake layers: Preheat the oven to 400°F (200°C). Make hazelnut paste by placing the hazelnuts in a clean, dry blender or food processor and blending until liquid.

Place the eggs, 1¼ cups (4.4 ounces; 125 grams) of the sugar, and the hazelnut paste in a medium-size mixing bowl and whip with an electric mixer on medium-high speed until creamy and light, about 1 minute. The hazelnut paste adds richness and moisture to the cake.

Place the egg whites in a large mixing bowl and whip with an electric mixer on medium speed until foamy. Make a French meringue by adding the remaining sugar 1 tablespoon at a time and whipping the whites to stiff but not dry peaks. Do not overwhip. The powdered sugar contains cornstarch, which helps stabilize the egg whites.

Use a rubber spatula to fold the hazelnut mixture into the French meringue in two additions, being careful not to deflate the batter. Gently fold in the melted butter, then the sifted flour, just until incorporated.

Spread about two thirds of the batter onto a parchment paper–covered baking sheet. Spread the remaining batter onto half of another parchment paper–covered baking sheet to make an 8 × 12-inch piece. It is easier to spread the batter in an even layer if you use an offset spatula: Lightly rest the edge of the spatula on the batter and gently push the excess toward the edges of the baking sheet. Dust the tops of the cake layers with powdered sugar for a nicer crust.

Bake until lightly and evenly browned on top, 6 to 8 minutes. Remove the cake layers from the oven and immediately unmold onto a wire rack to keep the heat of the baking sheet from continuing to bake them. Remove the parchment paper when the layers are completely cool. Set aside until ready to use.

While the cake is cooling, prepare the raspberry jam. Allow enough time for the jam to cool before you make the ganache. (A good-quality store-bought jam can also be used.)

Prepare the ganache: Make this 1 hour before you are ready to assemble the cake. It must be soft enough to spread easily. If you prepare the ganache too far in advance, it will harden too much as it cools. Pour the heavy cream into a 1-quart heavy-bottomed saucepan and cook over medium-high heat until bubbles begin to form around the edge of the pan. Place the chopped bittersweet chocolate in a medium-size bowl. Make a ganache by pouring the hot cream over the chocolate and letting it sit for about 30 seconds to disperse the heat and melt the chocolate. Gently whisk until smooth and homogenous. Set aside until ready to use. Do not refrigerate.

Cut the large cake layer in half to form two 8 × 12-inch pieces. You should now have three equally sized pieces of cake. Place one layer on a parchment paper–covered baking sheet. Spread half of the ganache over the cake layer, spreading it to the edges in an even layer. Cover with a second cake layer and evenly spread the raspberry jam to the edges. Top with a third cake layer and spread the remaining ganache evenly all the way to the edges. It is very important for this layer to be even, as it is the top of the cake. Place the assembled cake in the refrigerator to set for 1 hour while you prepare the chocolate garnishes.

Prepare the chocolate garnishes: Trace the template for the piano lid on the opposite page onto a piece of cardboard and cut it out with a sharp pair of scissors. Spread a ⅛-inch-thick layer of tempered bittersweet chocolate onto a piece of acetate. Let the chocolate harden until firm but not set, 4 to 5 minutes. With the tip of a sharp paring knife, cut the shape of the template into the chocolate sheet, making sure to cut all the way through the chocolate but not the acetate. Cut out a total of twelve lids. *In order for the lids to match the cakes, you will need to use the reverse side of the template when you cut six of the lids from the chocolate.* Cut twelve matchstick-size pieces of chocolate from the remaining chocolate on the sheet. These will hold the piano lids open. Place the chocolate sheet on a baking sheet in the refrigerator for about 5 minutes to finish setting.

Remove the chocolate from the refrigerator and cover with a clean sheet of parchment paper. Flip over both so that the acetate is on top. Peel off the acetate and separate the piano lids and sticks. The shiny sides will be the tops of the piano lids. Set the lids and sticks aside.

Spread tempered white chocolate in a very thin layer, about ⅛-inch thick, on a clean sheet of parchment paper. Draw the toothed scraper (see headnote) through the chocolate to create alternating lines. When the chocolate stripes are firm but not hard, use an offset spatula to spread a ⅛-inch-thick layer of tempered bittersweet chocolate over them. Let harden until firm but not set, about 5 minutes. With a sharp paring knife, cut out twelve $1/2 \times 3$-inch rectangles for the keyboards. Place the parchment paper on a baking sheet in the refrigerator for about 5 minutes to finish setting.

Remove the chocolate from the refrigerator and cover with a clean sheet of parchment paper. Flip over both so that the chocolate-covered parchment paper is on top. Peel off the parchment paper and separate the keyboards. Set aside until ready to use.

To assemble: Remove the cake from the refrigerator. With a hot chef's knife, trim about $1/4$ inch from each side for cleaner edges. (To heat the knife, run it under hot water and wipe it dry.) With a hot sharp paring knife, cut twelve pieces of cake in the shape of the template. *In order for the cakes to match the lids, you will need to use the reverse side of the template when you cut six of the pianos from the cake.* On the front of each piano, slice through the top layer of the cake to make a place for the keyboard. Now you can position the chocolate keyboards in place. (At this stage, the pianos can be stored in the freezer, well wrapped in plastic wrap, for up to two weeks.)

To make the seats, cut a small rectangle, about $1 \times 1\frac{1}{2}$ inches, from the remaining cake. Then separate the layers of the cake so the seat is half as high as the piano. Cut five more rectangles and separate them to make a total of twelve seats.

Place one piano in the center of each plate. Position a seat in front of each piano. A piano lid hinges on its long straight edge, so insert a matchstick-size piece of chocolate at the corner where the curved edge meets the keyboard and rest the chocolate lid on the matchstick so it appears to be open. Use a cornet (page 19) half-filled with dark chocolate to draw musical notes on the plate. Decorate with the sauces and serve.

Variation: Hazelnuts are not always easy to find. Almond flour can be found in most specialty shops, and you don't have to grind it yourself. If you prefer the taste of almonds or want to take a shortcut, substitute 1 cup (4.5 ounces, 125 grams) of almond flour for the hazelnut paste.

Autumn Leaves with Chocolate Mousse and Maple Syrup

10 SERVINGS

 ris's brother is quite an outdoorsman. He can track animals through the woods and identify plants and birds. One fall when we went home to Michigan to visit Rick and his family, I noticed that all of the trees in his yard had pails hanging from them. When I asked what they were for, he explained that he was collecting the sap to make maple syrup. When he gave me a taste of the finished syrup, I fell in love with the flavor. This dessert reminds me of northern Michigan on a cool October day.

For the leaves

Room temperature unsalted butter	*7 tablespoons*	*3.5 ounces*	*100 grams*
Powdered sugar	*¾ cup*	*3.5 ounces*	*100 grams*
Pastry flour	*¾ cup*	*3.5 ounces*	*100 grams*
Grated zest of 1 orange			
3 large egg whites			

For the nuts

Sliced blanched almonds	*Generous ⅓ cup*	*2 ounces*	*50 grams*
Light corn syrup	*2 tablespoons*	*1.5 ounces*	*45 grams*

To assemble

1 recipe Bittersweet Chocolate Mousse (page 139)			
Pure maple syrup	*1 cup*	*11.8 ounces*	*330 grams*

Prepare the leaves: Preheat the oven to 375°F (190°C). Place the butter, sugar, flour, and orange zest in a medium-size mixing bowl and beat with an electric mixer on medium speed until the butter is well incorporated and the mixture resembles wet sand. Gradually add the egg whites and continue to mix on medium speed until homogenous, about 1 minute. With a small offset spatula, spread the tuile batter over

the template (see below) on a nonstick baking sheet. Repeat until you have ten leaves, spacing the leaves about 1½ inches apart, as they will spread slightly when baked. Bake until lightly browned around the edges, about 5 minutes. Cool on a wire rack until ready to use. (At this stage, the leaves can be stored in an airtight container for up to five days.)

Prepare the nuts: Lower the oven temperature to 350° F (175° C). Place the sliced nuts and corn syrup in a 1-quart heavy-bottomed saucepan and place over low heat to liquefy the corn syrup. You only want to heat the mixture until the corn syrup is thin enough to coat the nuts evenly; this will take 2 to 3 minutes. Remove the saucepan from the heat. Using a large slotted spoon, allow the excess corn syrup to drain as you scoop the coated nuts onto a parchment paper–covered baking sheet. Be sure to spread them out in an even layer so they will toast evenly.

Bake until they are uniformly caramelized, 15 to 20 minutes. The nuts are well toasted when they are light brown on the inside. Keep an eye on them, because the sugar will burn very soon after it caramelizes. Remove the baking sheet from the oven and place on a wire rack. When completely cooled, break apart any nuts that are clustered together.

To assemble the dessert: Prepare the bittersweet chocolate mousse immediately before serving the dessert. It will be easier to make the quenelles (page 21) if you dip two large spoons in cool water and shake off the excess. This will keep the mousse from sticking to the spoons. Scoop a generous amount of chocolate mousse onto one spoon and make a quenelle by gently rolling the mousse between the two spoons to form an egg shape. Place two quenelles in the center of each plate. Place one leaf between each pair of quenelles. Sprinkle the nuts around the plate, drizzle with the maple syrup, and serve.

I make my own tuile stencil from a piece of plastic. You can buy heavy, pliable ⅛-inch-thick plastic at an art supply store. Use a pen to trace the outline of a maple leaf onto a square of plastic and cut it out with an X-Acto knife. The plastic piece with the cutout becomes your template and can be washed and used over and over again.

Frozen Finales

♦ ♦ ♦

TO MAKE SORBET, FRUIT is used in one of three forms: fresh puree, fresh juice, or commercially prepared frozen puree. No matter which you use, you need simple syrup. If you use fresh fruit, it is very important to select the ripest and best-quality fruit available. Unripened fruit does not have enough flavor and will not develop any more flavor once it has been picked, which will affect the sweetness of the sorbet. Depending on the ripeness of the fruit you use, it may be necessary to vary the amount of simple syrup slightly. For example, out-of-season mangoes will probably require more simple syrup to enhance their sweetness than those at peak season. Remember also that the fruit will have less flavor when it is frozen in a sorbet than it will at room temperature, and you'll want to compensate for that.

A refractometer is a very expensive piece of equipment used by winemakers to determine the amount of sugar in grapes. I have found that using a refractometer is an easy way to measure the sugar content in sorbet. It works by measuring light as it is reflected off the sugar crystals contained in the sorbet mix. This light registers on a Brix meter that ranges from 0 to 32 degrees Brix. The sweetness of sorbet should always be balanced between 24 and 26 degrees Brix. I balanced the sorbet recipes in this chapter with a refractometer.

Most ice cream machines work in the same way: The cold source comes from the outside of the container. The ice cream machine blade continually scrapes the sides of the container where the ice cream or sorbet mix has frozen and mixes the frozen particles throughout the mixture. The continuous motion of the blade keeps the ice crystals small. If properly spun, sorbet and ice cream should not be icy. The motion of the blade also traps air in the mix as it thickens, giving it increased volume.

The PACOJET is the only machine I know that works differently. At present it is available only to professionals, but a model for home use should be ready in 1998. (See my Web page—http://www.jacquestorres.com—for an update on availability.) With a PACOJET, you make a base, freeze it, and then spin only the number of portions you need. This machine is much more versatile because you can make anything, not just ice cream. The fast speed of the titanium blade ensures a very smooth, creamy end product.

In this chapter, you will usually have more than enough ice cream or sorbet for each recipe. There is no limit to the type of sorbet and ice cream flavor combinations you can make. Be creative. I've experimented with just about every possible flavor imaginable. One time I even made tobacco ice cream, but I have to say it is the most horrid tasting thing I have ever created.

Simple Syrup

2⅓ CUPS (24.5 OUNCES; 1700 GRAMS)

ugar retains the natural flavor of fruit. In sorbet, a sugar syrup, called simple syrup, is used to ensure that there are no undissolved sugar crystals. If you use granulated sugar, the sorbet may be grainy. Powdered sugar should not be used, because it contains cornstarch. I like to add a little lemon juice to simple syrup to boost the flavor of the fruit.

The idea is to add sugar, not water, to your sorbet mixture. If you use too much simple syrup, the sorbet won't freeze. If you add too little, it won't be sweet enough.

Granulated sugar	*2½ cups*	*17.5 ounces*	*500 grams*
Water	*Generous 1 cup*	*8.8 ounces*	*250 grams*
Juice of ½ lemon			

Combine all three ingredients in a nonreactive 2-quart heavy-bottomed saucepan and bring to a boil over medium-high heat. All the sugar crystals should dissolve completely. Remove from the heat and pour into a clean medium-size bowl. Let cool completely before using. If you are short on time, you can cool the syrup in an ice bath (page 3). Simple syrup can be stored in the refrigerator indefinitely if kept in an airtight container.

Cassis Sticks

18 PIECES

K ris and I really have an appreciation for Champagne. We try to bring its festivity to any occasion. I think the subtle flavor of cassis really complements the taste of Champagne. This is a very fast and easy way to add a simple touch of elegance to any dinner party or brunch.

Water	**²/₃ cup**	**5.3 ounces**	**150 grams**
Granulated sugar	**Generous ¹/₃ cup**	**2.5 ounces**	**75 grams**
Frozen whole cassis	**1 cup**	**5.3 ounces**	**150 grams**

Combine the water and sugar in a nonreactive medium-size saucepan and place over high heat. Bring to a boil and add the cassis. Stir gently to combine and remove from the heat. Pour the mixture into a 5 × 9-inch loaf pan or a rectangular shallow dish about the same size; it should make a layer about ½ inch thick. Place in the freezer until solid, about 2 hours. (At this stage, the mixture can be stored in the freezer, well wrapped in plastic wrap, for up to three weeks.)

To unmold, dip the pan in hot water for about 5 seconds. Run a sharp paring knife around the edges to loosen the sides of the frozen mixture from the pan. Center a small cutting board over the pan and flip over the board and pan at the same time so the pan is on top. Lift the pan. If the pan does not come off, you will need to dip it in water again. Use a serrated knife to cut the frozen mixture into ½-inch-wide strips about 3 inches long (or to fit in the glass you are using). Place one cassis stick in each glass and add Champagne. As the cassis sticks melt, they add a delightful fruity flavor to the champagne.

Variation: If you can't find cassis, use fresh blueberries.

Palette of Sorbets

8 SERVINGS

*I*n the summer, my hometown, Bandol, is filled with artists, boats, and tourists. All the artists display their works-in-progress on the long promenade that runs along the port. My dad loves ice cream more than just about anything else and his favorite store, Festival de Glace, is located on the promenade. When I am home, we head into town for ice cream cones, take a seat on the promenade, and watch the action. This dessert was inspired by those summer evenings, and I dedicate it to my dad and the artists.

If you are short on time, you can use store-bought sorbet. If you are going to make all of these sorbets, start a few days in advance to give them time to set. In each case, the sorbet should be spun until it is smooth and creamy, like soft-serve ice cream. If you poke the sorbet with the handle of a wooden spoon, it should just hold the shape of the indentation.

The weights given below are for the fruit after it is cleaned, peeled, pitted, or juiced. The volume measurements and number of pieces of fruits indicated are approximate. If you do not weigh the fruit, your sorbet may not be balanced.

For the grape sorbet

2 large bunches seedless grapes, stemmed	About 5¹⁄₂ cups	29.4 ounces	825 grams
Simple Syrup (page 267)	¹⁄₃ cup	3.5 ounces	100 grams
Water	²⁄₃ cup	5.3 ounces	150 grams

For the pineapple sorbet

1 small pineapple, peeled, cored, and chopped	About 3¹⁄₂ cups	16.5 ounces	500 grams
Simple Syrup (page 267)	²⁄₃ cup	7 ounces	200 grams
Water	Generous ¹⁄₄ cup	2.25 ounces	60 grams

For the raspberry sorbet

Fresh raspberries	About 4 cups	18 ounces	500 grams
Simple Syrup (page 267)	²⁄₃ cup	7 ounces	200 grams
Water	Scant ¹⁄₂ cup	3.5 ounces	100 grams

For the mango sorbet

2½ large mangoes, peeled, pitted, and chopped	About 2½ cups	17.5 ounces	500 grams
Simple Syrup (page 267)	⅔ cup	7 ounces	200 grams
Water	⅔ cup	5.3 ounces	150 grams

For the lemon sorbet

Juice of 7 large lemons, strained	1 cup	8.9 ounces	250 grams
Simple Syrup (page 267)	¾ cup + 1 tablespoon	8.7 ounces	250 grams
Water	Generous 1 cup	8.8 ounces	250 grams

For assembly

Bittersweet chocolate, tempered (page 9)		14 ounces	400 grams
Raspberry sauce (page 43 or 44; optional)			
Mango sauce (page 43 or 44; optional)			

Set 4 grapes aside to be used for the assembly of the palette.

Prepare the grape sorbet: When you look at the ingredients list, you will notice that I use more grapes by weight than any of the other fruit. That is because this sorbet is made with only the juice of the grapes. Use an immersion blender, food processor, or blender to process the grapes just until coarsely chopped; the consistency should resemble that of chutney. If you are using grapes with seeds, don't overblend, or the chopped seeds will make the grape juice bitter. Pass the grapes through a fine-mesh sieve placed over a medium-size bowl by firmly pressing the back of a ladle against the grapes and grinding them against the side of the sieve. Measure 2 cups (17.7 ounces; 500 grams) of juice and discard the remaining flesh and peels. Add the simple syrup and water to the grape juice and whisk until well combined. Spin the mixture into sorbet according to the directions for the type of ice cream machine you are using and store it in an airtight container in the freezer until ready to use.

Prepare the pineapple, raspberry, and mango sorbets: When making these sorbets, I don't strain the pureed fruit because I don't think it is necessary. I like the texture the fruit fiber gives to the sorbet. If you prefer a smoother sorbet, strain each puree through a fine-mesh sieve.

continued

The technique for making these three sorbets is exactly the same. The amounts of simple syrup and water change depending on the fruit's acidity and natural sweetness. Make the sorbets one at a time, following these steps: Puree the fruit until smooth with an immersion blender, food processor, or blender. Add the simple syrup and water and blend until well incorporated. Spin each mixture into sorbet and store each in an airtight container in the freezer until ready to use.

Prepare the lemon sorbet: The lemon sorbet is made from the juice of the fruit. I suggest you squeeze the lemons yourself and use fresh juice instead of using commercially prepared juice. Pour the lemon juice, simple syrup, and water into a medium-size bowl and whisk until well combined. Spin the mixture into sorbet and store in an airtight container in the freezer until ready to use.

Prepare the palette: Copy the template on page 274 onto a piece of cardboard and cut it out using a pair of scissors. Spread a $1/8$-inch-thick layer of the tempered chocolate onto a 16×24-inch sheet of parchment paper or acetate (page 2); I like to use acetate because the chocolate touching the acetate takes on a shine when it has set. Let the chocolate set slightly, 4 to 5 minutes. The chocolate should be firm enough to cut but it should not be hard. Trace the palette template onto the chocolate with the tip of a sharp paring knife, making sure to cut all the way through the chocolate. I like to use a 1-inch plain round cutter to cut out the finger hole. Use the tip of a $1/2$-inch plain decorating tip to cut five holes for the "paints" on the long curved edge of the palette. Cut out a total of eight palettes. Work quickly before the chocolate becomes too hard. When all eight have been cut, cover the chocolate sheet with another sheet of parchment paper and flip it over. Peel the paper or acetate off what is now the top. Remove the cut palettes and set aside.

Use a cornet (page 19) half-filled with tempered chocolate to make the paintbrushes. Pipe a $1/8$-inch-thick 4-inch-long line onto a clean sheet of parchment paper or acetate. Pipe an extra $1/2$-inch teardrop at one end of the chocolate line. Repeat these steps to make eight paintbrushes and set aside.

To assemble: Cut each of the reserved 4 grapes in half. Place one grape half, cut side down, in the center of each plate. Set each palette at an angle on the grape so the finger hole does not touch the plate. Slide the chocolate paintbrushes through the finger holes. Use a 1-inch mini ice cream scoop to scoop eight balls of sorbet from each flavor, placing one ball of each sorbet on each palette to resemble paints. I like to decorate the plates with raspberry and mango sauces. Serve immediately.

Variation: You can also cut the palettes from large slices of pineapple. Peel the pineapple (page 166). I find it easiest to cut the pineapple in half from top to bottom along either side of its core. You will end up with two "halves" without the core. Cut both halves into 1/2-inch-thick slices, slicing from top to bottom. The size of the pineapple will determine the number of slices you can cut from it. Lay each slice flat on your work surface and trace the template with a sharp paring knife. Use a 1-inch plain round cutter to cut out the finger hole and tip of a 1/2-inch plain decorating tip for the holes for the paints. Save the extra pineapple to use for the sorbet. Keep the pineapple palettes wrapped in plastic wrap and refrigerated until ready to use.

Nougatine Basket with Fruit Sorbets

1 BASKET; 8 TO 10 SERVINGS

The nougatine basket makes a stunning presentation. You can use any flavors of sorbet you like, but consider color in your choices. The most difficult part of this recipe is making the basket. You have to be *extremely* careful when you work with hot sugar because it can burn you. If you don't have the time to make the basket, see below for another presentation idea.

For the orange sorbet

Juice of 6 large oranges, strained	2 cups	17.9 ounces	500 grams
Simple Syrup (page 267)	²/₃ cup	7 ounces	200 grams
Water	Scant ¼ cup	1.75 ounces	50 grams

For the passion fruit sorbet

Passion fruit puree	1 cup	8.8 ounces	250 grams
Simple Syrup (page 267)	¾ cup + 1 tablespoon	8.7 ounces	250 grams
Water	Generous 1 cup	8.8 ounces	250 grams

For the strawberry sorbet

Medium-size fresh strawberries, hulled	1¾ pints	18 ounces	500 grams
Simple Syrup (page 267)	²/₃ cup	7 ounces	200 grams

For the nougatine basket

Granulated sugar	2½ cups	17.5 ounces	500 grams
Light corn syrup	Scant ½ cup	5 ounces	150 grams
Water	²/₃ cup	5.3 ounces	150 grams
Sliced blanched almonds, toasted (page 73)	2½ cups	14 ounces	350 grams
Vegetable oil for rolling	¼ cup	1.6 ounces	50 grams

For the caramel

Granulated sugar	½ cup	3.5 ounces	100 grams

continued

Prepare the sorbets: The technique for preparing the three sorbet mixtures varies slightly, but they are all spun into sorbet in the same manner. Spin them according to the directions for the type of ice cream machine you are using until smooth and creamy, like soft-serve ice cream. If you poke it with the end of a wooden spoon, the sorbet should just hold the shape of the indentation; it should not be hard or icy.

When making the orange and passion fruit sorbets, only the amount of simple syrup and water changes. Make each sorbet following these steps: Combine the fruit juice or puree with the simple syrup and water in a medium-size mixing bowl and stir until well mixed. Spin into sorbet and store in the freezer in an airtight container until ready to use.

The strawberry sorbet is different because it is made with the whole fruit and no additional water is added. I don't strain the seeds from the puree because I like the texture they add to the finished sorbet, but you can remove them by straining the pureed fruit through a fine-mesh sieve. Puree the strawberries using an immersion blender, food processor, or blender. Add the simple syrup and blend until well combined. Spin it and store in the freezer in an airtight container until ready to use.

Use a large ice cream scoop to shape balls of sorbet. Try to make them as round and as evenly sized as possible. Place the balls on a parchment paper–covered baking sheet and keep them in the freezer until you are ready to assemble the basket. Stacking two baking sheets on top of each other will help retain the cold. If the sorbet scoops are hard, you will be able to display the basket at room temperature for a longer period of time.

Prepare the nougatine basket: Hot caramel is used to make the nougatine. *Working with hot caramel is like playing with fire. It is very, very easy to burn yourself. Be extremely careful! The caramel is burning hot and sticky. It will stick to your skin and can cause a burn before you have the chance to remove it. Have a towel or bowl of ice cold water ready. If you get caramel on your skin, immediately wipe it off with the towel or submerge it in the cold water to cool it quickly. If you get hot caramel on your finger, never stick it in your mouth, or you will burn your mouth too.*

Cook the sugar mixture until golden brown.

Combine the sugar, corn syrup, and water in a 4-quart heavy-bottomed saucepan and place over medium-high heat. Cook until golden brown, 10 to 15 minutes. Add the toasted almonds to the caramel and stir until thoroughly combined. Remove the mixture from the heat and *carefully* pour it onto a nonstick baking sheet or into a lightly oiled or nonstick large frying pan. *Do not touch the nougatine because,*

Add the toasted almonds to the caramel and stir until thoroughly combined.

Pour the nougatine onto a nonstick baking sheet or into a lightly oiled nonstick frying pan.

Use a lightly oiled spatula to lift and fold the nougatine onto itself.

at this stage, the caramel will stick to your skin and may cause a burn. Use a lightly oiled large offset or heatproof rubber spatula to lift and fold the nougatine onto itself. This is done to cool it. If you don't turn it, the nougatine will cool unevenly and harden in spots. You can tell it is ready to be rolled when the nougatine is malleable like wet clay and no longer feels sticky if you lightly pat it with your hand.

Lightly oil a rolling pin and leave a little oil on your hands. This will keep the nougatine from sticking to your skin and causing a burn. Roll out the nougatine on a lightly oiled surface until it is about 1/2 inch thick. It is best to work on marble, but a Formica or wood surface will also work. If the nougatine hardens and becomes brittle while you are rolling it out, place it on a parchment paper–covered baking sheet, set in a 200°F (93°C) oven, and heat for 3 to 5 minutes so it softens slightly before continuing to roll. If the nougatine is sticky when removed from the oven, it is too hot and must be cooled slightly before rolling.

Use a sharp knife to cut out a 9 × 11-inch rectangle from the nougatine. Cut off the corners from the rectangle about 1 inch in from the point. Place all of the nougatine scraps in a pile on a parchment paper–covered baking sheet and place in a 200°F (93°C) oven to help it retain its heat.

Make the basket by placing the nougatine rectangle inside a lightly oiled medium-size glass or metal mixing bowl. Press it into the side of the bowl and smooth out any wrinkles as you shape the basket. Take the extra nougatine from the oven and, when it is not too hot, with lightly oiled hands, quickly roll it into a 12-inch-long 1-inch-wide cylinder. This will be the handle of the basket. Curve the cylinder to fit the basket base and lay it on a sheet of parchment paper. You will need to wait for the handle to cool, about 20 minutes, before the basket can be assembled. If it is still hot when it is attached to the basket, the handle will not hold its shape.

When the nougatine has cooled completely, lift the basket base from the bowl and place on a platter. Hold the end of the handle inside the basket to visualize where it will go. With a sharp paring knife, score the outside of each end of the handle and the inside of the basket to mark the spot where the two meet. This will give texture to the surfaces, which will help the handle stick to the basket. Make sure the handle and the basket are free of oil in those sections.

Cut out a 9 x 11-inch rectangle from the rolled-out nougatine.

Prepare the caramel: You need to make a dry caramel to glue the handle to the basket. Place a 1-quart saucepan over medium-high heat until the pan is warm but not hot. Add the sugar and cook, stirring occasionally, until all of it has melted and it is an even light golden brown. Remove the pan from the heat and quickly dip the side of each end of the handle in the caramel. Immediately place the handle in the basket to adhere. *Do not touch the caramel with your hands, as it is very hot and can burn you!* Hold the handle in place for a few minutes before letting it go. If it stays upright by itself for at least 5 minutes, it should hold until you are ready to serve. If necessary, dip the handle again in the caramel until it stays in place. (At this stage, the nougatine basket can be stored in the freezer for up to one week if well wrapped in plastic wrap.)

Make the basket by placing the nougatine rectangle inside a lightly oiled glass or metal mixing bowl.

To assemble: Remove the balls of sorbet from the freezer and place them in the fully cooled basket, piling them on top of each other in a decorative manner. Present and serve!

To make the handle for the basket, roll nougatine into a 12-inch long, 1-inch wide cylinder.

In New York, I can find all kinds of hollow plastic fruits. I cut them in half, fill each half with sorbet, stick the two halves together, and freeze. It is really fun to find the fruits that match the type of sorbet I am making. To unmold, I carefully dip the plastic in hot water. As the sorbet melts, it will easily pull away from the plastic mold. I place the sorbet "fruit" in the basket and serve. If you don't want to make the basket, arrange the sorbets on a decorative platter or bowl.

Chocolate Coconut Shells with Grand Marnier

I came up with this idea while lying on the beach at Little Dix Bay. I saw some island kids climbing the coconut trees to retrieve the fruit. They showed me how to clean a coconut and I was inspired when I saw the small interior coconut shell. I spent the rest of my vacation trying to cut fresh coconut with my Swiss Army knife!

I use Coco Lopez instead of pure coconut milk because it has the sweetness and flavor I want in this sorbet. It is also easy to find year-round.

For the granite

Water	*Generous 1²/₃ cups*	*14.3 ounces*	*400 grams*
Granulated sugar	*1 cup*	*7 ounces*	*200 grams*
Grand Marnier	*¼ cup*	*2 ounces*	*60 grams*

For the coconut sorbet

1 can Coco Lopez	*Scant 2 cups*	*15 ounces*	*425 grams*
1 can water	*Scant 2 cups*	*15 ounces*	*425 grams*

For the shells

Sweetened coconut flakes	*1 cup*	*3.3 ounces*	*95 grams*
Bittersweet chocolate, tempered (page 9)		*16 ounces*	*454 grams*

For the garnish

½ small pineapple, peeled, cored, and thinly sliced

Raspberry sauce (page 43 or 44; optional)

Mango sauce (page 43 or 44; optional)

An ice bath is used to cool down the granite. Prepare one in a 2-quart bowl (page 3) and place a clean, dry 1-quart bowl in it.

Prepare the granite: Combine the water and sugar in a 1-quart heavy-bottomed saucepan and bring to a boil over high heat. The sugar should completely dissolve. Remove the saucepan from the heat and pour the sugar syrup into the bowl placed in the ice bath. When cool, add the Grand Marnier and stir well to combine. (If you add the Grand Marnier when the syrup is hot, the alcohol will evaporate and you will lose the flavor.) Pour the granite mixture into a shallow dish and place in the freezer until solid, about 2 hours.

Prepare the sorbet: Combine the Coco Lopez and water in a medium-size mixing bowl and stir until well mixed. Spin the sorbet according to the directions for the type of ice cream machine you are using. The finished sorbet should be smooth and creamy, like soft-serve ice cream. Store in the freezer in an airtight container until ready to use.

Prepare the shells: While the sorbet is spinning, toast the coconut flakes; toasting the coconut intensifies the flavor. Preheat the oven to 400°F (200°C). Spread the coconut flakes on a parchment paper–covered baking sheet and place in the oven until lightly browned, about 5 minutes. The sugar in the coconut flakes can cause them to burn, so stir them every few minutes. Remove from the oven and set aside, allowing the flakes to cool until ready to use.

I use plastic dome molds to make the chocolate coconut shells, but you can use any 4-ounce rounded cups or molds. Tempered chocolate will retract from any non-porous surface (e.g., plastic, metal, or glass) if the mold is clean and dry. If you use a sheet of dome molds as I do (page 3) or a muffin pan, make sure your tempered chocolate is in a large, wide bowl. Use a ladle to fill sixteen molds with the chocolate to 1/2 inch from the top. Tap the sides of the molds with the handle of a knife or spatula to remove any air bubbles. Invert the molds over the bowl of tempered chocolate and allow the excess chocolate to drip back into the bowl. Scrape the edges clean with an offset spatula or chef's knife. Place a wire rack over a baking sheet and place the molds upside down on the wire rack until the chocolate begins to set, 4 to 5 minutes. If you use a paring knife to scrape the edges clean again at this stage, you will have nice straight edges on your finished shells.

Place the molds in the refrigerator for about 5 minutes. This will cause the chocolate to contract from the sides of the molds, making it easier to unmold. If you are using dome molds, you will be able to gently slide each shell out of the mold by pushing the edge of the shell on one side. If you use deeper molds, you may have to lift out the chocolate. To do so, rest your thumbs on the outside of each mold, place your first two fingers on the inside of the chocolate, and gently lift the chocolate from the mold. Do not press or pull too hard, or you will break the chocolate. You may need to apply this lifting pressure on all sides to loosen the chocolate from the mold.

Use a pastry brush to lightly paint the outside of each shell with tempered chocolate, then roll the outside of each shell in the toasted coconut while the chocolate is still wet.

To assemble: Center three pineapple slices on each plate, overlapping them slightly. Rest one chocolate shell on each bed of pineapple. Remove the coconut sorbet from the freezer. Use a large ice cream scoop or spoon to fill the shells with the sorbet. Remove the granite from the freezer. I shave the granite by scraping the tines of a fork across the frozen surface. Place about a tablespoon of shaved granite on top of the sorbet. I like to decorate the plate with dots of raspberry and mango sauces. Rest the empty shells on their edges against the full shells. Serve immediately.

Melon Sorbet Slices with Port Wine Sauce

8 SERVINGS

This dessert was created primarily because of my forgetfulness. One morning when I was taking my daily inventory, I found three overly ripe melons in the refrigerator. I cut them in half, discarded the seeds, and pureed the fruit with some simple syrup and a little port wine. I put the mixture in the ice cream machine and started my morning production. I remembered the sorbet a few hours later, at the height of the lunch service, when I needed to use the machine again. I was in a rush to clean out the machine and could not find anything in which to store the sorbet. My eyes fell on the melon rinds, and I thought, "Why not?" I filled each rind with the melon sorbet and stored them in the freezer. The next day I was trying to think of an interesting dessert for the daily special when I opened the freezer and saw the sorbet-filled rinds. I decided to slice them like a real melon and add some pignoli nuts to resemble the melon seeds. I made a little port wine sauce to decorate the plates, and served it. The restaurant patrons loved it and it became one of the classic desserts on my menu.

continued

Port wine	2 cups	16 ounces	460 grams
Granulated sugar	1/2 cup	3.5 ounces	100 grams

For the melon sorbet

1 large cantaloupe			
Simple Syrup (page 267)	2/3 cup	7 ounces	200 grams
Water	Generous 1/4 cup	2.25 ounces	60 grams
Port wine	1 tablespoon	0.6 ounce	18 grams

For the garnish

Pignoli nuts	1 tablespoon	0.3 ounce	8 grams
Fresh fruit (optional)			

Prepare the port wine sauce: Pour the port wine and sugar into a nonreactive 1-quart heavy-bottomed saucepan and cook over medium-high heat until it has reduced to about one third of its original volume and thickened slightly. Pour into a small, clean bowl and let cool before using. This sauce can be stored in the refrigerator in an airtight container for up to two weeks.

Prepare the melon sorbet: Thoroughly rinse the outside of the melon and pat it dry. Cut the cantaloupe into eight evenly sized wedges and discard the seeds. Use a sharp paring knife to remove the fruit from each wedge by sliding the knife between the rind and the flesh. Cut carefully, as you want the rind to be in one piece when you are finished. Lay the rinds on their sides (they hold their shape better like this) on top of a parchment paper–covered baking sheet and place in the freezer until frozen, at least 1 hour.

Make the sorbet while the melon rinds freeze. Slice the fruit into small pieces and puree with the simple syrup, water, and port wine. I like to use an immersion blender to puree but you can also use a food processor or blender. Spin the sorbet according to the directions for the type of ice cream machine you are using until it is smooth and creamy; it should have the consistency of soft-serve ice cream. It is really important for the sorbet to be the right consistency; otherwise you will not be able to shape it inside the melon rinds. If you poke the sorbet with the handle of a wooden spoon, it should just hold the shape of the indentation. Mold the sorbet immediately.

To mold the sorbet: Remove the frozen rinds from the freezer. Use a plastic scraper or metal spatula to fill the rinds with the sorbet so that they resemble slices of cantaloupe. It will be easier if you use a plastic scraper (page 6). Stack two baking sheets on top of each other to help retain the cold. Lay the slices on their sides spaced about 6 inches apart on the doubled baking sheet and place in the freezer until set, about 1 hour. Remove the slices from the freezer and set them upright. Heat a metal spatula in hot water, wipe off the excess water, and use the edge of the spatula to smooth the sides of the sorbet slices. Place three or four pignoli nuts in the center of each slice to resemble melon seeds. Return the slices to the freezer for at least 15 minutes, or until ready to serve. (The melon slices can be stored in the freezer for up to two weeks if wrapped in plastic wrap.)

continued

To serve, center one melon slice on each plate and drizzle with the port wine sauce. I like to decorate the plate with colorful fresh fruit.

Variation: During fig season, or whenever I can get really great figs, I like to add them to the port wine sauce. Cut the figs into quarters and add them to the sauce when it is almost ready. Cooking the figs slightly will impart their flavor to the sauce. Use as many figs as you like for a more or less strongly flavored sauce.

Frozen Strawberry-Vanilla Vacherin

8 TO 10 SERVINGS

This was the first cake I ever tried to make at home. Every time we had guests I made a frozen Vacherin, always changing the ice cream and sorbet combinations. My mom had one of those old-fashioned electric ice cream machines. The manufacturer's directions actually instructed you to place the machine in the freezer while it was still plugged into the electric socket: It was a pretty hilarious sight.

1 recipe Meringue Cake Layers batter (page 41)

For the vanilla ice cream
1/2 recipe Crème Anglaise (page 24)

For the sorbet
Strawberry Sorbet (page 275)

For the whipped cream and garnish

1/2 vanilla bean

Heavy cream	**1²/₃ cups**	**14 ounces**	**400 grams**
Granulated sugar	**3 tablespoons**	**1.4 ounces**	**40 grams**

1 large fresh strawberry (optional)

Preheat the oven to 200°F (93°C). Draw two 8-inch circles on a sheet of parchment paper by tracing around the outside of an 8-inch cake pan with a pen. Turn the paper over (so that the ink does not bake into the meringue) and place on a baking sheet. Prepare the meringue cake layers batter and place it in a pastry bag fitted with a ¾-inch plain tip.

To pipe the disks, hold the pastry bag at a slight angle about 1½ inches above the parchment paper. This height and angle allows the piped meringue to hold the full shape of the ¾-inch tip. Start at the center of the circle and pipe the meringue in a spiral to the edge of the outline. (I work counterclockwise because I am right-handed.) If the meringue breaks while you are piping it, just continue where it broke.

continued

If any air bubbles appear on the disk, go back and fill them in with the meringue left in the piping bag. It takes practice to get the disks perfectly round. Don't worry if yours are slightly misshapen; you can gently scrape away the imperfections after the disks are baked. Don't forget to sprinkle the disks with powdered sugar before baking.

Bake the meringue disks until they are firm to the touch, about 1 hour. If the meringue begins to take on color while baking, lower the oven temperature by 50°F (10°C). Remove the baking sheet from the oven and place on a wire rack until the meringue disks have completely cooled. If you have the time, turn off the oven and cool the meringue on the baking sheet in the oven. This will take about 1 hour and will allow the meringue to dry completely.

Prepare the vanilla ice cream: While the meringue disks are baking, prepare the crème anglaise and cool it in an ice bath (page 3). When the crème anglaise has completely cooled, make vanilla ice cream by spinning it in an ice cream machine according to the specifications of that machine. When finished it should be creamy and smooth, like soft-serve ice cream. If you spin it too long, it will become grainy and icy, making it difficult to mold in the cake pan. Store the ice cream in an airtight container in the freezer until ready to use.

Prepare the strawberry sorbet: The sorbet can be prepared and spun while the crème anglaise is cooling. Be careful not to spin it too long, just until it is smooth, creamy, and soft. Store the sorbet in the freezer until ready to use. If it seems to be getting too hard to spread easily, remove it from the freezer and place in the refrigerator for about 30 minutes.

To assemble the Vacherin: Cover the bottom of an 8-inch cake pan with a circle of parchment paper. Cut a strip of parchment paper the circumference and height of the cake pan and use it to line the side of the pan. This will make it easier to unmold the frozen Vacherin.

Place one of the meringue disks, flat side down, in the bottom of the cake pan. I use a plastic scraper (page 6) to cover the meringue layer and sides of the pan with a 1-inch-thick layer of the vanilla ice cream, but a large spoon or rubber spatula will work just as well. Fill the center with the strawberry sorbet and use an offset spatula to smooth the sorbet into an even layer, spreading it all the way to the top. Cover with the second meringue disk, flat side up. Press down slightly and place the cake pan in the freezer until frozen, at least 2 hours. (The Vacherin can be stored in the freezer for up to one week if well wrapped in plastic wrap.)

To unmold the Vacherin, dip the cake pan in a bowl of hot water for about 5 seconds. Center a plate over the Vacherin and flip the plate and the cake pan at the same time, so the pan is on top. Gently lift off the pan. If the cake does not release, it may be necessary to dip the pan in the hot water again. Once the cake pan has been removed, gently peel the parchment paper from the bottom and side. Place the Vacherin in the freezer while you whip the heavy cream.

Prepare the whipped cream and garnish: Use a sharp knife to slice the vanilla bean in half lengthwise. Separate the seeds from the skin by scraping the blade of the knife along the inside of the bean. Place the heavy cream, sugar, and vanilla seeds in a medium-size mixing bowl and whip the cream to stiff peaks with an electric mixer on medium-high speed. Remove the Vacherin from the freezer and use an offset spatula to spread a very thin, even coat of whipped cream over it. Fill a pastry bag fitted with a ¾-inch star tip with the remaining whipped cream and use it to decorate the top and side. Then make about six slices in the strawberry, cutting only three fourths of the way from the tip toward the hull and spread it into a fan shape. Place the fanned strawberry in the center of the Vacherin. I present the cake to my guests before I cut it.

It is easiest to cut the cake with a hot serrated knife. To heat the knife, dip it in a tall container filled with hot water before each cut and wipe off the excess water.

Variation: It is very easy to make pistachio- or coffee-flavored ice cream once you have made the crème anglaise. Simply add 1½ teaspoons pistachio paste or coffee extract to the crème anglaise after it has been strained, whisk to combine, and proceed with the recipe.

The frozen Vacherin can also be decorated with an Italian meringue (page 291) and gratinéed. Use a pastry bag fitted with a ¾-inch star tip to pipe the meringue onto the Vacherin. Place the Vacherin in the freezer for 30 minutes. Preheat the oven to 450°F (232°C). Place the Vacherin in the oven until the meringue is lightly browned, about 5 minutes. Watch the meringue closely, because it will burn quickly. Present and serve immediately.

Baked Alaska

This is a classic dessert. When ordered at a restaurant, it is usually flambéed in front of the guest. I think it is too dangerous to flambé things at home.

The cake layer is similar to an American pound cake, but almond paste is substituted for some of the butter. In French we call this almond cake *pain de gênes*, which means "bread from Genoa."

This dessert is easy to adapt to your own personal tastes and time limits. You can simply buy the pound cake and ice cream and assemble it. You can also use different flavors of ice cream instead of the chocolate and strawberry that I use.

For the chocolate ice cream

Whole milk	4 cups	34 ounces	970 grams
Unsweetened chocolate, chopped		7 ounces	200 grams
Granulated sugar	1½ cups	10.5 ounces	300 grams
8 large egg yolks			

For the strawberry ice cream

Whole milk	2 cups + 1 tablespoon	17.6 ounces	500 grams
Fresh strawberries, hulled and chopped	1¾ pints	18 ounces	500 grams
Granulated sugar	1¼ cups	8.7 ounces	250 grams
8 large egg yolks			

For the *pain de gênes*

Almond paste	¾ cup (very firmly packed)	7 ounces	200 grams
Granulated sugar	¼ cup	1.75 ounces	50 grams
Room temperature unsalted butter	½ cup + 1 tablespoon	4.5 ounces	125 grams
3 large eggs			
Grand Marnier (optional)	1 teaspoon	0.3 ounce	10 grams

| **Pastry flour** | ⅓ cup | 1.5 ounces | 40 grams |
| **Pinch of salt** | | | |

For the Italian meringue

Granulated sugar	¾ cup	5.25 ounces	150 grams
Water	¼ cup	2 ounces	55 grams
3 large egg whites			

First, prepare the ice creams and allow enough time for them to harden in the freezer. The technique used to make the ice cream bases is the same used to make crème anglaise. When you are making crème anglaise, the trick is to stop cooking before the eggs scramble. In the chocolate ice cream recipe, the unsweetened chocolate provides insulation for the eggs so they are not as likely to overcook. The strawberry ice cream base does not have that insulation and is more like a classic crème anglaise, which needs to be cooled over an ice bath. Have the ice bath ready before you begin (page 3).

Prepare the chocolate ice cream: Heat the milk and chopped chocolate together in a 2-quart heavy-bottomed saucepan over medium-high heat until bubbles form around the edge of the pan. While the milk is heating, combine the sugar and egg yolks and whisk until thoroughly incorporated and thick. Temper (page 22) the egg mixture by pouring about half of the hot milk into it and whisk well. Now pour the tempered egg mixture into the remaining hot milk and chocolate. Cook over medium-high heat until slightly thickened, stirring constantly with a heatproof rubber spatula. The mixture has finished cooking when it is thick enough to coat the back of the spatula, 3 to 5 minutes. Use the following method to tell if it is finished: Quickly dip the spatula into the hot mixture and hold it horizontally in front of you. With the tip of your finger, wipe a clean line down the center of the spatula. If the mixture holds and does not fill in the line, it is ready to be removed from the heat. If the line fills with liquid, the mixture must be cooked a little longer. Repeat the test every 30 seconds until the mixture is ready. At no time should the mixture begin to boil; if you see bubbles begin to form around the edge of the pan, remove it from the heat and whisk the mixture thoroughly to cool it down. Once the mixture has finished cooking, pour it into a clean bowl and set aside to cool. If you want to reduce the cooling time, you can cool the chocolate ice cream base in an ice bath.

Prepare the strawberry ice cream: While the chocolate ice cream base is cooling, prepare the strawberry ice cream base. The technique is the same as above: Heat the milk and chopped strawberries together in a nonreactive 2-quart heavy-bottomed saucepan over medium-high heat until bubbles form around the edges of the pan. While the milk is heating, combine the sugar and egg yolks and whisk until thoroughly incorporated and thick. Temper the egg mixture as described above, then pour the tempered egg mixture into the hot milk and strawberries. Cook over medium-high heat, stirring constantly with a heatproof rubber spatula, until thickened enough to coat the back of the spatula.

Remove the pan from the heat and pour the mixture into the bowl placed in the ice bath. Stir the mixture occasionally so it cools evenly. When it is completely cool, remove the bowl from the ice bath and puree the mixture until smooth with an immersion blender, food processor, or blender.

Spin the strawberry ice cream according to the directions for the type of ice cream machine you are using. The ice cream is ready when it is creamy and smooth, like soft-serve ice cream. Place the ice cream in an airtight container and store in the freezer until ready to use.

Spin the chocolate ice cream base in your ice cream machine and store in an airtight container in the freezer until ready to use.

Prepare the *pain de gênes*: Preheat the oven to 350°F (175°C). Combine the almond paste and sugar in a medium-size mixing bowl and beat with an electric mixer on medium-high speed until all, or at least most, of the sugar is incorporated, about 2 minutes. It is important to beat the mixture to soften the almond paste. Add the butter and continue to beat until the mixture gains volume and is very light in color, another 5 minutes. If you take the time to cream these three ingredients well, the *pain de gênes* will be light and airy. Add the eggs one at a time, incorporating each addition fully. (If you were to add all of the eggs at once, the mixture would become lumpy.) Add the Grand Marnier, flour, and salt and mix just until combined. Do not overmix, or the cake will be tough.

Spread the cake batter into a parchment paper-lined 10-inch cake pan and smooth the top with an offset spatula to make an even layer. The layer will only be ¼ inch thick. Bake until the cake is light golden brown and springs back when lightly pressed, 15 to 20 minutes. Remove from the oven and cool on a wire rack, then unmold and remove the parchment paper when the cake has completely cooled.

Use a 3-inch plain round cutter to cut seven circles from the cake layer and place them on a parchment paper–covered baking sheet.

Remove the ice cream from the freezer. Use an ice cream scoop to place one or two balls of ice cream on each cake circle. You can distribute the flavors any way you please. Place in the freezer until very hard, about 45 minutes. If you stack two baking sheets on top of each other, it will retain the cold and help harden the ice cream scoops. (At this stage, the cakes can be stored in the freezer, well wrapped in plastic wrap, for two weeks.) Store any remaining ice cream in an airtight container in the freezer to be eaten at a later date.

Prepare the Italian meringue: Pour the sugar and water into a 1-quart heavy-bottomed saucepan and place over medium-high heat. When bubbles begin to form around the edge of the pan, insert a candy thermometer. When the sugar reaches 245°F (118°C), begin to whip the egg whites.

Place the egg whites in a large mixing bowl and whip with an electric mixer on medium-high speed until foamy and slightly soft peaks.

When the sugar reaches 250°F (121°C), it has reached what is known as the soft ball stage (page 16). Pour it down the side of the bowl as you continue to whip the egg whites, being careful not to pour directly onto the beaters, or the hot sugar will splatter. Whip the meringue on medium speed until the outside of the bowl is warm but not hot, about 5 minutes.

Preheat the oven to 450°F (232°C).

To assemble: Place the meringue in a pastry bag fitted with a ¾-inch star tip. Remove the ice cream-topped cakes from the freezer and decorate with the Italian meringue. Return the decorated cakes to the freezer for 15 minutes.

Place the frozen desserts on the baking sheet in the oven and bake until the meringue takes on color, 2 to 3 minutes. Watch the cakes closely. Once it starts, the meringue browns very quickly. Remove from the oven and serve immediately.

Variation: Use a French meringue to decorate the frozen cakes instead of an Italian meringue. Omit the water called for in the Italian meringue. Whip the egg whites with an electric mixer at medium speed until foamy. Increase the mixer speed to medium-high and whip to stiff but not dry peaks while adding the sugar 1 tablespoon at a time.

While a French meringue is easier to prepare and takes less time, I use an Italian meringue as a safety precaution. A professional kitchen cannot take any risks with raw eggs and salmonella. The heat of the cooked sugar in the Italian meringue kills any bacteria in the eggs. If you use very fresh eggs, you should not have to worry about this possibility.

Strawberry Frozen Yogurt/ Banana Frozen Yogurt

8 SERVINGS

These two recipes are easy to prepare. To make this an even "healthier choice" dessert, use nonfat yogurt and omit the chocolate cups.

For the strawberry frozen yogurt

Medium-size fresh strawberries, hulled	Scant 1 pint	18 ounces	250 grams
Plain yogurt	2 cups	16 ounces	454 grams
Heavy cream	Scant ½ cup	3.5 ounces	100 grams
Granulated sugar	⅓ cup	2.4 ounces	70 grams

For the banana frozen yogurt

3 large bananas, peeled			
Plain yogurt	2 cups	16 ounces	454 grams
Heavy cream	Scant ½ cup	3.5 ounces	100 grams
Granulated sugar	Generous ⅓ cup	2.8 ounces	80 grams

For the presentation

Bittersweet chocolate, tempered (page 9)		12 ounces	340 grams

6 fresh strawberries, sliced, and 1 to 2 bananas, peeled and diced

Prepare the frozen yogurts: The technique for preparing both frozen yogurts is the same: Puree each type of fruit with the yogurt. I use an immersion blender, but you can also use a food processor or blender. Add the heavy cream and sugar and blend until well combined and smooth. Place each yogurt mixture in the ice cream machine and spin according to the directions for the type of machine you are using. The ideal consistency is creamy and smooth, like that of soft-serve ice cream. Store the frozen yogurt in airtight containers in the freezer until ready to serve. (It will keep for up to two weeks.)

Prepare the chocolate cups: To make the chocolate cups, I use a foam rubber cylinder 3 to 4 inches in diameter. Wrap the cylinder in plastic wrap and dip the bottom 2 to 3 inches into the bowl of tempered chocolate. Set it chocolate side down on a parchment paper–covered baking sheet. Place the baking sheet in the refrigerator until the chocolate sets, about 5 minutes.

To unmold, very delicately squeeze the foam cylinder inside the chocolate cup and very slowly lift it off the chocolate cup. The cup is very thin and will break easily. If it cracks, redip it in the tempered chocolate to strengthen it. Repeat to make 8 cups in all.

Place a chocolate cup in the center of each plate. Use an ice cream scoop to form balls of frozen yogurt and place them in the chocolate cups. I like to decorate the plates with sliced fresh fruit. You can also slice strawberries and dice bananas to sprinkle over the top of the frozen yogurt.

Frozen Strawberry Parfait

The day I learned how to make this recipe, I discovered that you don't need an ice cream machine to make a frozen dessert. You can use any kind of fruit puree. For this dessert, I used a six-cup heart-shaped mold.

½ recipe Classic Génoise batter (page 38)

For the simple syrup

Granulated sugar	½ cup	3.5 ounces	100 grams
Water	Scant ½ cup	3.5 ounces	100 grams
Framboise liqueur (optional)	1 tablespoon	0.4 ounce	12.5 grams

For the parfait

6 large egg yolks			
Granulated sugar	½ cup + 1 tablespoon	4 ounces	115 grams
Light corn syrup	Generous 2 tablespoons	1.6 ounces	50 grams
Water	¼ cup	2 ounces	55 grams
Heavy cream	1½ cups + 1 tablespoon	13.3 ounces	375 grams

6 medium-size fresh strawberries, hulled and pureed

For the decorations (optional)

White chocolate, tempered (page 9)		4 ounces	113 grams
Bittersweet chocolate, tempered (page 9)		4 ounces	113 grams

Preheat the oven to 400°F (200°C). Prepare the génoise batter and bake it on a parchment paper–covered baking sheet as specified in the recipe. Place on a wire rack until completely cooked. When cool, cut the génoise to fit the mold you are using. (If you don't have time to make génoise, use a good-quality store-bought pound cake.)

continued

Prepare the simple syrup: Combine the sugar and water in a 1-quart heavy-bottomed saucepan and bring to a boil over medium-high heat. Once all the sugar has dissolved, remove the pan from the heat and pour the syrup into a clean medium-size bowl to cool. When it is completely cooled, add the framboise liqueur and stir to incorporate. (If the liqueur is added while the syrup is still hot, the alcohol will evaporate.) Set aside until ready to use.

Prepare the parfait: Place the egg yolks in a large mixing bowl and whip with an electric mixer on medium-high speed for about 7 minutes. The whipped yolks will gain in volume, thicken, and lighten in color. Continue to whip while you cook the sugar.

Pour the sugar and water in a 1-quart heavy-bottomed saucepan and place over medium-high heat. When bubbles begin to form around the edge of the pan, insert a candy thermometer. When the sugar reaches 250°F (121°C), it has reached what is known as the soft ball stage (page 16). Make a *pâte à bombe* by pouring the sugar mixture down the side of the bowl as you continue whipping the egg yolks, being careful not to pour directly onto the beaters, or the hot sugar will splatter. Whip the *pâte à bombe* on medium speed until the outside of the bowl is warm but not hot, 3 to 5 minutes.

Pour the heavy cream into another medium-size mixing bowl and whip with an electric mixer on medium-high speed to soft peaks. (This is the stage at which the whipped cream has the most volume.) Using a rubber spatula, fold the strawberry puree into the whipped cream, being careful not to deflate it. Then make the parfait by folding the *pâte à bombe* into the whipped cream mixture. Be aware that if the *pâte à bombe* is too warm, it will melt the cream; if it is too cold, it will be difficult to incorporate.

Pour the parfait into the mold. Sometimes I use a pastry bag with a large opening (no tip). If you use a pastry bag, press gently, as the pressure of squeezing the parfait through a small opening can deflate it. Fill the mold almost to the top with the parfait.

Soak the piece of génoise with the simple syrup and place it syrup side down in the mold, completely covering the parfait. Place the parfait in the freezer until frozen, at least 2 hours. (At this stage, the parfait can be frozen well wrapped in plastic wrap for up to two weeks.)

Make the decorations, if you like: With a pen, draw a few hearts and birds on a sheet of parchment paper. Place a clean sheet of acetate (page 2) over the parchment paper. Fill some cornets (page 19) with the tempered chocolates. Trace around the lines of the hearts and birds with the bittersweet chocolate. Fill the inside of the tracings with the white chocolate. Let the chocolate harden until set; you can place the acetate in the refrigerator for 5 minutes to ensure that the chocolate sets.

Remove the parfait from the freezer and unmold by dipping the mold in hot water for 5 seconds. Center a flat plate over the mold and flip over both at the same time so the mold is now on top. Gently lift off the mold. It may be necessary to dip the mold more than once to release the parfait, but be careful not to let the mold get too hot, or the parfait will begin to melt.

Decorate the parfait with the hearts and birds. Present it to your guests as a whole dessert and then slice it with a hot knife. Heat the knife before each slice by dipping it into a tall container filled with hot water and wiping off the excess water.

For the Truly Adventurous

◆ ◆ ◆

YOU DON'T NEED TO go on a safari or white-water rafting to have an adventure. Start with these recipes and create some exciting desserts!

This chapter is for the more experienced baker. Some of the techniques will be familiar if you have already tried the other recipes in this book. Here we take those techniques and basic recipes one or two steps farther. It takes a lot of time, patience, and practice to perfect these skills, but I heartily encourage you to try them. I guarantee you will have fun experimenting and you will be amazed at the creations you can make. Use these recipes as guidelines and then create your own adventures. You never know—this might lead you to a new career!

Cookie Tree

1 COOKIE TREE

This presentation can be used to celebrate any season. The first time I ever made it, I decorated it with fake thousand-dollar bills. You could also personalize it with small pictures for an anniversary or birthday.

I like to use the optional cherries for their color. It will be much easier if you use two cherries connected by their stems to hang on the branches; I tried using single-stemmed cherries but could not figure out a way to hang them. You can buy branches at most florists or you can gather your own. Long branches make a more dramatic tree. If you use a vase, use a large, simple one made of clear glass so it does not draw attention away from the tree.

1 recipe Langues de Chat batter (page 75)		
Bittersweet chocolate, tempered (page 9)	*16 ounces*	*454 grams*
Plain tree branches		
Fresh cherries (optional)		

Preheat the oven to 400°F (200°C). Prepare the Langues de Chat batter but leave it in the mixing bowl instead of placing it in a pastry bag. Use a small offset spatula to spread the batter over a leaf template (see equipment photograph, page 4) placed on a nonstick baking sheet. Keep the thickness of the batter as even as possible, about 1/8 inch thick. Repeat until you have enough leaves to cover your branches.

Fill a cornet (page 19) half-full with tempered bittersweet chocolate. Draw the veins of the leaves by piping lines of chocolate down the center of each leaf and two to three lines on each side. Place the leaves in the oven and bake until lightly browned, 3 to 5 minutes. The chocolate veins will bake into the leaves, creating a more realistic look. Cool on a wire rack and set aside until you are ready to assemble the tree.

Use a very clean pastry brush to paint the branches with tempered chocolate until completely covered. Of course, this does not make them edible! You may need more than one coating. Place the coated branches on a sheet of parchment paper until the chocolate has fully set.

continued

Arrange the chocolate-coated branches in a vase. Use the tempered chocolate as "glue" to stick the leaves to the branches. There is no set pattern. Let your eye guide you as you randomly decorate the branches with leaves. My only advice is, don't clump the leaves together. If you are using cherries, hang them by their stems. Again, use as many or as few as you like, depending on the size of your tree.

Use the cookie tree as a centerpiece for the dinner table. When it is time for dessert, your guests can simply pick the cookies from the tree.

Croquembouche

12 SERVINGS

In France, a Croquembouche is the traditional way to celebrate very special occasions like weddings, a first communion, or Mother's Day. In the United States, sometimes I suggest it for second weddings. When Julia Child visited me on my television show, we made a Croquembouche together. It was especially meaningful to me to share the experience of making this classic French recipe with America's First Lady of culinary arts.

If you prefer not to make the nougatine, simply build the Croquembouche on a metal cake stand. Cut a lemon in half and rub it over the surface of the stand to ensure that the caramel adheres to it. I don't know why this works, but it does!

For the nougatine (optional)

Granulated sugar	1¼ cups	8.75 ounces	225 grams
Light corn syrup	3½ tablespoons	2.5 ounces	75 grams
Water	⅓ cup	2.6 ounces	75 grams
Sliced blanched almonds, toasted (page 73)	1¼ cups	7 ounces	175 grams
Vegetable oil for rolling	¼ cup	1.6 ounces	50 grams

For the pâte à choux

Water	Scant 1¼ cups	8.8 ounces	250 grams
Salt	1 teaspoon	0.25 ounce	5 grams

Granulated sugar	1 teaspoon	0.25 ounce	5 grams
Unsalted butter, cubed	½ cup + 1 tablespoon	4.5 ounces	125 grams
Bread flour	1¼ cups	7.5 ounces	175 grams
5 to 6 large eggs			

For the filling

Double recipe Pastry Cream (page 26), flavored

For the caramel

Granulated sugar	2½ cups	17.5 ounces	500 grams
Light corn syrup	Scant ⅔ cup	7 ounces	200 grams
Water	Scant ½ cup	3.5 ounces	100 grams

For the garnish (optional)

Angel Hair (page 48)

Prepare the nougatine, if desired: Hot caramel is used to make the nougatine. *Working with hot caramel is like playing with fire. It is very, very easy to burn yourself. Be extremely careful! The caramel is burning hot and sticky. It will stick to your skin and can cause a burn before you have the chance to remove it. Have a towel or bowl of ice cold water ready. If you get caramel on your skin, immediately wipe it off with the towel or submerge it in the cold water to cool it quickly. If you get hot caramel on your finger, never stick it in your mouth, or you will burn your mouth too.*

Combine the sugar, corn syrup, and water in a 4-quart heavy-bottomed saucepan and place over medium-high heat. Cook until golden brown, 10 to 15 minutes. Add the toasted almonds and stir with a wooden spoon until thoroughly combined. Remove the mixture from the heat and *carefully* pour it onto a nonstick baking sheet or into a lightly oiled or nonstick large frying pan. *Do not touch the nougatine because, at this stage, the caramel will stick to your skin and may cause a burn.* Use a lightly oiled large offset or heatproof rubber spatula to lift and fold the nougatine onto itself. This is done to cool it. If you don't turn it, the nougatine will cool unevenly and harden in spots. You can tell it is ready to be rolled when the nougatine has the consistency of wet clay and no longer feels sticky if you lightly pat it with your hand.

continued

Lightly oil a rolling pin and leave a little oil on your hands. (This will keep the nougatine from sticking to your skin and causing a burn.) Roll out the nougatine on a lightly oiled surface until it is about $\frac{1}{2}$ inch thick. It is best to work on marble, but a Formica or wood surface will also work. If the nougatine hardens and becomes brittle while you are rolling it out, place it on a parchment paper–covered baking sheet, set it in a 200°F (93°C) oven, and heat for 3 to 5 minutes to allow it to soften slightly before continuing to roll. If the nougatine is sticky when removed from the oven, it is too hot and must be cooled slightly before rolling.

Use a sharp chef's knife to cut a 10-inch circle from the nougatine, using a cake pan or a pan lid as a guide. This will be the base of the Croquembouche. Trim the edge of the circle until it is smooth. Place it on a sheet of parchment paper to keep it from sticking to the work surface and set aside on a flat surface to cool.

Prepare the *pâte à choux:* Preheat the oven to 400°F (200°C). Place the water, salt, sugar, and butter in a 4-quart heavy-bottomed saucepan and bring to a boil over medium-high heat. The butter should be completely melted by the time the mixture boils. Remove the saucepan from the heat, add the flour all at once, and incorporate it thoroughly with a wooden spatula.

Return the saucepan to the stove and cook over medium heat for about 3 minutes to dry out the choux paste. As it cooks, move the paste from side to side inside the saucepan with the wooden spoon. Turn it over onto itself so every side touches the bottom of the saucepan, allowing it to dry. Keep the paste moving as it dries, or it will burn. You will know the paste is dry enough when it begins to leave a thin film on the bottom of the saucepan.

Remove the saucepan from the heat and transfer the paste to a large mixing bowl. Mix with an electric mixer on low speed for about 2 minutes to release some of the steam. This will prevent the eggs from cooking and scrambling when mixed together with the paste. Continue to mix and slowly add the eggs one at a time, incorporating well after each addition. (Adding the eggs in this manner ensures that they will be evenly distributed throughout the batter.) After each egg is added, the paste will become loose and look separated. Don't worry; once each egg is well incorporated, the paste will become smooth and homogenous again. The number of eggs used will vary depending on how well the *pâte à choux* is dried. The drier it is, the more eggs you will need. After you have added 4 eggs, check the consistency by scooping a large amount of the paste onto the wooden spoon. Hold the spoon horizontally about one foot above the bowl and watch as the batter falls from the spoon back into the bowl. If it is pale yellow, smooth, moist, slightly elastic and sticky and takes 5 to 7 seconds to fall into the bowl, it is ready. If it appears rough and dry and falls into the bowl in one big ball, it needs more eggs. Add another egg and check the consistency again after it is well incorporated. If necessary, add one more egg. If the *pâte à choux* is too dry, it will not pipe well. If it is too wet, it will be loose and runny, and it won't hold its shape.

Place the batter in a pastry bag fitted with a $\frac{1}{2}$-inch star tip. Pipe the batter into $1\frac{1}{2}$-inch mounds (*choux*) on parchment paper–covered baking sheets about $1\frac{1}{2}$ inches apart, as they will spread slightly when baked. You will need about fifty *choux* for the Croquembouche. The Croquembouche will look nicest if all of the *choux* are the same size. (At this stage, the piped *choux* can be frozen. Place them in the freezer for about two hours, until hard. Remove from the freezer and completely cover with plastic wrap or place them in a zippered-top plastic bag. Return them to the freezer, where they may be stored for up to two weeks. Thaw in the refrigerator for about one hour before baking.)

Bake the *choux* for 15 minutes. Reduce the oven temperature to 350°F (175°C) and bake until golden brown and dry on the inside, about another 15 minutes. To check if the *choux* are ready, look inside the score marks made by the star tip. The color on the inside of these marks should be the same as the rest of the *choux*. To help the *choux* dry, you can open the oven door during the last 5 minutes of baking to let out the steam. (Baking the *choux* at a high temperature for the first 15 minutes produces enough steam to allow them to expand and rise. Reducing the temperature for the remaining baking time allows the *choux* to dry, become firm, and hold their shape.) The *choux* will continue to release steam as they cool, so let them cool completely on a wire rack before filling, or they will become soggy.

Prepare the filling: While the *choux* are baking and cooling, prepare the pastry cream. Since the pastry cream is one of the predominant tastes, I like to enhance its flavor with either framboise liqueur or grated orange zest.

When you are ready to fill the *choux,* place the pastry cream in a pastry bag fitted with a $\frac{1}{2}$-inch star tip. Make a small hole in the bottom of each *chou* with the tip of a paring knife. Insert the star tip into each hole and fill with pastry cream until the *chou* feels heavy. The weight of the filled *choux* will help hold the Croquembouche together. Set the *choux* aside while you prepare the caramel to "glue" the *choux* together. To make it easier to assemble the Croquembouche, group the *choux* in rows by size, starting with a row of nine, then a row of eight, etc., all the way down to one. Ideally your *choux* are all the same size, but if you have some that are larger, use them for the bottom row.

Prepare the caramel: Place the sugar, corn syrup, and water in a 1-quart heavy-bottomed saucepan and cook over medium-high heat until light golden brown. Remove the pan from the heat and carefully pour into a medium-size heatproof glass bowl. If you leave the sugar in the pan, the sugar will continue to cook and turn dark brown. A glass bowl will hold the temperature of the sugar. I put a towel under the bowl to keep the bowl from tipping over and to protect my hands from the heat of the glass. *Be careful when you work with the caramel. It is very hot and can burn! As always, when working with caramel, have a bowl of ice cold water next to you in case you get caramel on your hands.*

Set the nougatine circle on a platter. You are going to create a pyramid of *choux*. The challenge is to keep the form as you build the rows. Take the first *chou* in the row of nine and dip the bottom (the side with the hole) in the hot caramel (*watch your fingers!*). Immediately place it at the edge of the nougatine circle. Repeat with the remaining eight *choux* until all nine have been arranged in a circle. The caramel will anchor the *choux* to the nougatine, making a strong base. The next row is made with eight *choux*. Dip the top and one side of a *chou* in the caramel and position it so that the caramel-covered top faces out and the caramel-covered side sticks to the top of the first row. Repeat with the remaining seven *choux* to complete the row. Continue to build the Croquembouche in this manner with the remaining rows of *choux*. Dip the top and bottom of the last *chou* in the caramel and stick it in place right side up.

If you plan to make angel hair, do so immediately before serving the Croquembouche. Place the angel hair around the bottom and sides of the Croquembouche. The Croquembouche should be eaten the same day it is made. Usually I present the Croquembouche to my guests and then take it back into the kitchen to cut it. There is no graceful way to slice it. The easiest way to serve it is to slice it horizontally with a large serrated knife, separating the rows.

• • • For the Truly Adventurous • • •

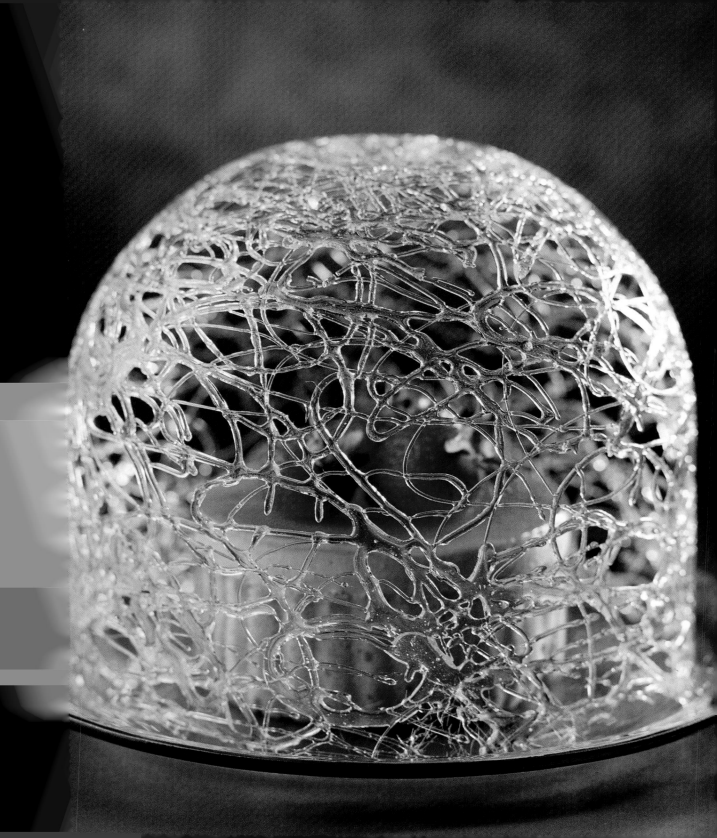

Sugar Cage

4 SUGAR CAGES

his small presentation gives any dessert great flair. I encourage you to try it. It is relatively easy to make once you get the hang of it. The hardest part is unmolding it from the bowl. I like to use a five-quart KitchenAid bowl, but you can use almost any stainless steel bowl and you can vary the size. With the KitchenAid bowl, the presentation resembles a birdcage. When you eat this yummy sugar cage, you liberate what is inside!

Remember, you are working with hot sugar, so be sure to have a bowl of cold water ready in case you get any of it on your skin. It is best to make sugar cages on a dry day, as humidity will melt the sugar. To be on the safe side, make your sugar cages no more than one to two hours before you are ready to use them.

Granulated sugar	**2½ cups**	**17.5 ounces**	**500 grams**
Light corn syrup	**Scant ⅔ cup**	**7 ounces**	**200 grams**
Water	**Scant ½ cup**	**3.5 ounces**	**100 grams**
Baking spray			

Place the sugar, corn syrup, and water in a 2-quart heavy-bottomed saucepan over medium-high heat. Insert a candy thermometer and cook the sugar mixture until it reaches 311°F (155°C), what is known as the hard crack stage (the sugar becomes brittle when it comes in contact with a cooler surface). Remove from the heat and *carefully* pour into a medium-size microwaveable glass bowl. If you leave the sugar in the pan, the sugar will continue to cook and turn dark brown. A glass bowl will hold the temperature of the sugar. I put a towel under the bowl to keep the bowl from tipping over and to protect my hands from the heat of the glass. (The sugar will stay liquid enough to work with easily for about 10 minutes; after that it will start to thicken. If this happens before you are finished, just pop the bowl in the microwave for 3 to 5 minutes, until the sugar is liquid enough to work with once again.)

Wash, dry, and lightly but thoroughly spray a clean, dry 5-quart KitchenAid bowl with baking spray. Dip the tines of a fork into the hot sugar. Carefully but quickly wave the fork over the inside of the bowl, allowing the sugar to drip off the

Try to distribute the strands evenly, making sure the sugar reaches all the way to the rim of the bowl.

Trim the edge of the cage with a sharp knife.

To unmold, gently pull the cage loose from the sides and bottom of the bowl.

Once the cage has released from the bowl, carefully lift it out.

fork in long, thin strands. Try to distribute the strands evenly on the side and bottom of the bowl, making sure the sugar reaches all the way to the rim of the bowl. When finished, you should still be able to see the bowl through the sugar.

Use a sharp chef's knife to trim the edge of the cage clean by scraping the blade of the knife along the rim of the bowl. Set aside to cool, about 5 minutes.

To unmold the cage, place your thumbs on the outside of the bowl and your fingers on the inside of the sugar cage. Gently pull the cage loose from the side and bottom of the bowl; you will be able to see the cage release from the inside of the bowl. You will need to apply this gentle pressure all around the inside of the bowl. Once the cage has released from the bowl, carefully lift it out and place it over the dessert. If the sugar is still too warm, the cage may begin to collapse. Sometimes I release the cage from the bowl but then leave it in the bowl until it has cooled completely. This will ensure that it keeps its shape. (At this stage, the cages can be stored, right side up, in an airtight container in a cool, dry place for one to two days.)

Pastillage Gazebo

1 DECORATED GAZEBO

@ friend of mine has a pastry shop in Antibes. About three years ago when I was visiting, one of the Styrofoam ceiling tiles came loose in the kitchen. He told me he had been trying to fix the tile for months. He tried using glue made especially for Styrofoam, but it didn't work. Since he was working with pastillage at the time, we decided to try fixing the ceiling tile with it. When I visited this past summer, he showed me it was still holding in place!

A pastillage presentation makes an elegant centerpiece for the table and it is a lot safer than working with caramel (hot sugar). I often use the gazebo on wedding cakes because I think it gives them a romantic flair. You can also use it as a presentation for petits fours. If you keep it away from humidity, it will keep for several months. Pastillage is edible, but it doesn't taste very good; it's really meant just for decoration.

Let the pastillage dry for a day or at least ten hours and be sure to dry all sides of each piece before assembling. The vinegar evaporates, helping the pastillage to dry.

You must use a stand mixer for this. A hand-held mixer is not strong enough. You can add food coloring to pastillage, but I prefer to paint it with an airbrush after it is dry because it is easier to control the color.

For the pastillage

8 gelatin sheets or 2²/₃ envelopes powdered gelatin

White vinegar	**Scant ¹/₂ cup**	**3.5 ounces**	**100 grams**
Powdered sugar	**8³/₄ cups**	**35 ounces**	**1,000 grams**
Cornstarch, plus extra if needed	**¹/₂ cup + 1 tablespoon**	**3.2 ounces**	**100 grams**

For the royal icing

1 large egg white

Powdered sugar	**1¹/₂ cups**	**6 ounces**	**175 grams**
Juice of ¹/₂ lemon, strained			

Prepare the pastillage: If you are using gelatin sheets, place them in a medium-size bowl with enough *very* cold water (about 1 quart) to cover. Cold water hydrates the

gelatin without letting it absorb too much liquid. If the gelatin absorbs too much water, the pastillage will be runny. Let stand for about 5 minutes to allow the gelatin to soften and hydrate. Remove the gelatin from the bowl and squeeze out the excess water with your hands. If you are using powdered gelatin, sprinkle the gelatin over ⅔ cup (5.3 ounces; 150 grams) of cold water. Let the gelatin bloom until it has absorbed all the water, about 2 minutes.

Pour the vinegar into a nonreactive 1-quart heavy-bottomed saucepan and place over medium heat until warm. Add the hydrated gelatin and stir until the gelatin dissolves and the mixture begins to simmer. The vinegar mixture needs to be hot when mixed into the sugar so that the pastillage will have a finer texture.

Place the sugar in the bowl of a stand mixer fitted with the paddle attachment. Mix at low speed as you *carefully* pour the hot liquid down the side of the bowl into the sugar. Add the cornstarch and continue to mix on medium speed. If the mixture looks soupy, it is because the gelatin absorbed too much water as it hydrated. To fix this, slowly add more cornstarch until the dough is no longer wet. The pastillage will be sticky. At this stage, it is best to let it rest for a minimum of 2 to 3 hours, or overnight. Store it, covered with plastic wrap, at room temperature in an airtight container.

After the pastillage has rested, transfer it to a work surface dusted with cornstarch and knead it slightly with your hands to judge the consistency. It should feel like clay. If it is too soft, slowly knead in more cornstarch, a couple of tablespoons at a time.

Divide the dough in half and set one piece aside. Use a rolling pin to roll out the other piece of the dough to a ¼-inch thickness. If the pastillage begins to stick to the rolling pin or to the work surface, dust the dough with more cornstarch.

Trace around a 10-inch circle for the bottom of the gazebo and an 8-inch circle for the other disks.

A gazebo is round on the bottom, so you will need to cut out a flat disk. I usually trace around a 10-inch cake pan. Gather the scraps together and roll out the dough again to a ¼-inch thickness. This time cut out two 8-inch circles. Set

To make the columns, twist each end of a piece of pastillage in opposite directions until tight.

Each column should be 1/2 inch thick and 5 inches long.

To make the domed top, place a circle of pastillage into a small bowl to shape it.

To make a bird, form the head, and then pinch the other end of the piece of pastillage to make a tail.

the three disks on a cornstarch-dusted baking sheet or wooden board to dry. Gather the scraps together and set aside.

To make the columns for the gazebo, divide the second piece of pastillage into four equal pieces. Use the palms of your hands to roll one piece on the cornstarch-dusted work surface until you have an even cylinder about 1/4 inch thick and 10 inches long. Fold it onto itself and twist it together until it is relatively tight, pulling slightly as you twist. You should now have a decorative column that is 1/2 inch thick and 5 inches tall. Repeat with the three other pieces. Make sure all four columns are the same height. Set these on the baking sheet to dry. Gather any scraps and add them to the scraps from the first piece.

The top of a gazebo is usually a dome shape. Roll out the pastillage scraps to a 1/4-inch-thick circle about 10 inches in diameter and place it inside an 8-inch bowl to shape it. Use a sharp paring knife to trim the edge flush with the rim of the bowl. Fill the dome with flour to help it keep its shape. Invert a plate over the center of the dome and flip over both at the same time. Remove the bowl. Uncovered, the dome will dry faster. Set aside to dry. Gather the scraps together to make the birds.

There are no specific directions for making the birds: Let your hands and eyes guide you as you free-form them. Have fun and be creative. I usually start by pinching a beak, forming a head, and then pinching the other end of the piece of pastillage to make a tail. Use the dull side of the blade of a knife to imprint tail feathers. Cut wings from pastillage that is rolled about 1/8 inch thick. I cut an almond shape and use the dull side of the blade of a knife to create feather marks. Use a little water to glue the wings to the birds. Set the birds upright on the baking sheet to dry.

Place any leftover pastillage in an airtight container with a damp cloth on top of the pastillage. This will keep the pastillage from drying. It can be stored this way for up to two weeks. When ready to use, knead it with your hands until it is pliable. If it is too soft, adjust the consistency by slowly kneading in a few tablespoons of cornstarch.

It is a good idea to flip the pieces (except the dome) every 6 hours to allow them to dry evenly and to keep the flat pieces from warping. When all the pieces are dry (after 10 to 24 hours), you are ready to assemble the gazebo.

Use a slightly damp dish towel to wipe any excess cornstarch from the pastillage pieces. Be very careful; they are fragile and will break easily. Gluing the pastillage together is the most important step. Make a cornet (see page 19) and fill it half-full with pastillage. Place the cornet in the microwave for about 10 seconds on high power. The pastillage will melt and become quite hot. If you don't have a microwave, place the pastillage (not the cornet) in a small pan and carefully heat it over medium-low heat until it liquefies. Use it to "glue" the pieces together, but be sure about your positioning because you cannot move the pieces once they are glued. Cut the end of the cornet with a sharp knife to make a very fine opening. Glue one of the 8-inch disks to the 10-inch disk. Then pipe a small amount of pastillage onto one end of each column and stick them in place on the 8-inch disk. Glue the other 8-inch disk on the top of the columns. Pipe pastillage around the top edge of this disk and glue the dome in place. If the pastillage inside the cornet hardens, reheat it in the microwave on high heat for about 5 seconds to liquefy it again.

Prepare the royal icing for the final decoration: Combine the egg white and sugar in a medium-size mixing bowl

Cut an almond shape for the wings. Use the dull side of the knife blade to imprint the tail feathers.

Use a little water to glue the wings to the birds.

Pipe a small amount of melted pastillage on the end of each column.

Use the royal icing to make decorations as you desire.

and whip with an electric mixer on medium speed until opaque and shiny, about 5 minutes. Add the lemon juice and continue whipping until completely incorporated, about 3 minutes. The lemon juice whitens the royal icing. The royal icing should be light, fluffy, and slightly stiff. You may need to adjust the consistency by adding more egg whites if the icing is too dry or more sugar if it is too wet.

Make another cornet and fill it half-full with royal icing. Cover the remaining icing with a damp cloth to keep it from drying while you work. It will be much easier to decorate the gazebo if you place it on a turntable. Use the royal icing to make decorations as you desire. Make as many cornets as needed to complete the design. Glue the small birds in place, and *Voila!*

The pastillage gazebo can be stored for several months at room temperature if protected from dust and humidity.

Special-Occasion/Wedding Cake

60 SERVINGS

Y ou can imagine how often I am asked to make special-occasion cakes. This is one of my favorite recipes. Making the cake is relatively easy, so you will have plenty of time to concentrate on the decorations.

One year, I was asked to make a surprise birthday cake for my friend Anne Traynor. I like to incorporate items from a person's personal life and use them to decorate the cake. She works for American Airlines and the party was in her office, so I asked her coworkers to send me all kinds of company knickknacks. You can imagine what they sent! I ended up making a cake that had an airplane suspended over a runway, with luggage tags, security stickers, ticket jackets, and passport holders decorating the base.

Make the cake and then use your imagination to customize it for any occasion.

Double recipe Classic Génoise batter (page 38)

For the simple syrup

Granulated sugar	**2¹/₂ cups**	**17.5 ounces**	**500 grams**
Water	**2 cups + 3 tablespoons**	**17.9 ounces**	**500 grams**
Dark rum	**¹/₄ cup**	**1.6 ounces**	**50 grams**

Double recipe Basic Buttercream 2 (page 32)

White rolling fondant (page 15) for a wedding cake		**6¹/₂ pounds**	**3000 grams**
OR			
Marzipan for an all-occasion cake		**2¹/₄ pounds**	**1000 grams**

For the royal icing

Powdered sugar	**3 cups + 1 tablespoon**	**12.25 ounces**	**350 grams**
2 large egg whites			
Juice of 1 lemon, strained			

continued

Prepare the génoise batter and bake it in buttered and parchment paper–lined cake pans as directed in the recipe. For a small wedding cake, I use three cake pans: one 6 × 3 inches, one 8 × 3 inches, and one 10 × 3 inches. Let the cakes cool completely.

Prepare the simple syrup: Place the sugar and water in a 1-quart heavy-bottomed saucepan and bring to a boil over medium heat. The sugar should completely dissolve. Remove from the heat.

Prepare an ice bath (page 3). Pour the simple syrup into a 2-quart bowl and let cool. When the syrup is cold, stir in the rum. (If you add the rum when the syrup is hot, the alcohol will evaporate.) Pour the syrup into a squeeze bottle or a small bowl and set aside until ready to use.

Prepare the buttercream as directed in the recipe. When the génoise, simple syrup, and buttercream are ready, you can assemble the cake.

The génoise from each cake pan must be sliced horizontally into three equal layers. To do this easily, mark the layers in the side of each génoise with a knife. Place one cake on a revolving cake stand. With a long serrated knife, begin to slice the cake as you turn the cake stand. This will keep the layer even as you cut it. When you have cut the cake all around, repeat the procedure, cutting in deeper until the layer is cut all the way through. Separate the layers by sliding each one onto a flat plate or cake board. This will make it easier to move them, as they are fragile and can break easily. Repeat with the remaining génoise. Set the flattest and most even layer of each cake aside to be used as the top of that tier.

Place each bottom layer on a cake board the same size as the cake. Soak these layers with about half of the simple syrup. Use an offset spatula to spread the buttercream between 1/4 and 1/2 inch thick on each cake layer, spreading all the way to the edge. Slide the middle génoise layers from the cake board onto the buttercream layers. Make sure they are well centered. Soak these layers with the rest of the simple syrup and cover with another layer of buttercream. The buttercream layers should be even so that the cake looks nicer when cut. Cover with the last layers of génoise and press down slightly to adhere. Use a large offset spatula to spread a thin coating of buttercream evenly over the top and sides of the tiers. If the cakes are slightly uneven, use the buttercream to make them flat.

continued

For the Truly Adventurous

You can cover this cake with either fondant or marzipan. I prefer the taste of marzipan, but if you need the cake to be white, use rolling fondant. The procedure for covering a cake with either of them is the same. While you can make your own fondant or marzipan, it is easier and less time-consuming to buy them as I do. For this cake, I used rolling fondant.

I like to use cornstarch rather than powdered sugar to roll out fondant because it has such a fine texture. To prevent the fondant from drying, you will only cover one cake tier at a time. For each tier, roll a piece of fondant to a $1/4$-inch thickness about 7 inches larger than the diameter of the tier. Roll the fondant around the rolling pin and unroll it over the top of the cake. Use your hands to smooth the fondant over the top and sides of the cake, removing any air bubbles. Trim the excess fondant from the bottom of the cake by cutting it flush against the cake board with a sharp paring knife. You can add this excess to the remaining fondant. The fondant scraps can be rerolled for the next cake tier as long as they are clean (i.e., no buttercream). When finished, set the covered tiers aside while you prepare the royal icing.

Prepare the royal icing: Combine the sugar and egg whites in a medium-size mixing bowl and whip with an electric mixer on medium speed until opaque and shiny, about 5 minutes. Add the lemon juice and continue whipping until it is completely incorporated, and the icing is light, fluffy, and slightly stiff, about 3 minutes. The lemon juice whitens the royal icing. You may need to adjust the consistency by adding more egg whites if the icing is too dry or more sugar if it is too wet. Royal icing can also be colored with food coloring, if desired.

In Europe, royal icing is used to decorate a wedding cake. Make a cornet (page 19) and fill it with a few tablespoons of royal icing. Cover the remaining royal icing with a damp cloth to keep it from drying. You can make any kind of decoration you desire: swags, dots, or any other design. Piping fine decorations with royal icing takes some practice, but you will improve with time. To train your hands and practice piping, try this exercise: Use a medium-point Magic Marker to draw the desired pattern on a sheet of parchment paper. Repeat the pattern several times to allow for practice. Place another sheet of parchment paper over the designs and tape both pieces to the work surface to keep them from moving. Use a cornet filled with royal icing to trace the pattern. When you feel you have had enough practice, place the cake in front of you and pipe the patterns onto the cake. Remember to fill in the seams and edges where the cakes meet.

For different widths of decorations, use several cornets and cut the ends into different-sized openings. With royal icing, if you make a mistake, you can just wipe it off! The royal icing will harden as it dries.

A fondant- or marzipan-covered cake can be stored well wrapped in plastic wrap in the refrigerator for up to two weeks. Don't wrap it until the royal icing is dry, or you will ruin the pattern. Allow it to stand at room temperature for about forty-five minutes before you remove the plastic wrap, or condensation will occur.

There are a few *trucs* (tricks of the trade) to remember when making a cake that will be stacked like a wedding cake. Keep the cake tiers on the cardboard cake rounds for support. Without them, the weight of the tiers will cause the cake to collapse. Wooden dowels cut to the height of each cake support the cake tiers. Make sure the dowels for each tier are cut to exactly the same length, or your cake will lean. Insert four dowels evenly spaced in the bottom layer so they are positioned midway between the center and edge of the cake. (For larger cakes, use five dowels; for smaller cakes, use three dowels.) This will help support the tier above it. Insert dowels in every tier except the top one. Place the dowels in the tiers before you begin to stack the cake. *Remember to remove them when you cut the cake; they are not edible!*

If you prefer a cake whose tiers are not stacked directly on top of each other, buy plastic columns at a specialty baking supply store. You will still have to place each tier on a cardboard cake round and insert wooden dowels to support the weight.

Be sure to keep the cake in a cool, dry place, or it will lean when the buttercream softens.

Flowers are widely used to decorate American wedding cakes. Usually, if the flowers are not fresh, they are made from gum paste. You can make your own gum paste flowers or buy them from a specialty baking supply store (see Sources, page 325). I would suggest buying them since they are very reasonably priced compared to the time and energy it takes to make them. Gum paste flowers can be reused for an anniversary celebration if stored in an airtight container. Remember to handle them with care, because they chip or break easily.

continued

If you have your own garden, pick some lovely blooms and use them to decorate the cake. Don't forget to use the natural greens to decorate around the base of the cake. Be sure you know which varieties of flowers and greens are safe to use; some are poisonous. Flowers that are safe to use include: apple blossoms, citrus blossoms, daylilies, English daisies, pansies, roses, tulips, lilacs, and violets.

I often use a small version of the Pastillage Gazebo (page 313) to decorate the top layer of a wedding cake. I think it is a nice alternative to the traditional bride and groom statues.

If the bride and groom are very fond of chocolate, you can decorate a wedding cake with white chocolate shavings. You will need a very large, smooth block of white chocolate and a very sharp knife to make the shavings. *Use extreme caution.* It will be easier if you hold the knife at a 45-degree angle and push the blade away from your body across the top of the chocolate block. You can also use a vegetable peeler to make smaller shavings. Use buttercream to cover the cake instead of marzipan or fondant, as the chocolate shavings will adhere to buttercream. Remember that the cake will be a creamy color rather than white.

There are many, many ways to decorate a wedding cake. Let your imagination be your guide and have fun with it. You may discover the next hot trend!

Sources

♦ ♦ ♦

Albert Uster Imports Inc.
9211 Gaither Road
Gaithersburg, MD 20877
800-231-8154
Specialty ingredients

Amco, a Leggett & Platt Company
800-621-4023
Stainless steel measuring cups and spoons
(also available through Williams-Sonoma)

Annieglass
310 Harvest Drive
Watsonville, CA 95076
800-347-6133
Handmade sculptural glass dinnerware

Broadway Panhandler
477 Broome Street
New York, NY 10013
212-966-3434
Cooking and baking equipment and supplies, other specialty items

Bridge Kitchenware Corp.
214 East 52nd Street
New York, NY 10022
212-838-6746
Pastry, baking, and other kitchen equipment

Dairyland USA
1300 Viele Avenue
Bronx, NY 10474
718-842-8700
Specialty ingredients

Dean & DeLuca
Catalogue information: 800-221-7714
Store locations: 212-431-1691
Specialty ingredients

De Choix Specialty Foods
(for the trade only)
58-25 52nd Avenue
Woodside, NY 11377
718-507-8080
Callebaut chocolate, specialty
ingredients

The Gourmet's Source
R.R. #1, Box 1142
Pittsford, VT 05763
802-483-2600
E-mail: Gourmet@gourmetsource.com
URL: www.gourmetsource.com
Specialty ingredients

Harry Wils & Co. Inc.
182 Duane Street
New York, NY 10013
212-431-9731
Specialty ingredients, chocolate molds

Hermès
800-387-5732
Circus Pattern China

King Arthur Flour Company
The Baker's Catalogue
P.O. Box 876
Norwich, VT 05055
800-827-6836
Flour, baking supplies, equipment

La Cuisine
323 Cameron Street
Alexandria, VA 22314-3219
800-521-1176
Equipment

Lillian Masamitsu-Hartmann
500-FIND-LIL (1-500-346-3545)
E-mail: cakes by lil@aol.com
Wedding and special-occasion cakes

The LS Collection
469 Broadway
New York, NY 10012
800-547-7557
Home furnishings and accessories

Matter & Sense
138 West 25th Street
New York, NY 10001
212-807-0805
Home furnishings, gifts, and accessories

NY Cake and Baking Distributors
56 West 22nd Street
New York, NY 10010
800-942-2539; 212-675-CAKE
Baking supplies, gum paste flowers,
equipment, cake-making supplies

Paris Gourmet Patisfrance
(for the trade only)
161 East Union Avenue
East Rutherford, NJ 07073
800-PASTRY-1

Pavillion Christofle
680 Madison Avenue
at 62nd Street
New York, NY 10021
212-308-9390
www.christofle.com
Flatware, china, holloware, table linens

Rosenthal USA Ltd
355 Michele Place
Carlstadt, NJ 07072
201-804-8000
China

Sweet Celebrations
7009 Washington Avenue South
Edina, MN 55439
800-328-6722
Specialty ingredients

Villeroy & Boch
800-Villeroy (845-5376) US
800-387-5732 Canada
Flatware, china

Wilton Industries
2240 West 75th Street
Woodridge, IL 60517
630-963-7100
Cake decorating supplies, dome molds

Index

♦ ♦ ♦

baking powder, 7
baking sheet, 2
    vs. cake pan, 39
baking spray, 7
banana(s):
    caramelized, 104–105, 249, 251
    frozen yogurt, 295–296
    in fruit sauce, 44
    moon cakes, 248–252
    mousse, 251
    tuiles, 246
basics, 23–48
    almond cream, 28–29
    angel hair, 48
    biscuit, 40–41
    buttercream 1, 31–32
    buttercream 2, 32–33
    chocolate sauce, 45–46
    crème anglaise, 24–25
    fruit sauce 1, 43
    fruit sauce 2, 44
    génoise, 38–39
    lemon curd, 29–30
    Linda's red raspberry jam,
        46–47
    meringue cake layers, 41–42
    pastry cream, 26–27
    quick puff pastry, 35–37
    sugar dough, 34–35
basket, nougatine, with fruit
        sorbets, 275–279
bavarian, 19, 154–155
    crème anglaise base of, 158–159
    for the mask, 158–159
    piña colada, 242–246
berries:
    fraisier, 195–199
    frozen parfait, 297–300
    frozen yogurt, 295–296
    in fruit sauce, 44
    ice cream, 290, 292

individual soufflés, 180–181
    for latte cotto, 132
    Linda's red raspberry jam,
        46–47
    meringue, 161, 163
    mousse, 255–256
    roasted, with vanilla ice
        cream, 172–173
    sorbet, 270, 271–273, 275–277,
        278
    strawberry-vanilla vacherin,
        frozen, 286–289
    syrups, 211, 223–224, 227,
        229, 254–255
biscotti, 72–74
    chocolate-dipped, 74
biscuit, 40–41
    disks, piping of, 155
    Manhattan, 227, 229
bittersweet chocolate, 8–9
    mousse, 139–141
bleached flour, 12–13, 39
blender, immersion, 3
bloom, 10–11, 19
blueberries in fruit sauce, 44
bomboloni, 56–59
book fold, 36, 66, 67
box, molding of, 118–119
bran, 12
bread flour, 13, 59, 70
brown sugar, 16
    air-drying of, 133
    caramelization of, 135
    for crème brûlée, 133–135
bubble wrap, design of, 124
butter, 7
    clarified, 8, 173
    in génoise, 39
    and gluten, 37
buttercream 1, basic recipe,
    31–32

buttercream 2, basic recipe,
    32–33

C

cage, sugar, 310–312
cake comb, 123
cake pan vs. baking sheet, 39
cakes:
    apricot charlotte, 152–155
    banana moon, 248–252
    biscuit for, 40–41
    the chocolate stove, 231–237
    frozen strawberry-vanilla
        vacherin, 286–289
    the Manhattan, 227–230
    meringue layers for, 41–42
    the piano, 257–261
    wedding/special-occasion,
        319–324
candied chestnuts, 8
candied grapefruit peels, 90–91
candy thermometer, 2
capelines, 218–222
caramel:
    -coated floating islands, 164
    dry, 279
    hot, warnings about, 277, 305
    nougatine basket, 275–279
    nougatine for croquembouche,
        304, 305–307
    overcooking and
        undercooking of, 151
    popcorn, 149–151
    sticking of, 304
caramelized:
    bananas, 104–105, 249, 251
    brown sugar, 135
    nuts, 96–99, 100
    pears, crêpes with, 176–179

grape (*continued*)
    sorbet, 270, 271
    terrine, 200–201
grapefruit, candied peels of,
    90–91

H

half-and-half, 14
halvah, 14
    frozen parfaits, 146–148
hard crack stage of sugar, 16, 32
hats:
    capelines, 218–222
    phyllo dough, 169–170
heavy cream, for crêpe batter,
    179
honey, 16, 17
hydration:
    of gelatin, 14, 136
    of yeast, 17

I

ice bath, 3
ice cream:
    chocolate, 290, 292
    coffee-flavored, 289
    pistachio-flavored, 289
    strawberry, 290, 292
    vanilla, 286, 288
ice cream machines, 266
icing, royal, 313, 317–318, 319,
    322–323
immersion blender, 3
ingredients, 7–18
    quality of, 1
    sources for, 325–326
    substitutions for, 18

invert sugar, 16
Italian meringue, 20, 33
    for baked Alaska, 291, 294
    for raspberry soufflés,
        180–181

J

jam, Linda's red raspberry,
    46–47

K

knives, chef's, 2

L

ladybug, the, 253–256
ladyfingers, piping of, 155
langues de chat, 75–76
latte cotto, 129–132
leaves, autumn, with chocolate
    mousse and maple syrup,
    262–264
lecithin, 14
lemon:
    candied peels of, 90–91
    curd, 29–30
    sorbet, 271–273
lemon juice:
    for fruits, 44
    to make caramel stick, 304
lime peels, candied, 90–91
Linda's red raspberry jam,
    46–47
line drawings in chocolate,
    121
liqueur, framboise (raspberry), 14

M

macaroons, old-fashioned,
    84–85
maceration, 20
mandoline, 3
mango sorbet, 271–273
Manhattan, the, 226–231
Manhattan biscuit, 227, 229
Manhattan cream, 227–230
maple syrup, autumn leaves
    with chocolate mousse
    and, 262–264
marbleizing of chocolate,
    119–120
mascarpone cheese, 14
mask, the, 156–160
    as mold for chocolate, 120
measures, 3
melon sorbet slices with port
    wine sauce, 283–286
mendiants, 100–102
meringue:
    baking of, 42
    cake layers, 41–42
    coating of, 163
    egg yolk and, 41
    for floating island,
        161–164
    French, 20, 40, 127, 294
    Italian, 20, 33, 180–181, 291,
        294
    raspberry, 161, 163
    scraper for, 241
meringue powder, 14
    albumin in, 112
milk, 14
    half-and-half, 14
milk chocolate, 9
    mousse, 151
mille-feuilles, 50

mimosa aspic, 202–204
mixers, 3
molded chocolate sculpture,
    118–121
molds:
    baba (*timbale*), 62
    box, 118–119
    bubble wrap, 124
    dome, 3
    glass, 121
    plastic, 118, 121, 125
    stainless steel, 121
moon cakes, banana, 248–252
mousses:
    apricot, 218, 220–221
    banana, 251
    bittersweet chocolate, 139–141
    chocolate, autumn leaves with
        maple syrup and, 262–264
    milk chocolate, 151
    raspberry, 255–256
    two-tone, 139
    white chocolate, 136–139

N

Napoleons, 50–52
nonreactive pans, 21
nougatine:
    basket with fruit sorbets,
        275–279
    for croquembouche, 304–309
nuts:
    almonds, 7
    autumn leaves with chocolate
        mousse and maple syrup,
        262–264
    candied, 8
    caramelized, 96–99, 100
    chocolate-coated, 98–99

chocolate-covered, 94–95
coated in corn syrup before
    toasting, 94–95
with cocoa powder coating, 99
mendiants, 100–102
pistachio, 15
with powdered sugar coating,
    99
toasting of, 73
whole roasted peaches with,
    174–175

O

offset spatula, 3
oil, 14
orange:
    candied peels of, 90–91
    sauce, 112
    sorbet, 275–277
ovens, 6
oxidation, 21, 44

P

PACOJET, 266
paillason, 214–217
pain au chocolat, 64–69
pain de gênes, 21, 290, 293
palette of sorbets, 270–274
palmiers, 86–87
pans, *see* equipment
parchment paper, 6
parfaits, 21
    frozen halvah, 146–148
    frozen strawberry, 297–300
passion fruit:
    crème brûlée, 218–220
    sorbet, 275–277

pastes:
    almond, 7
    pistachio, 15
    praline, 15
pastillage gazebo, 313–318
pastries, 49–70
    baba au rhum, 60–63
    bomboloni, 56–59
    book fold of, 66, 67
    croissants, 64–69
    double fold of, 66, 67
    pain au chocolat, 64–69
    puff, *see* puff pastry
    temperature of, 59
    see also dough
pastry bag, 6
    filling of, 141
    holding of, for piping biscuit,
        155
    for piping creams into tarts,
        185
pastry brush, to spread glazes,
    185, 247
pastry cream, 26–27
pastry flour, 13
pâte â bombe, 21, 31
    gelatin added to, 145
pâte à choux, 304–305, 307–308
pâton, 21
peaches, whole roasted, with
    fresh almonds and
    pistachios, 174–175
peaks:
    soft, 21, 128
    stiff, 21, 42
peanut butter cups, 116–117
pears, caramelized, crêpes with,
    176–179
pectin, 17
petits fours, *see* cookies and
    petits fours